The Unmasking of English Dictionaries

When we look up a word in a dictionary, we want to know not just its meaning but also its function and the circumstances under which it should be used in preference to words of similar meaning.

Standard dictionaries do not address such matters, treating each word in isolation. R. M. W. Dixon puts forward a new approach to lexicography that involves grouping words into 'semantic sets', to describe what can and cannot be said and providing explanations for this. He provides a critical survey of the evolution of English lexicography from the earliest times, showing how Samuel Johnson's classic treatment has been amended in only minor ways. Written in an easy and accessible style, the book focuses on the rampant plagiarism between lexicographers, on ways of comparing meanings of words, and on the need to link lexicon with grammar. Dixon tells an engrossing story that puts forward a vision for the future.

R. M. W. DIXON is Professor and Deputy Director of the Language and Culture Research Centre at James Cook University, North Queensland and a Fellow of the British Academy. His books include *Australian Aboriginal Words in English: Their Origin and Meaning* (2nd edition 1995); *A Semantic Approach to English Grammar* (2nd edition 2005) and *Making New Words: Morphological Derivation in English* (2014). He is the author of the classic three-volume text *Basic Linguistic Theory* (2010–2012) and has published grammars of languages from Amazonia and Fiji, and of several of the original languages of Australia.

Books by R. M. W. Dixon

BOOKS ON LINGUISTICS
Linguistic Science and Logic
What *is* Language? A New Approach to Linguistic Description
The Dyirbal Language of North Queensland
A Grammar of Yidiñ
The Languages of Australia
Where Have All the Adjectives Gone? And Other Essays in Semantics
and Syntax
Searching for Aboriginal Languages: Memoirs of a Field Worker
A Grammar of Boumaa Fijian
A New Approach to English Grammar, on Semantic Principles
Words of Our Country: Stories, Place Names and Vocabulary in Yidiny
Ergativity
The Rise and Fall of Languages
Australian Languages: Their Nature and Development
The Jarawara Language of Southern Amazonia
A Semantic Approach to English Grammar
Basic Linguistic Theory, Vol. 1, Methodology
Basic Linguistic Theory, Vol. 2, Grammatical Topics
Basic Linguistic Theory, Vol. 3, Further Grammatical Topics
I Am a Linguist
Making New Words: Morphological Derivation in English
Edible Gender, Mother-in-law Style and Other Grammatical
Wonders: Studies in Dyirbal, Yidiñ and Warrgamay
Are Some Languages Better than Others?
"We Used to Eat People": Revelations of a Fiji Islands
Traditional Village

with Alexandra Y. Aikhenvald
Language at Large: Essays on Syntax and Semantics

with Grace Koch
Dyirbal Song Poetry: The Oral Literature of an Australian
Rainforest People

with Bruce Moore, W. S. Ramson and Mandy Thomas
Australian Aboriginal Words in English: Their Origin and Meaning

The Unmasking of English Dictionaries

R. M. W. Dixon

Language and Culture Research Centre
James Cook University Australia

CAMBRIDGE
UNIVERSITY PRESS

CAMBRIDGE
UNIVERSITY PRESS

University Printing House, Cambridge CB2 8BS, United Kingdom

One Liberty Plaza, 20th Floor, New York, NY 10006, USA

477 Williamstown Road, Port Melbourne, VIC 3207, Australia

314–321, 3rd Floor, Plot 3, Splendor Forum, Jasola District Centre,
New Delhi – 110025, India

79 Anson Road, #06-04/06, Singapore 079906

Cambridge University Press is part of the University of Cambridge.

It furthers the University's mission by disseminating knowledge in the pursuit of
education, learning, and research at the highest international levels of excellence.

www.cambridge.org
Information on this title: www.cambridge.org/9781108421638
DOI: 10.1017/9781108377508

© R. M. W. Dixon 2018

First published 2018

Printed in the United Kingdom by Clays, St Ives plc

A catalogue record for this publication is available from the British Library.

ISBN 978-1-108-42163-8 Hardback
ISBN 978-1-108-43334-1 Paperback

Contents

Abbreviations and Conventions

-	affix boundary
=	clitic boundary (see pages 12–14)
/... /	encloses a phonological form, made up of a string of phonemes (see page 10)
*	reconstructed form in a proto-language
♦	unacceptable sentence or phrase
DAE	Dictionary of American English
ME	Middle English
NP	noun phrase
OE	Old English
OED	Oxford English Dictionary
PIE	Proto-Indo-European (see pages 147–8)
RP	Received Pronunciation (see page 10)

Abbreviations for syntactic functions (see pages 179–80)

A	transitive subject function
O	transitive object function
S	intransitive subject function

At first mention, dictionaries are generally accorded their full title, in italics; for example, *Webster's Ninth New Collegiate Dictionary*. Later mentions generally use a shorter form, with no italics: for example, Ninth Collegiate.

Prologue: The Work in Advance

A dictionary should tell you when to use one word rather than another. A word must not be regarded as an isolated item. It is a node in the structural framework of the language.

Towards the end of the first millennium, Anglo-Saxon scholars working with Latin texts would write the Old English equivalent below a Latin word. These 'glosses' were gathered together, and put in order. For the next 500 years they served as the first dictionaries, Latin to English. For each Latin word, an equivalent in English was provided; this was its 'definition'. In 1587 Thomas Thomas gave, for the Latin word *lassitūdo*, the English meaning *wearines* (this was one of the spellings used at the time).

The first monolingual English dictionaries – commencing in 1596 – dealt just with 'hard words' (those of foreign origin) and explained them in terms of Germanic forms. The second such dictionary, by Robert Cawdrey in 1604, included:

> **lassitude**, wearines

The Latin head word **lassitūdo**, in the bilingual dictionary, had been replaced by the cognate English word, **lassitude**, in Cawdrey's monolingual dictionary. The Romance word *lassitude* – borrowed into English from French in the middle of the sixteenth century – was 'defined' in terms of adjective *weary* and suffix *-nes(s)*, which derives an abstract noun (both are of Anglo-Saxon origin).

A bilingual dictionary gives translation equivalents between two languages. A Latin sentence including the word *lassitūdo* could be translated by an English sentence with *wearines*. A monolingual dictionary is a quite different matter. It aims to elucidate the meaning of a word (the **head word**, shown in bold type here) in terms of other words of the same language.

We may get a single word following the head word, as with '**lassitude**, wearines'. Does this imply that the words *lassitude* and *weariness* have the same meaning, that each could be substituted for the other? Why should we need two words if they mean the same?

In fact, it is *never* the case that two words have exactly the same meaning. There is always a difference – even if sometimes only slight – concerning what they refer to, the circumstances in which they are likely to be used, and the pragmatic effects of their use. The function of a monolingual dictionary should be to discuss and compare words with similar meanings, explaining when to use one and not the other.

Lassitude is a fascinating word, linking physical and mental conditions – bodily fatigue on the one hand, and lack of interest or enthusiasm on the other. It has partly overlapping meanings with *tiredness* and *weariness*, and also with *langour* and *lethargy*. In order to know when to use *lassitude*, rather than a word of related sense, a dictionary user should be able to consult an account of the similarities and differences of meaning between *lassitude* and its congeners, their grammatical possibilities, and the interpersonal consequences of selecting one word over another.

By and large, the dictionaries we have today fail to provide this information. In the present book, I will show that this is due to a misconceived methodology. Developing and refining the principles of 'glossing', from a thousand and more years ago, has led to the idea that the meaning of a word – considered as a discrete figment – can be adequately rendered by a 'definition'. In some circumstances, it is suggested that the definition could be substituted for the head word in a sentence, with no significant shift in meaning.

Treating each word as a self-contained entity is the FIRST of three radical faults afflicting present-day lexicography. Each word must be placed within its semantic milieu, the set of words with related meanings. And each such set must be located within the interlocking framework of the entire vocabulary. Words must also be linked to grammar; different nuances of meaning may imply different structural possibilities (and vice versa).

For example, *want* and *wish* have compatible meanings; one can say either *I wish to apply for that position* or *I want to apply for that position*. But, alongside *I wish that I had applied for that position*, it is not permissible to say ♦*I want that I had applied for that position*. The grammatical possibilities correlate with meaning differences, and this must be brought out in a dictionary. (*Want, wish (for)*, and *desire* are discussed in chapter 12.)

Finish and *cease* both relate to something which was – but no longer is – happening. One can say either *That bank ceased trading last June* or *That bank ceased to trade last June*. However, with *finish* only the first alternative is possible – *That bank finished trading last June* but not ♦*That bank finished to trade last June*. This grammatical difference reflects a fundamental contrast in meaning for the two verbs. (Chapter 3 has a fullish discussion of *cease, finish*, and their congeners.)

Lexical meaning and grammatical properties are intertwined; each helping to characterise the other. Grammar cannot be properly studied without close attention to the semantic proclivities of grammatical slots, and the kinds of lexical words which may fill them. Contrariwise, the contrastive meanings of words (from a certain semantic set) determine their grammatical functions. Each grammatical construction carries a meaning, and each lexical word has a meaning; these will combine together to show what can be said, and why.

We began by stating that a dictionary should assist the reader in deciding when to use one word rather than another. This aim cannot be achieved through just a list of lexical words, generally in alphabetical order, with a short 'definition' provided for each (and an indication of whether the word is a noun, verb, adjective, or whatever). Lexicon and grammar are interlocking facets of language. In order to learn how to speak and understand a language, equal consideration must be paid to these two components, and to their semantic linkages. Not paying anything like adequate attention to grammar constitutes the SECOND major failing of present-day lexicography.

We can loop back to the early monolingual dictionaries. In the seventeenth century, the head words were forms which had been borrowed from French and Latin during the previous couple of centuries. They were defined in terms of a quite different set of words, those inherited from Old English (plus a few words taken over in the Middle Ages from other Germanic tongues). At that time, the purpose of a dictionary was to explain 'hard words'.

At the beginning of the eighteenth century, the concept expanded. A dictionary should now cover all words in the language, even common adjectives such as *little* and *small*. That is, Germanic words were now included, and they were defined in terms of ... well, in terms of other Germanic words. Nathan Bailey's dictionary from 1730 was the best of its era. But some definitions for the most frequent words were not really very helpful. For example:

> **little,** small
> **small,** little in Size, or in Number

Little and *small* may be used interchangeably in some contexts, but by no means in all. In Bailey's time, as today, *little sister* meant younger sister (irrespective of size). One may say, *Only a little snow fell last night. Small* is not permissible here. On the other side of the coin, only *small* may be used in *The dresses were all of a small size* and *Only a small number of people were killed in the avalanche*. (Chapter 6 deals with *little* and *small* plus, of course, *big* and *large*.)

Beside being only partial, these two entries of Bailey's are uninformative. If the reader was already familiar with one of the words *little* and *small*, they would get a rough idea of the meaning of the other. If they knew neither, they would simply be bewildered.

Things haven't improved all that much over the centuries. A large modern dictionary lists the following lead senses:

> **choose,** select out of a greater number
> **select,** choose, esp. as the best or most suitable

Select, taken from Latin in the latter part of the sixteenth century, and the Anglo-Saxon word *choose* are here defined in terms of each other.

What the reader needs – to be able to decide what to use when – is explicit comparison of the meanings and functions of the words. *Choose* has a wide general meaning, whereas *select* is a hyponym of it. That is, the meaning of *select* is included within that of *choose*. In virtually every instance, *select* can be replaced by *choose*; for example, *They selected/chose the films to be shown at the festival*. However, there are many uses of *choose* where *select* would not be possible. For instance, when followed by *between*, as in: *She couldn't choose between the diamond ring and the ruby earrings*. And only *choose* can take a TO complement clause, as in: *She chose to close the meeting early*.

Suppose that a foreign learner wanted to know how to use the verb *ask*, and consulted a medium-sized dictionary from the mid-twentieth century. The trail of enquiry goes:

> **ask**, call for an answer to
> **answer**, reply to
> **reply**, make answer, respond, in word or action (to)
> **respond**, make answer (especially of congregation making set answers to priest, etc.); perform answering or corresponding action

The entry for *ask* refers the learner to *answer*. That leads to *reply*, which bounces back to *answer*; but it also mentions *respond*. However, the *respond* entry scarcely helps, simply circling back to *answer*.

If every word can be defined in terms of every other word, where to start and where to stop? One solution would be to recognise a small set of 'basic words' which would not themselves be defined but could be used in the definitions of non-basic words. The definitions would of course have to be succinct, and not umpteen lines long. In the mid-twentieth century there were a handful of dictionaries which adopted a 'defining vocabulary' of 1,500 to 2,000 words; all other words were defined in terms of these. However, words on the defining vocabulary were also accorded definitions and these showed the same old circularity (see pages 204–10).

We mentioned the recurrent suggestion that, in many circumstances, a definition should be substitutable in a sentence for its head word, with no significant shift in meaning. This is sometimes feasible. For example:

> **widow**, woman who has lost her husband by death and has not married again

In place of *Maria is a widow*, one could say, *Maria is a woman who has lost her husband by death and has not married again*. However, this doesn't extend very far. When our foreign learner hears *Little Jimmy has a new dog* and wishes to know what this is, they look up the dictionary:

> **dog**, any four-legged flesh-eating animal of the genus *Canis*, of many breeds domesticated and wild, kept as pets or for work or sport

The entry is encyclopaedic and instructive, but it can not be substituted into *Little Jimmy has a new –*. As another instance, the definition *call for an answer to* is not substitutable for head word **ask** in, for example, *Tom asked Bill for a cigarette* or *Robin asked Hilary to come to the party*. The same applies for most of the definitions quoted in this volume. I am not suggesting that a definition *should* be substitutable for its head word, but am simply pointing out that this is something which has often been suggested, and that it only occasionally succeeds.

Whether a definition is substitutable or not is a minor matter, something of a distraction. The main point at issue is that, in all modern-day dictionaries, definitions are haphazard, unsystematic and unprincipled. Anything is defined in terms of anything else, and – as with the *ask* and *answer* example – it often leads round in a circle, taking you back to where you started, and not much wiser for the journey.

Relying on definitions is the THIRD shortcoming of present-day lexicography. This ties in with the first one, dealing with each word as an autonomous entity. The way a word is used can only adequately be explained – and understood – by placing it within its semantic and grammatical homeland. This involves matching it against words with similar and opposite meanings, and examining the contexts in which each of these may be used, with well-chosen examples illustrating semantic nuances and subtleties. There will be links from one semantic set to others, and from one grammatical configuration to a related one.

A few years ago, a leading lexicographer explained his plan of attack for a new dictionary – 'Letters A and B will be my responsibility, Ivan will do C, Vanessa D and E, and then I'll chip in again with F, G and H.' A better plan would have been for one person to deal with verbs of motion, another with verbs of speaking, a third with value adjectives, and so on. A set of similar words (for example, *lovely, beautiful, pretty, handsome*, and the like) should be the province of a single lexicographer, who would examine the contrasts between them. As a final step, the entries could be collated into a single alphabetical listing, to make a conventional dictionary.

Constraints on dictionary-making include time, expertise, money (to pay for the time and expertise) and size. As a book, a dictionary has to be of a size that can be afforded and easily used. Space is always at a premium. Each entry is a compromise between informativeness and succinctness.

However, the world has moved on. Computers can accomplish complex tasks in no time at all. During the last few decades, they have been of immense help to lexicographers in compiling and searching corpuses, laying down a foundation on which definitions are based.

With computers, space limitations dissolve. Things need no longer be presented as a list, in a single dimension. The semantic and grammatical superstructure which characterises a language can be encoded as a multi-dimensional matrix.

Open the 'dictionary file' on your computer, and enter *little*. You will be directed to the semantic set centred on *big* and *little*, *large* and *small* (see chapter 6). There will be sidelinks to sets dealing with *short*, *long*, and *tall*; *deep* and *shallow*; *wide* and *narrow*; and more besides.

There will be characterisation of the words in a semantic set within an overall conceptual template, comparing and contrasting them in terms of structural frames and pragmatic implications. No 'definitions', in the traditional sense; no round-in-a-circle peregrinations.

The plan of this volume is as follows. First, there are chapters on 'How the language is made up' and 'What a dictionary needs to do'. There follows a narrative on the evolution of English dictionaries, step by step – from the early glossing, through dictionaries of 'hard words' to those which dealt with all words (including, inappropriately, grammatical elements such as *the* and *this*). The historical account is interwoven with discussion of types of semantic organisation; with the tradition of copying or part-copying from predecessors (often held to be the only suitable methodology), and with the role of grammar.

Dictionaries came of age with Samuel Johnson, distinguishing different senses of words and including illustrative examples 'from the best writers'. Johnson's methodology underpinned the massive and magisterial *Oxford English Dictionary*, which commenced at the end of the nineteenth century. But then progress halted. During the last century, dictionary-making has been virtually untouched by the emerging science of linguistics. Advances in the understanding of semantics and grammar stand apart, not considered relevant for the grand old tradition of lexicography (treated almost like a branch of history).

Interspersed within the general story are preliminary accounts of four semantic sets – that including *finish*, *cease*, and *stop* in chapter 3; *big* and *little*, *large* and *small* in chapter 6; *fast*, *quick*, *rapid*, *swift*, *slow*, and *speed* in chapter 9; and *want*, *wish (for)*, and *desire* in chapter 12.

The final chapter recapitulates proposals made throughout the book, setting out the blueprint for an innovative – and, indeed, revolutionary – approach to dictionary-making.

1   How the Language Is Made Up

A language is not just a conglomeration of words. It is a complex system of mental organisation, with structures and systems flowing one into the other. Each section of the organisation depends upon other sections, and is in part determined by them. Grammar provides the infrastructure, and lexical words fill grammatical slots. The resulting product enables people to communicate – to work together, to compose songs and stories, to construct scientific argumentation, to express their emotions, and many things besides.

It is a little like a physical organisation. There will be sectors for purchasing raw materials, for manufacturing, for packaging, for sales, for advertising, and so on. Each sector is linked to the others. The salespeople provide feedback to packaging on what appeals most to customers. Advertising extols the purity of the raw materials used. Within the organisation there are people – filling roles, doing jobs, checking, and planning.

It would not be informative to say that the company consists essentially of a set of people, with an organisation being built around them. It is the organisation that is prior, and suitable people are chosen to make it work. Similarly for language. It would not be informative to state that a story, say, consists of a collection of words with grammar being wrapped around them. The story has a structure. Connected paragraphs are made up of coordinated sentences, each with predicate and subject; the latter will have a central element (the head) and an optional set of modifiers. Lexical words are chosen to fill slots in the structure (a bit like people in the manufacturing company).

As an illustration, there are two basic grammatical frames in which adjectives may occur: after the copula verb *be* (this is called 'copula complement' function) and modifying a noun within a noun phrase. *Happy* and *content* are adjectives with similar meanings. But to know how to use them properly, one must be aware of how they operate within the overall grammatical organisation of the language.

Happy is used in both frames:

> The manager was happy with the decision reached
> She was a happy manager

In contrast, *content* occurs as copula complement:

    The manager was content with the decision reached

But *content* may not be used to modify a noun; that is, it is not acceptable to say ♦*She was a content manager*.

Now consider two more adjectives with similar meanings, *lone* and *isolated*. Both may modify a noun:

    There was a lone house on the plain
    There was an isolated house on the plain

But only *isolated* may function as copula complement:

    The house on the plain was isolated

That is, one does not say ♦*The house on the plain was lone*.

It is not enough to state that a word is an adjective, with a certain meaning. The grammatical framework of the language must first be established in order to understand the ways in which each adjective may be used. And similarly for every other kind of word.

We can now examine a pair of verbs, *give* and *donate*. They involve three participants: Donor, Gift, and Recipient. *Give*, with a general meaning, occurs in two grammatical frames:

    The philanthropist$_{DONOR}$ gave £500,000$_{GIFT}$ to [the hospital]$_{RECIPIENT}$
    The philanthropist$_{DONOR}$ gave [the hospital]$_{RECIPIENT}$ £500,000$_{GIFT}$

Donate refers to a particular type of giving, where the Recipient is a worthy cause. It can occur in the first construction available for *give*:

    The philanthropist$_{DONOR}$ donated £500,000$_{GIFT}$ to [the hospital]$_{RECIPIENT}$

but not in the second one. That is, ♦*The philantrophist$_{DONOR}$ donated [the hospital]$_{RECIPIENT}$ £500,000$_{GIFT}$* is not an acceptable sentence for most speakers.

A dictionary should explain the meaning of each word, and the grammatical contexts in which it may be used. These are linked. For example, *donate* focuses on the magnitude of the Gift (others will be giving to the same Recipient) and, in view of this, the noun phrase referring to the Gift must be in direct object function, immediately after the verb.

A language consists of two independent but interlocking parts: lexicon (or vocabulary) and grammar. Plus phonology, which codes meanings into sounds – these are uttered by a speaker, heard by a listener, and decoded by them back into meanings. And orthography, the representation in writing of phonology.

A language makes up a single large system, each part of which only has significance with respect to the whole. Taking it one step further, a language does not exist in a vacuum. It is a social phenomenon, reflecting the way of life of its community of speakers, mirroring the world in which they live. This determines the grammatical possibilities, the assemblage of lexical words and their meanings, and how these knit together. (Exemplified by the way in which *donate* can be used.)

In the remainder of this chapter we characterise grammar and lexicon (illustrating grammar with discussion of comparative constructions and complement clauses), then discuss phonological and orthographic representations, and the multi-faceted nature of 'word'. The final section deals with two approaches to language description – vocabulary prior, or an integration of grammar and vocabulary.

Grammar and Lexicon

The grammatical template of a language deals with types of main clause. An intransitive clause has a verb plus a subject noun phrase (NP), as in *The boy yawned*. A transitive clause has a verb plus a subject NP and an object NP, as in *The pensioner has eaten lunch*. In various circumstances, a transitive clause may omit the object NP; one could just say *The pensioner has eaten*. However, a subject NP can never be omitted.

There are also subordinate clauses, one important type being relative clauses. We can start with two simple clauses:

(1)   I saw the dog
(2)   The dog chased the cat

The second of these can be incorporated into the object NP of the first:

(3)   I saw [the dog [which chased the cat]~RELATIVE.CLAUSE~]~OBJECT.NP~

Here, the relative clause helps to specify which dog it was that I saw.

The relative clause is introduced by *which*. One of the arguments of the relative clause must be identical to the head (or central element) of the NP in which it occurs. In (3) it is the subject of the relative clause, *the dog*. Alternatively, it could be the object, *the cat*, as in:

(4)   I saw [the cat [(which) the dog chased]~RELATIVE.CLAUSE~]~OBJECT.NP~

It is interesting that *which* must be included in (3) but may be omitted from (4). Why is this? In (3), *which* has two functions: (a) introducing the relative clause; and (b) filling the subject slot in the relative clause. We noted that a subject must be stated in each clause. It is in view of property (b) that *which* must be retained in (3); the relative clause must have a subject.

In (4), *which* has the same function (a) but a different (b): referring to the object of the relative clause. As already seen, an object may sometimes be omitted and this explains why *which* is optional in (4). (The relative clause here does have a stated subject, *the dog*.) Hearing *I saw the cat the dog chased*, a listener knows – from their intuitive knowledge of English grammar – that this is a relative clause construction, with the *which* omitted.

Another facet of grammar is affixes. A regular verb takes one of the inflectional suffixes *-s*, *-ed*, *-ing*, or nothing. There can be derivational affixes; for instance, *pre-Christmas* and *post-Christmas* involve prefixes being added to a noun, *Christmas*, to derive adjectives. These have opposite meanings, 'before' and 'after', respectively, and a word can include only one of them.

Two prefixes with similar meaning are *super-* (based on *super* 'over, above' in Latin) and *over-* (an inheritance from an Old English prefix with the same meaning). Some adjectives take one of the prefixes and some the other: there are *super-natural*, *super-human* and *over-fed*, *over-developed*. A few words can take either prefix, with a slight but significant difference in meaning; *super-* is 'to a high degree' and *over-* 'too much, more than is desirable'. If you move into a new house and describe the neighbours as *super-friendly*, this implies that their behaviour is desirable and useful. But if they are *over-friendly* it implies that they act in a way which you find intrusive and unacceptable. A word may include either of these prefixes, but not both at once.

Grammar works with small systems of terms. Some are affixes and others separate words. There are a limited number of terms in each system, such that each can be identified as not being any of the others.

For instance, English has demonstratives, whose primary meaning is to point to something in the context of speaking: *Would you like this cake?* (pointing to one nearby); *No, I'd rather have that one* (pointing to a cake at the other end of the table). Demonstratives deal with 'near/far' and 'singular/plural', making up a closed system. 'I'm thinking of a demonstrative. It is not *this*, *that*, or *those*, what is it?' The answer is *these*. There are precisely four terms in the demonstrative system; if something is not the first, second, or fourth, it must be the third.

Some of the slots in the grammatical infrastructure of the language are filled by grammatical items, such as demonstratives, articles and pronouns. Others are filled by lexical words – nouns, verbs, and adjectives. Grammatical systems each contain a limited number of forms, and they are closed. That is, new items cannot easily be added to them; no new demonstrative, article, pronoun, interrogative word, preposition, etc.

In contrast, lexical words fall into large open-ended (not closed) classes. New nouns, verbs, and adjectives are constantly being added to the language. A lexical class consists of words with the same grammatical profile. *Apple* and *pear* are both nouns, with the same basic structural possibilities. Similarly for adjectives *clever* and *stupid*, verbs *walk* and *run*, and so on.

Grammatical forms – such as *pre-*, *post-*, *this*, *the*, and *you* – are fully speci-fied in terms of the interlocking structures and systems of the grammar; noth-ing else remains to be said about them. Complementary to the grammar is a dictionary, which contrasts and explains the meanings of words in the open lexical classes.

Terms in a grammatical system are mutually exclusive; they cannot occur together. That is, a word cannot include the two prefixes *pre-* and *post-*, nor can an NP include the two demonstratives *this* and *that*. There is no such constraint on lexical words. *Large* and *small* have opposite meanings (a bit like *pre-* and *post-*), but it is not too difficult to think up a situation in which they may co-occur. Suppose that Ingrid shows Pablo her collection of small lacquered boxes from the East. Pablo picks up one and remarks: *This is a pretty large small box!*

The dictionary picks things up where grammar leaves off. The grammar is a complex system, with constructions, affixes, and grammatical words. What is the lexicon? Simply a set of words? No, absolutely not. Just like grammar, the lexicon is a complex system, but one of a rather different nature. Each lex-ical word enters into a series of relationships, linking it to items with similar meanings, with opposite meanings, with compatible meanings but different grammar, and so on.

As a brief illustration, we can take as a starting point the verb *dislike*. Its links include:

- Verbs which are less common than *dislike* and have a more specialised mean-ing, such as *loathe*, *abhor*, and *detest*. For example, *I loathe insincerity* conveys much stronger emotions than *I dislike insincerity*.
- Verb *hate*, which is more common than *dislike*, and has a wider meaning. Any instance of *dislike* can be substituted by *hate*, producing an acceptable sentence with similar but modified meaning. However, *hate* may not be sub-stituted by *dislike*; not, for instance, in *I'd hate to have to tell your daughter the bad news*.
- Verbs with an opposite meaning to *dislike*, *hate*, *loathe*, *abhor*, and *detest*. They include *like*, *love*, and *enjoy*.
- Branching out from these positive verbs is *prefer*. The sentiment *Mary prefers London to Berlin* implies *Mary likes London more than she likes Berlin*.
- Leading off in another direction from *like*, there is the verb *please* which effectively interchanges subject and object with respect to *like*. One could say either (a) *Robin likes Mary's dancing*, or (b) *Mary's dancing pleases Robin*. A difference is that for (a) Mary may not have been aware that Robin was watching her dance, whereas (b) implies that Mary was doing it on purpose in order to try to please Robin.

This provides a sample of the kinds of linkages which knit together the lexical system.

The next two sections briefly describe two important construction types in English grammar – comparatives and complement clauses. Each will be referred to in later chapters.

Comparative Constructions

The basic comparative construction involves comparing two entities in terms of the degree of a gradable property relating to them. One of the entities is taken as the STANDARD of comparison; the other, which is being compared against the standard, is the COMPAREE. The property is the PARAMETER of comparison and there is an INDEX, showing the type of comparison. For example:

	COMPAREE	INDEX	PARAMETER		STANDARD
(1)	Simon	is	more	famous	than	Gordon
(2)	Gordon	is	less	famous	than	Simon

This is a copula sentence, with copula verb *is*. The comparee is copula subject and the parameter is copula complement, with the standard being marked by preposition *than*.

For negative comparison, the index is always *less*. But for positive comparison the index varies. Some adjectives require *more* before them, as in (1), while others take suffix *-er*. For example, with *quiet*:

	COMPAREE	INDEX	PARAMETER	INDEX		STANDARD
(3)	Max	is	–	quiet	-er	than	Basil
(4)	Basil	is	less	quiet	–	than	Max

A few adjectives do not, by virtue of their meaning, form a comparative; for example *first* and *opposite*. Of the great majority which do, some only occur with *-er*, some only with *more*, while a third set may take either. For example, *Beatrice is clever-er than Doris* and *Beatrice is more clever than Doris* are equally acceptable. This is not a random matter; there are clear principles involved. Whether an adjective takes *-er* or *more* depends on how long its form is, which sound it ends in, and whether it already includes a suffix. The essential principles are:

I   **Adjectives taking -er:**
    monosyllabics, e.g. *quiet, fat, brave, new, slow, rude*
    unanalysable disyllabics ending in vowel /i/, e.g. *heavy, pretty, happy, busy*

II **Adjectives taking either -er or more:**
    unanalysable disyllabics ending in a vowel other than /i/, e.g. *yellow, clever*
    disyllabics which end in suffix *-y* or *-ly*, e.g. *cloud-y, luck-y, friend-ly, man-ly*

III **Adjectives taking** *more*

> disyllabic or longer words ending in a consonant, e.g. *famous, superb, public, difficult, splendid*
>
> trisyllabic and longer words ending in a vowel, e.g. *ordinary, necessary*

No grammar is ever completely tidy and there are a handful of exceptions to these principles – disyllabic adjectives ending in consonants which take *-er*. These include *stupid, polite*, and *common*.

There is an explanation for two of the exceptions. If we have a pair of adjectives with opposite meanings, they are likely to behave in the same way.

Clever and *stupid, rude*, and *polite* are such pairs. We can see that *clever* and *rude* take *-er* by virtue of their form; it is likely that *stupid* and *polite* also take *-er* by analogy. No similar explanation can be offered for *common*, except that it is a rather common word. This is just an exception. Most things can be explained within a grammar, but not quite everything.

Adjectives form superlatives on the same principles as comparatives, taking *-est* in place of *-er, most* rather than *more*, and *least* in place of *less*. (The origins of *more, most, less*, and *least* are explained in pages 71–2.) There are three adjectives which have irregular forms: *good* with *better* and *best, bad* with *worse* and *worst*, and *far* with *farther* and *farthest* (or *further* and *furthest*).

If a dictionary is to fully inform its users how to use words, it should provide information on acceptable comparative indexes for each adjective.

Complement Clause Constructions

For some verbs, subject and object must be noun phrases (NPs); for example, *eat, chase, wipe*. Others may have either an NP or what is called a 'complement clause' in object function. For example:

They will soon announce [the election result]$_{\text{NOUN.PHRASE}}$
They will soon announce [that the Green party has won]$_{\text{COMPLEMENT.CLAUSE}}$

English has three main varieties of complement clause, marked by complementisers *that, -ing*, and *(for) to*, respectively. They have contrasting meanings.

- *A* THAT *clause describes a fact.* The complement clause commences with *that*, as in:

    I know [that John built the hen-coop]

- *An* -ING *clause describes an activity.* The verb of the complement clause takes suffix *-ing*, as in:

    Fred watched [John build-ing the hen-coop]

- *A (FOR) TO clause describes a potentiality (purpose or intention).* If complement clause and main clause have different subjects, *for* is placed before the complement clause subject, and *to* before the complement clause verb, as in:

  I had intended [(for) Tom to build the hen-coop]

The *for* may optionally be omitted from this sentence. If the two clauses have the same subject then this subject is omitted from the complement clause, together with *for*, as in:

  I had intended [to build the hen-coop]

Which complement clause type(s) a given verb occurs with depends on the meaning of the verb and on the meaning of the complement clauses. In chapter 3 there is explanation of why *finish* only takes an -ING clause but *cease* both -ING and TO varieties; and chapter 12 explains why *wish* may take THAT and (FOR) TO complement clauses whereas *want* only occurs with TO clauses.

 Some verbs may take all three varieties, with quite different implications. This can be illustrated with *like*.

- *Like* may relate just to the subject's feelings about the fact of a certain thing happening (they may not be at all interested in the internal details of the event). A THAT complement clause is then appropriate, as in:
  John likes it [that Mary sings the blues each Friday evening]
  (because she goes out, and he can watch football on TV)

- Or *like* may relate to the subject's feelings about some activity as it unfolds; -ING is then the appropriate complement choice:
  John likes [Mary singing the blues]
  (he could listen to her all night)

- Or, the main clause subject might have good (or bad) feelings about the complement clause subject's getting involved in an activity (without necessarily enjoying the activity per se); a (FOR) TO complement will then be used:
  John would like [(for) Mary to sing the blues]
  (because he thinks her voice is just right for that style – although in fact his own preference is for opera)

It is interesting to survey the grammatical potentialities for other verbs from the same semantic set as *like*, mentioned a little while back. All can, of course, take a plain NP as object. In addition, there are complement clause possibilities as follows:

- -ING, THAT, and (FOR) TO clauses with *like, love, prefer, hate*
- just -ING and THAT clauses with *dislike, loathe, abhor, enjoy*
- only -ING clause with *detest*

Why, one may ask, should *like, love, prefer*, and *hate* take a TO clause but not *dislike*? One can say *I'd like/love/prefer/hate [to watch cricket today]*, but not ♦*I'd dislike [to watch cricket today]*. The answer lies with derivational prefix *dis-*; it appears that no *dis-* word may occur with a TO complement clause.

Either *Jacob continued [painting the wall]* or *Jacob continued [to paint the wall]* is acceptable, but only *Jacob discontinued [painting the wall]*, not ♦*Jacob discontinued [to paint the wall]*. Similarly, *agree* and *allow* can take a TO clause, but *disagree* and *disallow* cannot. It appears that the prefix *dis-* is incompatible with a potentiality sense.

The verb *detest* refers to an activity, not to a fact or a potentiality. For this reason, it can only take as object an NP, or an -ING complement clause; for example, *Mary detests [insincerity]* or *Lucy detests [being photographed]*.

Complement clauses most often occur in object slot, but there are some verbs which accept them in subject function. As mentioned before, *please* reverses subject and object with respect to *like*. Corresponding to the *like* sentences just exemplified, we can have *[That Mary sings the blues] pleases John*, *[Mary singing the blues] pleases John*, and *[For Mary to sing the blues] would please John*.

Plainly, if a dictionary user is to learn how to use a verb appropriately, they must be told what type(s) of complement clauses it may be used with, and in which circumstances.

We now examine the way in which grammatico-lexical information is communicated from speaker to listener – the sound system.

Orthography and Phonology

Mankind has been around for at least 100,000 years (maybe much longer) and for just about all of that time human languages have had sophisticated grammars and extensive lexicons. Writing was invented only about 5,000 years ago. Then, for a long period it was the prerogative of just a few educated people. Until the last few centuries, only a small proportion of people in England habitually wrote more than their name or a brief message (if that).

Today, almost everyone can read and write with fair fluency, but spoken language is still the predominant mode. We talk and listen much more than we write and read. And for most people, the hours spent listening to TV, radio, and films greatly outnumber those spent with a book, magazine, or newspaper.

Speaking is the essence of language use with writing being a secondary manifestation – for communicating when out of earshot, and for producing a permanent record. The purpose of writing is to represent speech through an orthography. In the world today, writing systems differ in how efficient they are. Spanish, for instance, has an almost perfect orthography, with one letter for each contrastive sound, or 'phoneme'. If you can pronounce a word you know how to spell it, and if you can spell it you know how to say it. For example, the spelling *altura* 'height' represents phonological form /altura/. (Slant brackets, /... /, indicate a phonological form, made up of a string of phonemes.) The ways in which phonemes are organised, to make up words and higher units, is called 'phonology'.

English orthography is of a very different nature. Typically, one phoneme may be written by different letters in different words, and a single letter may represent a multitude of sounds. Consonants pose some difficulty. One letter may represent different phonemes in different words. For example:

- Letter *g* may represent the 'hard *g*' sound, /g/, as in *gain* /gein/, or the 'soft *g*' sound, /dʒ/, as in *giant* /dʒaiənt/.
- Digraph *th* is used both for the voiced apico-dental fricative /ð/, as in demonstrative *this* /ðis/, and for the corresponding voiceless sound /θ/, as in adjective *thin* /θin/.

Looking at things the other way round, a phoneme may be represented by different letters in different words. For example:

- Phoneme /s/ is written as *s* in *please* /pliːs/; and as *c* in *niece* /niːs/.
- Phoneme /z/ is written as *z* in *lazy* /'leizi/; and as *s* in *rose* /rouz/.
- Phoneme /ʃ/ is written as *sh* in *shoe* /ʃuː/; as *s* in *sure* /ʃuə/; and as *c* in *ocean* /'ouʃən/.
- Phoneme /ʒ/ is written as *s* in *pleasure* /'pleʒə/; and as *g* in *beige* /beiʒ/.
- Phoneme /tʃ/ is written as *ch* in *chain* /tʃein/; and as *t* in *nature* /'neitʃə/.
- Phoneme /dʒ/ is written as *j* in *jam* /dʒam/; as *g* in *gem* /dʒem/; as *d* in *soldier* /'souldʒə/ (or /'soudʒɛ/); and as *dg* in *lodger* /'lɔdʒə/.

Vowels are a nightmare in English. The Latin-based orthography used for English has five vowel symbols. But the sound system of Standard British English (what is called 'Received Pronunciation' or 'RP') has seven short and five long vowels, plus eight vowel sequences or diphthongs. They are, with a sample word for each:

SHORT VOWELS	LONG VOWELS
/i/ as in *bit* /bit/	/iː/ as in *beat* /biːt/
/e/ as in *bet* /bet/	
/a/ as in *bat* /bat/	/aː/ as in *barter* /baːtə/
/ɔ/ as in *bottom* /'bɔtəm/	/ɔː/ as in *bought* /bɔːt/
/u/ as in *book* /buk/	/uː/ as in *boot* /buːt/
/ʌ/ as in *but* /bʌt/	
/ə/ as in *batter* /'batə/	/əː/ as in *Bert* /bəːt/

DIPHTHONGS

/ei/ as in *bait* /beit/	/ɔi/ as in *boy* /bɔi/
/ai/ as in *bite* /bait/	/iə/ as in *beer* /biə/
/ou/ as in *boat* /bout/	/eə/ as in *bear* /beə/
/au/ as in *bout* /baut/	/uə/ as in *boor* /buə/

Fourteen of the vowels and diphthongs are illustrated in the frame /b–t/. For /u/ we need /b–k/ and for four of the diphthongs /b–/. The unstressed short vowel /ə/ (called 'schwa') does not occur in a monosyllable.

Things might look reasonably tidy from the tabulation just given. In fact, they are not. For example:

- Letter *a* is used to write vowel phoneme /a/ in *fan* /fan/, /a:/ in *father* /'fa:θə/, /e/ in *many* /'meni/, /ɔ/ in *want* /wɔnt/, /ɔ:/ in *talk* /tɔ:k/, and even /i/ in *village* /'vilidʒ/.
- Proceeding from the opposite direction, vowel phoneme /ɔ/ is represented by letter *o* in *dog* /dɔg/, by *a* in *want* /wɔnt/, by *ou* in *cough* /cɔf/, by *ow* in *knowledge* /'nɔlidʒ/, and by *au* in *laurel* /'lɔrəl/.

Many other examples could be quoted along these lines.

Surely every grammar should frame its discussion in terms of actual phonological forms, rather then the eccentric orthography. Almost none do, except for an odd comment here and there. Surely a dictionary should give phonological as well as orthographic representation for every word; some do and some don't.

Relying on orthography can obscure regular patterns within the language. For example, there is a suffix which makes nouns out of verbs. There is a regular rule for applying it to a set of verbs ending in /t/ or /d/ – replace the final /t/ or /d/ by /ʃən/. This is illustrated by:

VERB		NOMINALISATION	
SPELLING	FORM	FORM	SPELLING
desert	/di'sə:t/	/di'sə:-ʃən/	desertion
permit	/'pə:mit/	/'pə:mi-ʃən/	permission
intend	/in'tend/	/in'ten-ʃən/	intention
extend	/iks'tend/	/iks'ten-ʃən/	extension

The phonology is straightforward but, as can be seen in the rightmost column, this is obscured by orthographic irregularity. In the first row, *ion* is simply added after the final *t*. In the second, final *t* is replaced by *ssion*. In the third row, *d* is replaced by *tion*, and in the final row *d* is replaced by *sion*. The final /-ʃən/ is thus written as *tion*, *ssion*, *tion*, and *sion*, respectively.

A typical word in English has one syllable with primary stress (shown by '
before it) and the remaining syllables unstressed. A stressed syllable can have
any of the vowels and diphthongs except for /ə/. The vowel of an unstressed
syllable can be either /ə/ or /i/. (It will be seen that /i/ is the only vowel found
in both stressed and unstressed syllables.)

The syllable with primary stress can be at any position within a word; it is the
first syllable for *caterpillar* /'katəpilə/, the second for *important* /im'pɔːtənt/,
and so on. Longer words may also include a syllable with secondary stress
(shown by ˌ before the syllable); these may also involve any vowel or diphthong other than /ə/. Secondary stress is typically found on some affixes – for
instance *re-state* /ˌriː'steit/ – and in many compounds – such as *grandfather*
/'grandˌfaːðə/ and *caveman* /'keivˌman/.

Some affixes cause stress to shift within a lexical root to which they are
added, with a previously stressed syllable becoming unstressed. When this
happens, the general principle is that stressed /iː/ or /i/ becomes unstressed /i/,
as when noun *speed* /spiːd/ takes suffix *-ometer* /-'ɔmətə/, giving *speedometer*
/spi'dɔmətə/. And all other vowels and diphthongs become /ə/. As an illustration of this, consider suffix *-ic* /-ik/, which normally requires stress to go on the
syllable preceding it. When added to *atom* /'atəm/, this gives *atomic* /ə'tɔmik/.
Stressed /a/ in the first syllable has becomes unstressed /ə/, and in the second
syllable unstressed /ə/ has become stressed /ɔ/.

This overview of English phonology has been schematic and far from comprehensive. But it is a sufficient basis for discussion of that most important
topic: what are the varieties of words in English, and which of them should be
included in the dictionary?

What Is a Word?

An orthographic word is what comes between two spaces in writing. But when
we examine speech – the way in which the language is used in everyday life –
the characterisation of words is far less straightforward.

There are a number of grammatical elements which are written as if they
were distinct words but are generally pronounced as part of a following or preceding full word.

One could say *to the woods* as /'tuː'ðiː'wudz/ (three words, each with primary stress) but it would only be pronounced in this way by someone dictating
slowly or by a partly-taught foreigner (using a 'spelling pronunciation'). The
normal way of saying it is /tə=ðə='wudz/. Definite article *the* /ðiː/ and preposition *to* /tuː/ lose their stress, have their vowels replaced by the short central
vowel /ə/, and are attached to the following lexical word *woods* /'wudz/. These
are called 'clitics', (from the Greek word for 'leaning'); they have no stress
themselves and so 'lean on' – and become part of – an adjacent word which

does bear stress. The boundary of a clitic is shown by '=', in contrast to an affix boundary, which is shown by '-' (as in *wood-s* /'wud-z/).

Clitics which attach to a following word, such as *the* /ðə=/ and *to* /tə=/, are called 'proclitics'. Those which attach to a preceding word are 'enclitics', for instance *him* /=əm/ in *Hit him!* /'hit=əm/.

The following sentence consists of twenty orthographic words.

(1) He should have guid-ed her to the house or those hut-s of your father for a bit of a laugh

As it would be pronounced in fluent speech, there are just eight words with primary stress (these are underlined); two are grammatical words – *he* and *those* – and six are lexical words – *guided, house, huts, father, bit,* and *laugh.* There are also nine proclitics and three enclitics. The phonological form of the sentence is:

(2) 'Hi:=ʃəd=əv 'gaid-id=ə tə=ðə='haus ə='ðouz 'hʌt-s əv=yə='fa:ðə fər=ə='bit əv=ə='la:f

There are in English more than fifty grammatical items that are generally clitics but which *do* have a full form, with a vowel other than /ə/ and primary stress. However, the full form is used only in special contrastive situations. For example, in *I said he's going to the market, not coming from it*, prepositions *to* and *from* would be /'tu:/ and /'frɔm/, respectively; but in a non-contrastive context they would be /tə=/ and /frəm=/.

All grammatical forms which are reduced to clitics are monosyllabic, except for preposition *upon* (full form /ə:pɔn/ reducing to /əpən=/). The unstressed clitic vowel is /ə/ in most cases, /i/ in a few/.

Proclitic reductions include:

I Articles:
- *a,* as in *a bit* /ə='bit/ and *a laugh* /ə='la:f/ in (2);
- *the,* as in *the house* /ðə='haus/ in (2);
Also *an* and *some.*

II Ten prepositions:
- *to,* as in *to the house* /tə=ðə='haus/ in (2);
- *for,* as in *for a bit* /fər=ə='bit/ in (2);
- *of,* as in *of your father* /əv=yə='fa:ðə/ and *of a laugh* /əv=ə='la:f/ in (2);
Also *at, from, till, than, as, by,* and *upon.*
    Note that there are other monosyllabic prepositions which do not reduce, such as *up, down, in, out, on, off.* And, except for *upon,* there is no reduction of disyllabic prepositions such as *below, between, about, among* (and many more).

III Conjunctions:
- *or,* as in *or those* /ə='ðouz/ in (2);
also *and* and *but.*

IV Possessive pronouns:
  - *your,* as in *your father* /yə='faːðə/ in (2);
  Also *his, her, its, our, their,* and *my.*
V Auxiliary verbs:
  - *are* may be reduced to /ə=/ as in *the men are going* /ðə=men ə=gouiŋ/;
  Also *be, been* and (just in interrogative use) *do* and *does.*

Enclitic reductions include:

VI Object pronouns:
  - *her,* as in *guided her* /'gaid-id=ə/ in (2);
  Also *me, you, him, it, us,* and *them.*
VII Auxiliaries: forms of *be* and of *have* – as in *he should have* /'hiː=ʃəd=əv/
  in (2);
  Also modal verbs such as *would, will, shall, can, could, must,* and *should* –
  as in *he should* /'hiː=ʃəd/ in (2).

Some reductions in speech are often (but not always) shown as abbreviated forms in writing. For example, *'ll* for *will,* *'d* for *would,* *'s* for *is,* *'re* for *are.* The negator *not* undergoes a different kind of reduction shown in writing by *won't* /'wount/ for *will not* /'wil 'nɒt/, and *don't* /dount/ for *do not* /'du 'nɒt/.

In summary, a language consists of:

(a) Grammatical constructions, such as main clause, relative clause, possessive phrase.
(b) Grammatical affixes (marked by '-'). Each of these is associated with a particular word class (occasionally with more than one class), and is an integral part of the word to which it is attached. For example, plural suffix *-s* on *hut* and verbal suffix *-ed* on *guide* in (1).
(c) Grammatical items which can be a full word (with stress) but are most often reduced to be clitics (marked by '='), without stress of their own. A clitic can generally attach to a wide range of words.
(d) Grammatical items which are always full words, with stress. For example, *he* and *those* in (2).
(e) Lexical words (also called lexemes), such as *guide, house, hut, father, bit,* and *laugh* in (2). Each of these will have a number of forms; for example, *laughs, laughed, laughing, laughter.*

The grammar deals with (a–d). Systems of affixes, clitics and grammatical words are fully specified within the interlocking parameters of the grammar. Nothing else needs to be said about them.

Where the grammar leaves off, the dictionary should take over, providing a semantic characterisation of (e) lexemes, and explaining their grammatical possibilities as a consequence of their lexical meanings.

Two Approaches

Dictionary and grammar are intricately integrated, such that each can only be properly considered in relation with the other.

When a linguistic scholar works on a previously undescribed language from the Americas, or Africa, or Asia, or Australia, or a Pacific Island, they devote attention to both lexicon and grammar. It would be impossible to make any headway on one without taking full account of the other.

For well-known languages the situation is quite different. There is a coterie of lexicographers, working on dictionaries, and a cohort of grammarians – with minimal overlap of the two groups, and precious little constructive communication between them. This works to the detriment of both. Grammarians would benefit by not just describing, say, types of complement clauses, but by studying what verbs occur with each and the semantic underpinnings for this. On the other side, the gains for dictionary-makers would be immense. By contrasting the meanings of words within a given semantic set, and their distinct but overlapping grammatical possibilities, a coherent picture will emerge of when to use one word rather than another. And that, surely, should be the purpose of a dictionary.

We can distinguish two approaches to the comprehensive description of a language:

I   Start with words. Provide a definition for each word, on an individual basis. Regard grammar as something more-or-less extraneous, which gets wrapped around the words.

II Simultaneously consider grammatical constructions and the lexical items which may inhabit them, each serving to characterise the other.

As the chapters of this book will recount, the established dictionary-making tradition is firmly of type **I**. This is encapsulated in *A Handbook of Lexicography: The Theory and Practice of Dictionary-Making* by Bo Svensén. Slightly less than one page is devoted to 'Dictionary and Grammar' and it begins:

Grammar can be regarded as a set of rules. The grammatical information given in a dictionary can be taken as a description of how the [head word] functions in relation to these rules.

But the grammatical information given is minimal – word class, and perhaps transitivity value for verbs – and ad hoc, without any cognisance of the full interconnected parameters of the grammar.

To return to the analogy with which this chapter began, it is rather like saying that a manufacturing company consists of a set of individual people, with the organisation being draped over them. Rather than that the company is the basic entity, and it is the people employed there who make it work.

As we shall demonstrate, in some detail, approach **I** has gradually developed, over the past millennium and a half – from the early lists of textual glosses into the massive dictionaries of today. There has been no revolution, and one is sorely overdue.

The following chapters make the case for approach **II**, with sample illustrations of how it can operate.

2 What a Dictionary Needs to Do

A language, spoken by living people, is continually evolving. Old words and old construction types fade from use, and new ones develop. A word is accorded a novel referent, as when a device for operating a computer came to be named *mouse*. This new sense is really different, and speakers debate as to whether its plural should be *mice*, the same as for the small furry animal, or the regular form *mouse-s*. A lexicographer will note the alternatives and watch, as time passes, to see which prevails.

Some writings on language are 'prescriptive', laying down regulations concerning how it is proper to speak (is now, and will be for all time). The scientific approach is to study language as it is used, in a similar way to how a biologist studies the ways of animals, and a geologist the characters of rocks. Grammars and dictionaries should be descriptive documents – not saying how things *should be*, but rather portraying how things *actually are* (in a standard, or other, dialect). Someone will consult a dictionary to learn how to use one word rather than another. They want to know how it is employed by the language community today (rather than being told by some prissy pedant what should pertain).

Most dictionaries give the pronunciation of each word, in terms of a phonemic alphabet, sometimes noting dialect differences. For instance, *provost* is said as /ˈprɔvəst/ in England but as /ˈprouvəst/ in the USA.

Etymologies are an interesting extra. Knowing where a word came from, and the original meaning, can assist in understanding its present-day import. For example, the fact that *indemnity* 'protection against damage or loss' comes from negative prefix *in-* added to the Greek word *damnum* 'loss, damage'. Historical information may help explain modern-day irregularities such as why many speakers may not say ◆*littler* and ◆*littlest* (but must use *smaller* and *smallest* instead); see chapter 6. Knowledge of gradual meaning shift over the centuries helps to explain the present-day senses of *want*, as described in chapter 12.

Form and Function

Each word has two aspects. These are its form, or internal composition, and its function, which is the way it is used within higher units of language – phrase, clause, sentence, discourse. Study of the ways in which words function is called 'syntax' (as it was in ancient Greece). From the late nineteenth century, the term 'morphology' has been used for investigation of the structure of words. (This is an extension of a slightly earlier use of 'morphology' dealing with the structures of plants and animals, and is based on the Greek word *morphé* 'form'.) The parts of a word are called 'morphemes'; for instance *un-tru-th-ful-ness* consists of five morphemes: derivational prefix *un-*, root, *tru(e)*, plus derivational suffixes *-th*, *-ful*, and *-ness*.

Morphology and syntax merge into each other, with a morphological element marking a syntactic role. In *John's hat*, morpheme *-'s* is a suffix to *John* and it indicates a syntactic relation of possession between *John* and *hat*. Within the sentence *John likes [Mary singing the blues]*, morpheme *-ing* is a suffix to *sing*, and it marks *Mary singing the blues* as a complement clause functioning as the object of main verb *likes*.

A word is built up in the following way:

- Start with an unanalysable root which belongs to a certain word class.
- Optionally, apply one or more derivational affixes, each of which produces a stem; this may be of the same or different word class as the preceding root or stem.
- Apply an inflection appropriate for the word class of the final stem.

This can be illustrated for *un-tru-th-ful-ness*:

DERIVATION	FORM	STATUS	WORD CLASS	PROPERTIES
	true	ROOT	adjective	takes comparative index *-er*
suffix *-th*	*tru-th*	STEM	count noun	takes plural suffix *-s*
suffix *-ful*	*tru-th-ful*	STEM	adjective	takes comparative index *more*
suffix *-ness*	*tru-th-ful-ness*	STEM	non-count noun	
prefix *un-*	*un-truth-ful-ness*	STEM	non-count noun	

A simple stem consists just of a root, with no derivational affix. *True* is a monosyllabic adjective and forms a comparative with suffix *-er*, as in *Mary gave a truer account of the incident than John.* Adding suffix *-th* produces stem *tru-th*, which is a count noun; that is, it can take plural suffix -s, as in *I'm going to tell you a few home truths*. The further derivational suffix -*ful* produces stem *truth-ful*, which is an adjective of a different kind from *true*. One speaks of a *true story* but of a *truthful person*. Since it is disyllabic and ending in a consonant, *truthful* forms a comparative with *more*, as in *Mary is more truthful than John*.

Derivational suffix -*ness* creates stem *truth-ful-ness*, an abstract noun referring to something which cannot be counted (it does not take plural -*s*); for example, *Truthfulness is a trait to be esteemed*. Then there is the prefix *un-*; unlike -*th*, -*ful*, and -*ness*, this does not change word class but simply adds a negative meaning. In fact, *un-* could be added at any stage in the derivation, since we do have adjective *un-true*, noun *un-tru-th*, and adjective *un-tru-th-ful* in addition to noun *un-tru-th-ful-ness*.

After the derivational suffixes (if any) have applied, an inflection appropriate to the word class is added, to create a full word. English has much less inflection than a language such as Latin or German, but it is important. A count noun, for instance, must bear one of the two number inflections; this is either suffix -*s*, for plural, or a zero suffix, for singular. For example, *magnet-s* refers to more than one of these metal objects, and *magnet* to just one. The zero suffix (or, if you prefer, the lack of an explicit suffix) here indicates singular number.

Applying derivational suffix -*ise* (an alternative form is -*ize*), we get verb stem *magnet-ise* 'make into a magnet'. To be a functioning word, this must take one of the inflectional suffixes applying to verbs in English. These are -*ing* after auxiliary *be*, as in *He is magnet-is-ing it*; or past tense -*ed*, as in *He has magnet-is-ed it*; or -*s* for present tense with a 3rd person singular subject, as in *He magnet-ise-s things for a living*; or zero inflection for present tense with any other subject, as in *We magnet-ise things for a living*. Note that the absence of a non-zero suffix on *magnet-ise* carries a definite meaning: present tense with a subject other than 3rd person singular, just as the plain form of noun *magnet* indicates singular number.

There is also the morphological process of compounding: two roots may form a compound stem, to which derivations and inflections apply as to a simple stem. For example, *class-conscious* with derivation *class-conscious-ness*.

Derivation

The dictionaries we have today focus on morphology. Verb inflections are generally predictable so that there is no need to mention them except in the case of irregularities (for example, *give*, *gave*, *given* and *sing*, *sang*, *sung* in place of what would be regular forms *give-d* and *sing-ed*). A dictionary user may need to know whether a given noun is 'count' (taking plural suffix -*s*) or not, but this information is only sometimes provided.

All derivations based on a given head word should of course be stated and explained; here, dictionaries vary greatly. If a derivation has different stress or vowel quality from the head word, then it is almost always listed separately, and a meaning provided. For example, *atom* /'atəm/ and *atomic* /ə'tɔmik/. But if the derivational process simply adds an affix, with no alteration to the vowels or stress of the root, then dictionaries – by and large – serve us less well.

No two words ever have exactly the same meaning. Yet many dictionaries seem to imply that they do. We typically find *bachelorhood* and *bachelordom* simply listed, with a comma between them, at the end of the entry for *bachelor*. Or else separate entries are listed with one derivation 'defined' as synonymous with the other. But suffixes *-dom* and *-hood* have distinct meanings (as described in the grammar) and so do these two words:

- *bachelorhood* – the state a man is in when not married
- *bachelordom* – the collection of all unmarried men, and the sort of lifestyle they follow

Some nouns form adjectives by means of suffix *-ic*, some with *-ical*, and others with both. There is always a difference. Dictionaries do typically distinguish *historic* from *historical*. But they lump together *geographic* and *geographical*, *philosophic* and *philosophical*. The meanings are not identical. People speak of a *geographic fact* but a *geographical study*, or a *philosophic point* but a *philosophical discussion*, alongside a *historic decision* but a *historical account*. In essence, the *-ic* adjective describes a TYPE of point, fact or decision while *-ical* relates to the MANNER or NATURE of a study, discussion or account.

Some lexical roots have been handed down from Old English while others were borrowed – predominantly in mediaeval times – from Romance languages. The same applies for derivational affixes. Frequently, the two go together: a Germanic affix on a Germanic root and a Romance affix with a Romance root. Romance derivational suffix *-ous* and Germanic *-y* have a similar meaning, roughly 'characterised by'. Almost all nouns which take *-ous* are of Romance origin; for example, *furi-ous*, *humour-ous*, *danger-ous*. The majority of those taking *-y* were inherited from Old English, including *angr-y*, *smell-y*, *mood-y*. There is just a handful of Romance roots with *-y*, such as *chanc(e)-y*, *risk-y*, and *fault-y*.

Generally, a noun will take either one suffix or the other. *Thunder* provides a rare exception, with *thunder-y* (or *thundr-y*) and *thunder-ous*. None of the half-dozen current dictionaries which I have consulted distinguishes the meanings of the two derivations. But there is a difference (as there always is):

- *thunder-y* 'featuring thunder', as in *Thundery weather is forecast for next week*
- *thunder-ous* 'with a noise like thunder', as in *Her performance was greeted with thunderous applause*

One would be unlikely to hear *thunderous weather* or *thundery applause*.

If there are two derivations with similar meanings, it is not sufficient to say that they are almost the same (or to imply that they are exactly the same). The difference may be subtle but it can be a critical matter for indicating to a dictionary user what word to use in which circumstances.

Only Half the Story

Current dictionaries concentrate on morphology (although they don't cover it fully) and pay scant attention to syntax. But some grammatical features span the two facets of grammar. Comparative constructions, for instance, involve the index of comparison being a morphological element, suffix *-er*, for some adjectives, but a syntactic construction with grammatical word *more* for others. Similarly for superlatives with *-est* and *most*.

How does a dictionary deal with this? Well, if an adjective takes *-er* and *-est* this is stated (under *fat* there are listed *fatter*, *fattest*, and so on). If it doesn't take *-er* and *-est*, then nothing is said.

But, as we saw in the previous chapter, adjectives which form comparatives and superlatives fall into three sets:

I   Those which only take *-er* and *-est*, e.g. *quiet, fat, heavy, pretty*
II Those which take either *-er* and *-est* or *more* and *most*, e.g. *clever, lucky, stupid, common*
III Those which only take *more* and *most*, e.g. *famous, superb, ordinary*

A dictionary specifies *-er* and *-est* forms for adjectives of sets I and II. Reading the dictionary in association with a grammar, one could infer that an adjective for which no *-er* and *-est* forms are stated must belong to set III, taking just *more* and *most*. This is correct. But what one can't know from the dictionary entries is which adjectives only take *-er* and *-est* (set I) and which may employ either technique (set II). Not enough information is given to enable the dictionary user to learn the different possibilities for, on the one hand, *quiet* (only *quiet-er* and *quiet-est*) and, on the other hand, *clever* (either *clever-er* and *clever-est* or, as an alternative, *more clever* and *most clever*). Only half the story is there.

One important type of derivation is creating a noun stem from a verb root. Such nominalisations can have several meanings, which include:

• Describing a unit of activity, e.g. *announce-ment, perform-ance*. These are count nouns and can take plural suffix *-s*, as in *announce-ment-s, perform-ance-s*.

• Describing an extended activity, e.g. *understand-ing, guid-ance*. These are not count nouns and do not take plural *-s*.

Verbs in a single semantic set do not necessarily all form nominalisations in the same way, or have the same meanings. Consider nouns formed from some of the verbs of the 'liking' set (mentioned on page 8):

VERB	COUNT NOUN	NON-COUNT NOUN
like	like	lik-ing (for)
love	love	love (for)
hate	hate	hat-red (of)
dislike	dislike	dislike (of)
prefer	–	prefer-ence (for)
loathe	–	loath-ing (of)
abhor	–	abhor-rence (of)
detest	–	detest-ation (of)

Four of the verbs occur as count nouns with the same form, and can be used in the frame *Mary has three pet – s*. That is:

Mary has three pet likes/loves/hates/dislikes

Corresponding to all eight verbs there are non-count nominalisations (involving a variety of derivational suffixes). These can occur in the frame *John has a strong – for/of cheddar cheese*. That is:

John has a strong liking/love/preference for cheddar cheese
John has a strong hatred/dislike/loathing/abhorrence/detestation of cheddar cheese

Note that the positive words generally take preposition *for*, and the negative ones *of*.

A critical point is that *like* and *hate* have different count and non-count forms (*like* and *hate* as against *lik-ing* and *hat-red*) but that *love* and *dislike* have the same form. (There is a derivation *lov-ing* but it is of a quite different character, being an adjective.)

Standard dictionaries do give the nominalised forms and state whether a word can be both verb and noun. But they do not distinguish between count and non-count nominalisations, or specify that *love* and *dislike* may be either, but *like* and *hate* only the former. Some information is provided for the dictionary user, but not enough for them to know exactly how to use each word. Once again, we have morphological forms without the necessary concomitant syntactic information. Only a part of the story is told.

Dictionaries specify whether a lexical head word or derivation is noun, verb, adjective, or adverb. This is seldom sufficient, especially in the case of adverbs, which have varying syntactic possibilities.

Adverbs are formed from many adjectives by adding derivational suffix *-ly*. Going back to derivations based on *true*, earlier in this chapter, we can add:

- From adjective *true* is formed adverb *tru-ly*.
- From derived adjective *tru-th-ful* is formed adverb *tru-th-ful-ly*.

Truly and *truthfully* are both adverbs but with rather different possibilities. *Truly* may be placed at the beginning of a clause, or before the verbal element, or at the end (with slight differences of emphasis). For example:

> Truly I don't mind looking after mother
> I truly don't mind looking after mother
> I don't mind looking after mother truly

In contrast, *truthfully* is restricted to the end of a clause:

> James spoke truthfully

Adverbs from the same semantic set may vary in their possible placement. Consider:

> $\boxed{W}$ they $\boxed{X}$ walked $\boxed{Y}$ away $\boxed{Z}$

Adverb *rapidly* may be included at any of the four positions $\boxed{W}$, $\boxed{X}$, $\boxed{Y}$, or $\boxed{Z}$. One can say *Rapidly they walked away* or *They rapidly walked away* or *They walked rapidly away* or *They walked away rapidly*; the same applies for *swiftly* and *slowly*. But adverb *fast*, although it has a similar meaning to *rapidly* and *swiftly*, may only be included at the end of a clause, in position $\boxed{Z}$. (These forms are discussed further in chapter 9.)

As a further illustration, consider the frame

> $\boxed{X}$ she is $\boxed{Y}$ speaking $\boxed{Z}$

Adverb *now* may occur in all three positions, $\boxed{X}$, $\boxed{Y}$, and $\boxed{Z}$. *Certainly* can be in $\boxed{X}$ and $\boxed{Y}$ but not $\boxed{Z}$, and *well* in $\boxed{Z}$ but not $\boxed{X}$ or $\boxed{Y}$.

There is a fuller discussion of the syntactic possibilities for adverbs on pages 181–3.

The section on adverbs in any grammar should describe their possible positionings in clause structure, and the semantic implications of each (see chapter 13). But it is not the role of a grammar to provide an exhaustive list of which adverbs may be used in which slot. There are many hundreds of adverbs in English. The grammar provides the framework and it is then incumbent upon the dictionary to state the placement possibilities for every adverb in its alphabetical listing. The predominant failure to do so means that, in this respect, dictionaries are only telling a minor part of the story.

Then there are complement clause constructions. We noted in the previous chapter that *like* takes -ING, THAT, and (FOR) TO clauses, *dislike* just the -ING and THAT varieties while *detest* is restricted *to* -ING complement clauses. If a dictionary user is to learn how to use the language, this information should be made available; it is not there in a standard dictionary.

Dictionaries deal with words. We have seen how they provide a good deal of information (although not enough) on word structure but appear unconcerned about word function. Then there is the matter of meaning. As one proceeds through the alphabetical listing, each word – considered in isolation – is provided with a definition. What this doesn't do is tell readers how and when to use one word rather than another with a similar meaning.

Investigating Meaning

When the renowned anthropologist Bronislaw Malinowski was working in the Trobriand Islands, just off New Guinea, he wrestled with the problem of translating words between languages, of characterising the meaning of a word. This could only be achieved, he maintained, 'by placing it within its context of culture, by putting it within the set of kindred and cognate expressions, by contrasting it with its opposites, by grammatical analysis and above all by a number of well-chosen examples'.

The referents of words divide up the world. Opposite meanings are fairly straightforward; for example, *pull* as against *push*. Then there may be a number of specific terms included within the meaning of a general one (they are hyponyms of it). Relating to *pull* there are *tug*, *jerk*, *pluck*, *drag*, and *tow* (among others) while for *push* we have *shove*, *thrust*, and *ram*. Each of these has meaning with respect to others in its set.

Basic colour terms should be mutually exclusive. A language learner will only be able to use the word *brown* in an acceptable manner if they appreciate where its zone of reference gives way to that of *green* in one direction, and of *red* in another. There can be fuzzy areas between colours: *brown* then *greeny-brown*, then *browny-green*, then *green*. To say simply 'green is the colour of grass' is fine if one only wants to talk about grass, but is of less help when choosing a matching shade of paint.

Consider a set of words describing vocal communication: *mumble*, *mutter*, *shout*, *talk*, and *whisper*. Of these, *talk* is the most general term, with the others relating to it in varying ways.

- *Whisper* is used for talking in a low voice without allowing the vocal cords to vibrate, and *mumble* for talking indistinctly so that it is hard to make out the words. Both describe a kind of talking; one can say *talk in a whisper*, or *talk in a mumbling way*.
- In contrast, one would be unlikely to say *talk in a mutter*. Muttering is an alternative to talking normally – it is typically used by a person for complaining about something in a deliberately low voice, so that not everyone can hear. The muttering person may be venting their frustration but in such a way that the person complained about does not hear it and get annoyed.

- *Shout* is used for talking loudly; one could say *He can only talk in a shout.* A shout can involve language or just some emotive noise. There are specialised hyponyms, illustrated by *yell in anger, scream in pain, holler out a warning.*

Verb *speak* can often be substituted for *talk* but they are far from synonymous. If one *speaks to the manager* about something it is likely to be a complaint (perhaps about a minion's unspeakable rudeness) whereas *talking to the manager* may be friendly interaction. As a general capability, someone may *speak French,* but on a particular occasion they will *talk in French.* A person can *speak the truth* and a group may *talk it over.* And so on.

This is a sampler of how meanings of words may link together in some places and diverge in others. A dictionary user needs to be aware of the significant difference between *mumbling* and *muttering* (despite these two words sounding similar), something that can be shown by following Malinowski's suggestion of considering a word 'within the set of kindred and cognate expressions'. The technique is illustrated for *finish, cease,* and *stop* in the next chapter, and for further semantic sets in chapters 6, 9, and 12.

The traditional way of making a dictionary involves a great deal of copying. Firstly, look up the entries for a given word in several other well-thought-of dictionaries. The lexicographer uses their judgement to blend these together, sometimes extending them (but sometimes not; see the lengthy discussion in chapter 10). They may look for instances of the word in a corpus or two, and thereby amend the entry. The dogma goes: it is silly to keep on 're-inventing the wheel'. Earlier dictionaries have definitions for the word (probably copied in part from one another). This is what the meaning *is;* all that is needed is a little fine-tuning. Thus, everything stays more-or-less the same from dictionary to dictionary in what is (no doubt considered to be) the best of all possible worlds.

Alternatively, one can relegate tradition to the background and start all over again, working from first principles and with a fresh viewpoint. Do not depend on what has gone before. Do not have *a priori* notions. Do not be prejudiced by what other people have said. Simply let the semantics and syntax of a set of words talk to you, and reveal its basic patternings.

This alternative technique for investigating meaning is as follows.

- Firstly, the lexicographer must have a native or near-native-speaker knowledge of the language, since the method involves making critical judgments of acceptability and felicity.
- Select a set of related words. The lexicographer examines each word in turn, considering the senses they know of, and the grammatical possibilities for each. Properties of the individual words in the semantic set are continually being compared.

- Consult a representative textual corpus and identify canonical examples of each word in the corpus. Investigate (by the lexicographer's own judgment) whether other words from the set may be substituted for a given word in each of its frames. If they can be substituted, this will sometimes involve little difference in meaning, but other times there will be a significant difference (the nature of this difference is likely to be crucial).
- Work out a conceptual template for the set of words in terms of a handful of critical notions (particular to this semantic set). There is discussion of the idea of 'critical notions' on pages 119–20.
- After completing the task, working from first principles, it is of course appropriate to see what earlier scholars have said about the words under investigation. The lexicographer has not relied on previous work, but it would be perverse not to benefit from it, at a pre-final stage.

The next section provides a brief illustration of this technique, and in particular the idea of substitution, for the two words *help* and *assist*.

Help and *Assist*

We give here an example of distinguishing the meanings and uses of two words with similar meanings, by noting the contexts in which both may be used (and the slight differences in meaning) and those in which just one may be used.

The words considered are:

- *Help* /help/ – verb *help* goes back to Old English *helpan*, with the same meaning; nouns *help* and *helper* /'helpə/ developed in Middle English times.
- *Assist* /ə'sist/ – verb *assist* and nouns *assistance* /ə'sistəns/ and *assistant* /ə'sistənt/ were all borrowed from Romance into Middle English. (It comes from prefix *ad-* plus *sistere*, a form of the verb 'stand' in Latin, and this goes back to Proto-Indo-European verb *stā-* 'stand'.)

These have similar meanings, and there are many contexts in which either can be used, with minor difference in meaning. Each of the following sentences occurred with the first-cited word, but the other (added in parentheses) seems also to be acceptable. First, examples with verbs *help* and *assist*:

(1) After a lifetime of helping (assisting) others, she has retired
(2) Julia's daughter will assist (help) her in selecting new curtains
(3) We will assist (help) in every way possible

And now three with nouns *help* and *assistance*:

(4) The unemployed miners are asking for help (assistance)
(5) They need all the help (assistance) they can get
(6) She thanked all her colleagues for their assistance (help)

The Romance form *assist* is regarded as slightly more refined than the Germanic form, *help*. Where both are possible, *assist* may be preferred within a formal context:

(7) The Government is prepared to extend limited financial assistance to those unemployed miners who have a family to support

Financial help would be perfectly possible here, but *financial assistance* is a little posher (*financial aid* would be posher still). This is also why *assistance* was used in (6); *help* would be equally appropriate but sounds a trifle crude.
    The basic meaning of *help* is:

make things better or easier

For example:

(8) She took a deep breath to help (to) control her feelings
    (to control her feelings better)
(4) The unemployed miners are asking for help
    (to make their lives better/easier)
(9) She helped the cripple with getting into bed
    (made it easier for him)
(10) It helped (to) clarify his understanding
    (made him understand more clearly (better))

Help is a general term, with *assist* a hyponym, providing further specification. For just about every sentence with *assist* or *assistance*, *help* can be substituted for it. The reverse does not apply; for example, *assist* may not replace *help* in (8) or (10).
    If one hears 'X assists Y', there is the implication that there is a formal difference between the two participants: Y is more powerful, more important, or more senior than X. Often X has a secondary role, and Y the primary role. There is no such implication for 'X helps Y'.
    Consider:

(11) Jim Moffatt is assisting Professor Jensen with her book

One infers that the Professor is doing the actual writing of the book, with Jim Moffatt making this easier for her by looking up references, making the index, checking proofs, etc. If *help* were used in place of *assist* here, it would suggest that Professor Jensen is writing some of the chapters and Jim Moffatt the remainder.
    If *assist* is used in sentence (2) it implies that Julia is the main person in the furniture-choosing exercise, with her daughter perhaps offering ancillary advice about the colour scheme. In contrast, if (2) used *help*, it would imply that the two of them have a fairly equal role in the choosing.

The agentive nominalisations derived from these two verbs clearly reinforce their meanings:

- *Assistant* always indicates a secondary function; in (11) Jim Moffatt is Professor Jensen's assistant. It can function as noun or as modifier, as in *assistant manager, assistant secretary*.
- Whereas *assistant* is a very common word, *helper* is comparatively rare. It is basically a noun (scarcely ever a modifier) and is used when one does not want to impute a lower status to the helper. For example, the gnomes helping to prepare Christmas gifts for children could be called *Santa's helpers*. At a formal function, the organiser might have *a bevy of assistants*. At a church bazaar, there are likely to be *a number of helpers* for the vicar.

Whereas *assist* is pretty well restricted to somewhat formal situations, *help* has a wide use. One can say *He asked for help* or *He asked for assistance*. But only *help* (not *assistance*) is likely to be used in:

(12)   She screamed for help

Similarly for the cry of a drowning person: *Help me!* or just *Help!* Or, urging the onlookers: *Help him!*

Grammatical possibilities are different for the two verbs. *Help* is commonly used with a TO complement clause in its object slot, as in (8), (10) and:

(13)   Father's advice didn't help Max (to) improve his game
(14)   The poultice helped her (to) get to sleep

Interestingly, the *to* of a TO complement clause may be optionally omitted after *help*. (The only other verb which behaves like his is *make*; this obligatorily omits the *to* from a TO complement clause in an active sentence but includes it in a passive sentence – *She made him run* and *He was made to run*.)

Assist very seldom takes a complement clause. If one wanted to employ *assist* in (13) or (14), the sentences would have to be rephrased (and *help* would still be possible):

(13')   Father's advice didn't assist/help Max in improving his game
(14')   The poultice assisted/helped her with getting to sleep

There is a special sense of *help* to do with serving up a meal, as in *Mother helped Simon to another piece of pie* (a *helping* of pie), or *Simon helped himself to a third helping*.

This discussion has briefly illustrated how to explicate the meanings of similar words by studying contexts in which one has been used, checking whether the other may be substituted for it and, if so, what the difference in sense might be. Needless to say, the write-up of a semantic set will present the results in a systematic manner, rather than recapitulating the procedure followed in arriving at them.

There is a good deal more which could be said about the meanings and functions of *help* and *assist*. The aim here has been to illustrate the methodology involved.

We can now shift focus to another semantic set. To set the stage, a large modern dictionary has the following entries:

> **finish**: bring to an end, come to the end of, complete
>
> **cease**: stop, bring to or come to an end
>
> **stop**: (a) put an end to ... (b) cease from motion or speaking or action... (c) close or block up (a hole or leak etc.)

The relevant sense of verb ***complete*** is given as simply *finish*.

Other dictionaries provide similar information.

The next chapter studies the semantic set centred on *finish*, *cease*, and *stop*.

3   Semantic Set: *Finish, Cease*, and *Stop*

We here focus on three verbs with comparable meanings:

- *finish* /ˈfiniʃ/ was borrowed into Middle English from French *finiss-*, a development from Latin verb *finir*, 'to end, limit, set bounds to'.
- *cease* /siːs/ came into Middle English at about the same time, from French *cesser*, emanating from Latin *cessāre* 'to cease, be inactive', this being a frequentative form of *cēdere* 'yield'.
- *stop* /stɒp/ goes back to the Old English verb *stoppian* (only attested with intensive prefix *for-* as *for-stoppian*) 'to close up'. It has a range of meanings in the modern language, including the following three senses:
  - *stop₁*, transitive verb relating to an activity, shown either by an -ING complement clause, as in *We stopped singing (when the pianist fell ill)* or a noun referring to an activity, as in *We stopped the recital (when the pianist fell ill)*. There is also a causative version of this sense, as in *The headmistress stopped us singing/the recital*.
  - *stop₂*, intransitive verb describing interruption of motion, as in *They stopped (in order) to look at the map* and *We'll stop for the night at the inn*. This also has a causative version, as in *The policeman stopped the speeding motorist/ the thief*.
  - *stop₃*, transitive verb with concrete object, as in *She stopped (up) the hole in the dam* (this continues the Old English sense 'to close up').

We are here primarily concerned with the *stop₁* sense, although *stop₂* cannot be overlooked since it interferes with the grammatical possibilities for *stop₁*.

These three verbs have similar meanings, all relating to something which had been done and is no longer being done. Their contrasting meanings are exemplified in:

(1) John has finished [reading *Pilgrim's Progress*]ₒ
     (he has read to the end of the book)
(2) John has stopped₁ [reading *Pilgrim's Progress*]ₒ
     (he finds it heavy-going and is taking a break, but intends to resume reading it later on)

(3) John has ceased [reading *Pilgrim's Progress*]$_O$
     (he got tired of the book part-way through and has no plans to read
     any more)

The essential difference between these verbs is:

- Verb *finish* has 'object orientation'. In (1), the referent of the object of the verb, *Pilgrim's Progress*, has been fully read; that is, there is nothing left to read.
- In contrast, verbs *stop*$_1$ and *cease* have 'subject orientation'; John has made a decision not to continue reading the book, on either a temporary or a permanent basis.

The three main varieties of complement clause construction were outlined on pages 7–9. A THAT clause describes a fact – as in *I heard [that Mary had a baby]* – and is not appropriate with *finish*, *cease*, or *stop*$_1$. An -ING clause describes an activity and all three verbs may have an -ING complement clause in their object slot, as illustrated in (1)–(3). A TO clause relates to a purpose or intention on the part of the subject. *Finish* has object orientation; it is thus not eligible for a TO complement clause. However, since *cease* and *stop*$_1$ have subject orientation, they should be able to take a TO complement clause, as an alternative to an -ING one. In fact, *cease* does accept a TO clause – instead of (3) one could say *John has ceased [to read* Pilgrim's Progress*]*. But *stop*$_1$ may not occur in this construction. The reason for this will be given in a few pages' time.

The semantic and grammatical characteristics of *finish* can now be outlined, followed by those for *cease* and *stop*.

Finish

As in example (1), *finish* typically takes an -ING complement clause, referring to an activity. If it is clear from the context of speaking what activity is involved, the verb of a transitive complement clause may be omitted. For example:

(4) John has finished (reading) Pilgrim's Progress
(5) Mary has finished (sending out) the invitations
(6) Tom will soon finish (chopping) the firewood

One noun may be in object function for several verbs after *finish*, as in:

(7)   Anna Jenkins has just finished (writing) a spy story
(8)   Anna Jenkins has just finished (illustrating) a spy story
(9)   Anna Jenkins has just finished (translating) a spy story
(10) Anna Jenkins has just finished (binding) a spy story
(11) Anna Jenkins has just finished (filming) a spy story
(12) Anna Jenkins has just finished (reading) a spy story

On hearing *Anna Jenkins has just finished a spy story*, it would be unclear what she had been doing to it if you knew nothing about her. If you know she is a writer then the underlying structure (7) would be inferred, if an illustrator (8), if a translator (9), if a book-binder (10). If Anna were a film director or cinematographer or something else to do with movies, then (11) would be inferred. If none of these, then (12) is the most likely interpretation, since just about everyone reads books.

An elliptical sentence such as *Anna Jenkins has just finished a spy story* must be understood as referring to a particular activity, described by the omitted verb. If two such sentences are coordinated, the same activity must be involved (that is, they must have the same underlying verb). For example, on hearing

(13)   Anna Jenkins has just finished a spy story and Russell Dawes has just finished a romance

one infers that they have been doing the same thing to the spy story and the romance, respectively – both writing, or both illustrating, or both translating, etc. Sentence (13) would scarcely be said if Anna Jenkins had been *writing* a spy story and Russell Dawes *reading* a romance.

Sentences (4–13) illustrate verbs which can be omitted from an -ING complement clause after *finish*, if their identity could be inferred from the context. However, this is only possible when the verb describes a typical activity applying to the object. One can omit the verb from *He's finished (picking) the apples, He's finished (eating) the apples, She's finished (sewing) the dress*, and *They've finished (drinking) their coffee*, but scarcely from *They've finished firing inefficient workers, They've finished counting the audience*, or *We've finished choosing new furniture*.

If *finish* occurs with a concrete noun, then it is likely to be the reduction from an -ING complement clause. For instance, *Edna has finished the wall* might be said if she had finished building it or finished painting it (and we can infer from the context which of these it is).

As an alternative to an -ING complement clause describing an activity, *finish* may take as object an abstract noun describing an activity; for example, *She has finished the job, They have finished their packing, Fred has finished his dinner*. Rather more common than this is for *finish* to be used intransitively with an activity noun as subject, as in *The fight finished when Jason James was knocked out, Dinner finishes at eight o'clock*, and *The game isn't finished until the referee blows his whistle*.

Rain, as a verb, takes subject *it*; thus, *It has finished raining*. Alternatively, *rain* can be used as a noun, in intransitive subject function: *The rain has finished*.

Adverb *up* has the sense 'do fully' as in *Clean up the room!* and *Break up the statue of the deposed leader (into lots of little bits)!* It may be used after *finish* – typically with a verb of consumption – to emphasise the idea of 'doing fully'; for example, *He finished up the beer. Finish* may also be followed by *off*, typically referring to something which was already partly done, as in *There was just one piece of pie remaining, and the schoolboy finished it off.*

Finish may take an object referring to a period of time, as in *They finished the season (off) with a win* and *We finished the day (off) with a feast.* Alternatively, the noun referring to time can be an intransitive subject: *The season finished with a win, The day finished with a feast.*

Used as a noun, *finish* can relate to the closing stages of an activity, as in *The race had an exciting finish* (alternatively, one could say *They finished the race in an exciting manner*, or *The race finished in an exciting manner*). A rather different sense of the noun is to refer to the result of a finished activity – *After all that polishing, the surface had a shiny finish.*

Derived adjective *finishing* may relate to the way in which an activity finished – *He put on a fast finishing spurt* – or to the place at which something finishes – *The judge stood abreast of the finishing line.*

Complete is primarily an adjective – as in *The complete works of Charles Dickens* – but also functions as a transitive verb whose meaning overlaps with that of *finish*. It refers to some definite and significant piece of work. *Complete* can substitute for *finish* in (4–11) since each of these refers to making something, but not in (12) since reading a book is an entirely passive activity.

Whereas *finish* can be used both transitively and intransitively, as in:

(14)   Anna Jenkins finished her book with an epigram
(15)   Anna Jenkins' book finished with an epigram

complete can be substituted for *finish* in (14):

(16)   Anna Jenkins completed her book with an epigram

but there is no correspondent to (15) with *complete* used intransitively. That is, ♦*Anna Jenkins' book completed with an epigram* is not acceptable.

Another difference between the two verbs is that *complete* (but not *finish*) can be used for adding the final component(s) to something, as in *You must complete the form by filling in each box*, and *The director completed the cast with an actor we'd never heard of.*

Stop and *Cease*

We can now examine *stop$_1$* and *cease*. First, attention must be paid to the second sense of *stop*, an intransitive verb referring to interruption of motion. This can be introduced through a digression.

There are two construction types which are similar on the surface but in fact have quite different structures and meanings. We can compare:

(17)   Bill went (in order) to swim
(18)   Bill intended [to swim]$_O$

Sentence (17) involves two intransitive clauses *Bill went* and *Bill swim*, linked by coordinator *in order to*, which typically reduces and becomes just *to*. In contrast, (18) has transitive verb *intended*, whose object slot is filled by complement clause *to swim*. Main clause and complement clause have the same subject, and its second occurrence is omitted. (Alternatively, they may have different subjects, and the complement clause subject is then preceded by *for*, as in *Bill intended [for Hilary to swim]$_O$.*) Note that the *to* in (18) can not be expanded to *in order to* (that is, one cannot say ♦*Bill intended in order to swim*).

Although the sentences *Bill went to swim* and *Bill intended to swim* appear to have the same structure, their meanings are quite different. They can be distinguished through knowing that *go* is an intransitive verb which cannot take a (FOR) TO complement clause, whereas *intend* is a transitive verb which typically has a (FOR) TO clause in its object slot.

An important point for the discussion here is that a clause with intransitive verb *stop$_2$* may be conjoined to a following clause by means of the conjunction *in order to*, which can be reduced to just *to*:

(19)   Robin stopped$_2$ (in order) to look at the scenery
(20)   Robin stopped$_2$ (in order) to eat

A few pages back, it was explained that since *finish* has object orientation, it may not take the Potential type of complement clause, marked by (FOR) TO. However, *stop$_1$* and *cease* have subject orientation, and they should be able to take a Potential complement clause, as an alternative to the Activity type illustrated in (2–3). The two possibilities can be illustrated for *cease*:

(21)   He gradually ceased [believing in God]$_O$ during the war years
(22)   He ceased [to believe in God]$_O$ when his daughter died

Sentence (21) refers to an activity, the gradual loosening of a faith, whereas (22) describes the rather sudden and definite realisation of a potentiality.

By virtue of its meaning (one cannot cease something for someone else), *cease* can only take a potential clause where main clause and complement clause subjects are identical, and omitted from the second clause.

Let us now compare the grammatical behaviour of *cease* with that of *stop$_1$*.

We will see soon that *stop$_1$* has more of a volitional nuance than *cease*, so that we should expect it to occur pre-eminently with a Potential TO complement clause. It does not do so, and is restricted to the Activity type, as in (2). This is because of interference from its homonym, $stop_2$. Compare:

(23)   Robin ceased [eating]$_O$ Activity -ING complement clause
(24)   Robin ceased [to eat]$_O$ Potential TO complement clause
(25)   Robin stopped [eating]$_O$ transitive $stop_1$ plus Activity -ING
                                         complement clause
(26)   Robin stopped to eat   intransitive $stop_2$ plus *(in order) to*
                                         conjunction

The verb *stop* in (25) must be interpreted as $stop_1$, a transitive verb with an -ING complement clause in object function. But (26), *Robin stopped to eat*, is always interpreted as the intransitive verb $stop_2$ followed by conjunction *(in order) to*, as in (20). The intransitive verb $stop_2$ thus usurps the possibility of a TO complement clause after transitive $stop_1$, confining this verb to an -ING complement clause.

Finish, with its object orientation, focuses on the object of an -ING complement clause. If the nature of the activity can be inferred from the referent of this object phrase, together with the listener's general understanding of the situation involved, then the complement clause verb may be omitted, as in (4–12). (Note that this omission is also possible for *start* and *begin*.) In contrast, omission of a complement clause verb is not possible after $stop_1$ or *cease*. For example, *reading* may be omitted from (1) but not from (2) or (3). As another example, one can say *She's finished decorating the Christmas tree* or just *She's finished the Christmas tree*, but *decorating* may not be omitted from *She's stopped$_1$/ceased decorating the Christmas tree*. The subject orientation of $stop_1$ and *cease* requires statement of the activity which the subject is involved in.

Stop$_1$ and *cease* have similarity of meaning, but show important differences. In essence:

- ***Stop$_1$*** often (but not invariably) implies volition on the part of the subject, and may refer to a definite (perhaps sudden) action, perhaps only on a temporary basis.
- ***Cease*** is typically used of something which has been happening continuously for some time but is no longer happening, and perhaps will never happen again.

This contrast is brought out in:

(27)   Hattie Fisher has stopped campaigning
                (during the period of mourning)
(28)   Hattie Fisher has ceased to campaign
                (for good)

There are a number of contexts for which *stop₁* is possible, but *cease* may not be used, and vice versa. There is also quite a bit of overlap, which can exemplify the contrasts of meaning (and also that between -ING and TO complement clauses for *cease*). For example:

(29)   Dr Fell stopped annoying me
                 (he realised that what he was doing annoyed me, and didn't do
                 it any more)
(30)   Dr Fell's behaviour gradually ceased annoying me
                 (over time, I became used to it)
(31)   Dr Fell's behaviour ceased to annoy me
                 (once I realised that it was the result of a chronic illness over
                 which he had no control)

In (29) Dr Fell had been doing something which annoyed me and then voluntarily didn't do it any more. In (30) and (31) it was Dr Fell's behaviour which annoyed me. This didn't change but I just got used to it after a time, in (30), or I realised I should make allowances after learning about his illness, in (31).

   Although *cease* can take both TO and -ING complement clauses, the TO variety is the most frequent. As already stated, *stop₁* only accepts the -ING kind. Typically, one may hear either of:

(32)   Nicolas Hicks stopped₁ being an MP when he lost his seat at the election
                 (but he will stand again at the next election)
(33)   Nicolas Hicks ceased to be an MP when he lost his seat at the election
                 (and he has now retired from public life)

It is also possible to say, with the same meaning, *Nicholas Hicks ceased being an MP when he lost his seat at the election*, but this would be less common.

   Like *finish*, both *stop₁* and *cease* may be used intransitively, with an activity noun as subject. We can compare:

(34)   The trade negotiations finished
                 (a deal was reached)
(35)   The trade negotiations stopped₁
                 (for the weekend, but talks will resume on Monday)
(36)   The trade negotiations ceased
                 (there was no hope of a deal being reached)

and:

(37)   The rain has finished
                 (the clouds have disgorged all their precipitation and gone away;
                 it is unlikely that there will be any more rain today)
(38)   The rain has stopped₁
                 (but there are still dark clouds, and the rain will probably start
                 again soon)

(39) The rains have ceased
      (that was the last storm of the wet season, and the dry season is now upon us)

We can now illustrate some sentences in which only *cease* may be used (not *stop₁*), since reference is to something which had been happening continuously and will never happen again:

(40) When Major Smythe dies, the agreement will cease and be void
(41) When she ceases to reside on the island, all her entitlements will cease
(42) After the entire population of Carthage had been deported, the city ceased to exist

Both *stop₁* and *cease* may be used in a statement such as:

(43) Eventually, the child ceased to cry
(44) Eventually, the child stopped₁ crying

However, a corresponding imperative is likely to be restricted to *stop₁*, since this relates to the volition of the person crying:

(45) Stop₁ crying!

The response to this could be:

(46) I cannot stop₁ crying

This also relates to volition, so that only *stop₁* is possible. (♦*I cannot cease to cry/crying* is entirely infelicitous.)

Where both *cease* and *stop₁* are possible, the choice between them may relate to style of speech (or of writing). *Cease* sounds posher and may be preferred in more formal registers with *stop₁* being used in indecorous speech. A highfalutin alternative to (45) could be:

(47) For pity's sake, child, cease your infernal crying!

We can now examine causatives. Since *finish* describes the referent of the object argument being fully dealt with, it is not amenable to being causativised. In contrast, *stop₁* refers to something being done at the subject's volition and a causer may be introduced to control this volition. Compare:

(48) Fred stopped₁ chopping firewood
(49) John stopped₁ Fred (from) chopping firewood

Another example is:

(50) Prince Igor stopped₁ his daughter (from) marrying a gypsy

Note that *from* may optionally be added after the underlying subject in causative constructions such as (49) and (50).

It is interesting that although *cease* is like *stop₁* in having subject orientation, it cannot be used as a causative. That is, *ceased* can be substituted for *stopped₁* in (48) but not in (49) or (50). This may be (at least in part) because *stop$_1$* has a stronger implication of volition than *cease*.

In place of a complement clause, *stop$_1$* may have an activity noun in object function:

(51)   The government stopped$_1$ the building of a new stadium

However, this is ambiguous between (a) the government was building a new stadium themselves and stopped doing so, and (b) a causative sense: someone else was building a new stadium and the government stopped them from doing so. Note that *cease* could scarcely be substituted for *stop$_1$* in (51).

Prevent (from) has an overlap of meaning with the causative sense of *stop$_1$*; for example, it could be substituted for *stop$_1$* in (49) and (50). A difference is that *John stopped$_1$ Fred (from) chopping firewood* could be used either (a) if Fred was part-way through the job and John wouldn't let him do it any more, or (b) if John wouldn't let Fred commence the task, whereas *John prevented Fred (from) chopping firewood* only has meaning (b).

Stop$_2$, the 'interruption of motion' sense, can also be used causatively; alongside *The train stopped$_2$* one can say *The driver stopped$_2$ the train*. When used as a noun, *stop* has the second sense; it can mean a place to stop, as in *They waited at the bus stop*, or the activity of stopping, as in *The train came to a complete stop*.

Definitions from two large modern dictionaries were quoted at the end of the previous chapter:

> **finish:** bring to an end, come to the end of, complete
> **cease:** stop, bring to or come to an end
> **stop:** (a) put an end to ... (b) cease from motion or speaking or action... (c) close block up (a hole or leak etc.)

Note that the definitions for *finish* and *cease* show overlap, that *cease* is defined in terms of *stop*, and *stop* (b) in terms of *cease*.

These scarcely do justice to the semantic and grammatical characters of the three verbs, and they certainly do not provide adequate information to a dictionary user concerning when and why to use one verb rather than another.

This chapter has provided a first outline of the semantic set *finish, cease,* and *stop*. When incorporated within an online dictionary/thesaurus, there would be cross-references to sets dealing with related verbs such as *complete, conclude, terminate, end, close, quit, desist, discontinue, leave off, check, halt,* and also *start, begin,* and *commence*.

The first three chapters have explained how a language works, outlined the tasks that a dictionary should confront, and provided a brief illustration of one semantic set. We can now embark on a more-or-less chronological account of how present-day dictionaries came to be the way they are – the gradual development out of bilingual glossaries, copying, some innovations, more copying, a little further refinement, and then marking time.

4 Explaining Hard Words

In the fifth and sixth centuries CE, England was invaded by the Angles, Saxons, and Jutes, Germanic tribes speaking mutually intelligible dialects. The language they developed in the new land was called Anglo-Saxon (later referred to as Old English, OE). Viking tribes, speaking Old Norse (closely related to Anglo-Saxon) arrived in the ninth century; the words they contributed to the vocabulary included *gate, haven, husband, root,* and *skin.* There was some Latin influence on Anglo-Saxon with the arrival of Christianity towards the end of the seventh century; among loans from Latin into OE were *sock, hymn, priest, history, butter,* and *kitchen.*

Christianity brought literacy, and thence a literature in OE. There was prose and poetic composition, both religious and secular – notably the *Anglo-Saxon Chronicle* and *Beowulf.* But works written in Latin were of major importance, and there arose a need for assistance in reading them. Students would scratch a 'gloss' above or below a hard word in the Latin text (or in the margin) explaining it. Most of the glosses were simpler Latin words – so this was like an embryo monolingual dictionary – but some were in Old English, and a few in Old French – so this was the foundation for a bilingual dictionary.

Glosses written in a particular text would be of use to another scholar reading the same text, but nothing more. So glosses were gathered together in general lists, for common use. A handful of such 'glossaries' are known from OE times. Some are arranged by semantic fields, others in a rough alphabetical order. Often this just involved grouping together all words, commencing with 'A', then all with 'B', and so on (words being given in any order within each letter). Sometimes attention was paid to the first two letters: all those beginning with 'AB', then with 'AC', 'AD', 'AE', and so on.

What is believed to be the oldest glossary – from the early eighth century – is preserved in only one copy, in the library of Corpus Christi College, Cambridge. The 'Corpus glossary' has 8,712 head words, about three-quarters of which are explained in Latin, and the remainder in OE. Three entries of the latter sort are:

LATIN	OLD ENGLISH
sorix	mūs
cepa	ynnilaec, cipe
soccus	socc, slebescoh

A single equivalent was given for *sorix* 'mouse' but two OE words were offered for the others. *Cepa* (or *caepa*) was 'onion' in Latin with *ynnilaec* and *cipe* being alternative names in Old English for the vegetable. The Latin word *soccus* referred to 'a light shoe or slipper (as used among the Greeks)'. Two English translations were offered, *socc* 'sock' and *slebescoh* (also written as *slēfescoh* or *slīefescoh*) 'slipper', a type of *scoh* 'shoe'. The English word *sock* was a loan from Latin *soccus* into Old English, and this appears to be its earliest occurrence in writing.

Almost three hundred years later, the English abbot Aelfric (c955–c1010) produced the first grammar of Latin written in English and appended after it a Latin-to-OE glossary. This was intended for teaching Latin to Benedictine monks at Cerne Abbey in Dorset. The glossary was a handy size, of about 1,320 words, and it was arranged into eighteen semantic fields, including 'Family relationships', 'Weather, universe', 'Birds', 'Fish', 'Wild animals', 'Herbs', 'Trees', and 'Human vices'. That concerned with 'Parts of the human body' includes:

LATIN	OLD ENGLISH	
sanguis	blod	'blood'
caro	flæsc	'flesh, body, living creature'
cutis	hyd	'hide'
pellis	fell	'skin'
scapula	sculdra	'shoulder'
dorsum	hrycg	'back'

Then the integrity of OE – and of the English nation – was disturbed by another invasion from the continent of Europe: that of William the Conqueror, from Normandy.

Bilingual Dictionaries

After 1066, the Saxon ruling class was almost entirely replaced by Normans. A dialect of French called Anglo-Norman became the language of administration. This continued until the King of England lost his French possessions at the beginning of the thirteenth century. By the end of the fourteenth century, English had once again become the official language of government.

The historical stage of the language from the twelfth until the end of the fifteenth century is known as Middle English (ME). Whereas there had been a standard form of OE, with a burgeoning literature, in its early period ME split into a number of regional varieties, each with its own spelling conventions. Written materials were confined to local dialects, and there was little attention to school instruction or glossaries.

ME underwent profound grammatical changes, losing much of its nominal and verbal inflection, and the gender system (except for sex-based forms of the 3rd person singular pronoun). There was immense vocabulary augmentation. It is estimated that around 10,000 words were borrowed from French (or directly from Latin, which was still the major language of culture) into ME, about three-quarters of which are still in use today. Some replaced Anglo-Saxon terms but most were in addition to them. However, grammatical forms and organisation, and the most commonly used words (including strong verbs with their irregularities) maintained the profile of a strongly Germanic language.

By the late fourteenth century, English was again being used in law courts and taught in school. There were fine works of literature such as *Piers Plowman* and Chaucer's *Canterbury Tales*. A number of substantial bilingual dictionaries, mostly between Latin and English, were prepared during the fifteenth century. Then came the introduction of printing in 1476.

A Latin-English dictionary with the engaging title *Hortus Vocabulorum*, 'Garden of Words', was published in 1500 (part of an earlier manuscript version is known from 1430). It had around 27,000 Latin head words, each with inflection and gender (for nouns) and these were arranged by semantic field. The first English-Latin dictionary, called *Promptorium Parvalorum sive Clericum*, 'Storehouse [of words] for children or clerics', came out as a manuscript in 1440 and was printed in 1499 (there were five later editions, until 1528). It had more than 10,000 entries, arranged in two alphabetical lists, for *nomina* (nouns) and *verba* (verbs).

Sample entries from the *Promptorium* deal with two senses of the noun *balle* (modern *ball*):

ENGLISH	LATIN
balle of play:	pila, -e, fem
balle of eye:	pupila, -e, fem

The declension of the Latin nouns is shown by *-e*, and their gender as feminine.

The *Promptorium* dealt not only with English words of Anglo-Saxon origin but also with the flood of forms recently taken in from French and Latin, for example:

ENGLISH	LATIN
eloquent, or wel spok man or woman:	eloquens, -tis; omnia gen

The declension of the Latin adjective was shown by *-tis*, and 'omnia gen' indicates that it can be of all three genders (agreeing with the gender of the noun it modifies).

The interesting question here is why it was thought necessary to explain the meaning of the word in English (a well-spoken man or woman; that is, an eloquent person) before providing the Latin translation equivalent. The reason must be that *eloquent* was a rather recent loan into English (the first attestation in the OED is from 1393). It was a 'hard word' which might not yet be fully familiar to all speakers of English, hence the explanation in terms of familiar Anglo-Saxon words.

Many bilingual dictionaries followed. The most influential one during the early part of the sixteenth century was *The Dictionary of Sir Thomas Elyot knyght* (1538). Produced at the behest of Henry VIII, Elyot appears to have made little use of earlier Latin-English compilations such as the *Hortus Vocabulorum*. Instead, he basically adapted the head words from a 1535 mono-lingual Latin dictionary by Ambrogio Calepino. Elyot's work, which was (roughly) alphabetical, is notable for the title being in English, rather than Latin, and for its including the word 'dictionary'.

It is instructive to look at Elyot's entries for the three words which we quoted from the *Corpus Glossary* of 800 years earlier:

LATIN	ENGLISH
sorex, ricis,	a ratte, or a fielde mouse
caepe,	an oynyon
soccus, & socculus,	a socke, which women and players in Comedies onely ware

The OE words for 'onion', *ynnilaec* and *cipe*, had been replaced by *oynyon* (in its spelling of the time), a borrowing from French *oignon* (first attested in the OED from 1356 to 1357). *Socculus* is the diminutive form of *soccus* 'light shoe or slipper'. In Latin, *ricis* after *sorex* indicates the declension for this word.

The early glossaries had explained Latin terms through OE words, which were predominantly of Germanic origin (*sock* was one of a smallish number of exceptions). By the sixteenth century, a large portion of English vocabu-lary consisted of fairly recent loans either from French or directly from Latin. These were in many instances clear cognates of Latin head words in a diction-ary such as that of Elyot, and with similar meanings. It is instructive to enquire how these were dealt with.

Consider the following entries from the Elyot compilation:

LATIN	ENGLISH
circumspectus,	circumspect
fama,	fame or renome, somtyme opinion
omnipotens, tis,	allmyghty
agilitas,	nymbleness, dexteritie

Circumspect had been taken into English directly from Latin (first noted in 1422) and it was appropriately given as a translation equivalent of its

Latin progenitor. *Fame* had been an earlier loan from French (attested from 1225) and was included by Elyot among the English equivalents for the Latin original. The interesting point is that *omnipotent* (from 1330) and *agility* (from 1425) were well established in English, yet were not used in the translations for Latin head words *omnipotens* and *agilitas*. The Germanic terms *allmyghty* and *nymbleness* were preferred. Plus rather surprisingly, the recent loan from French *dexteritie*. The earliest mention of this in the OED is 1527 (a hundred years later than *agility*, and just eleven years before the publication of Elyot's volume), although it is likely to have been in circulation somewhat earlier.

There was a flurry of lexicographic activity in England during the sixteenth century, dealing with French, Italian, Greek, and Welsh as well as Latin. Several English-Latin dictionaries typically reversed the sequence in Elyot – placing the English before the Latin. Compare an entry in Elyot:

LATIN   ENGLISH
pullatio,   hatchynge of chyckens

with the corresponding one in Richard Huloet's *Abecedarium Anglo-Latinum*. ('English-Latin ABC') of 1552:

ENGLISH   LATIN
hatchynge of chickens,   pullatio

At Trinity College, Cambridge, in the 1550s, John Baret had his students translate English prose into Latin. Growing tired of their continually coming to ask him the Latin equivalents of English words, he had them each day copy out a few pages from Elyot's dictionary (the one they had available) putting the English before the Latin. 'Thus within a yeare or two they had gathered togither a great volume, which (for the apt similitude betweene the good scholars and diligent Bees in gathering their wax and honey into their Hive) I called them their Alvearie [beehive]'. The work expanded and in 1573 Baret published *An Alvearie or Triple Dictionarie, in Englishe, Latin and French*.

After Elyot's death, in 1546, his dictionary was revised and expanded by Bishop Thomas Cooper, who in 1565 published his own *Thesaurus Linguae Romanae & Britannicae*. This remained the standard Latin-English work for twenty years, until it was superseded by the *Dictionarium Linguae Latinae et Anglicanae* (1587), compiled by Thomas Thomas, who was University Librarian at Cambridge.

Thomas's entries were, on the whole, fuller than those of Elyot. For example. Thomas gave:

LATIN   ENGLISH
circumspectus,   wise, prudent, circumspect, which advisedly considereth
                         what hee ought or what hee hath to doe
omnipotens, tis,   almighty, omnipotent

Elyot's simple *circumspect* for Latin *circumspectus* is expanded, with the cognate term still being included. And for *omnipotens*, the cognate adjective *omnipotent* was added to Elyot's *almighty*.

Thomas's bilingual dictionary was hugely influential, fourteen new editions being issued (until 1644). It was also a major base for the general listings of 'hard words', which could be called the first monolingual dictionaries of English.

Before turning to these, it will be useful to briefly comment on specialised inventories of English words – with explanations of their meanings – which appeared after the advent of printing.

Early Word Lists

By 1600, more than seventy lists of English words had been published, each focusing on a particular area. They ranged from ten terms (from 1583) for apothecaries' weights (for example, 'A graine is a barely corne taken in the midst of the eare') to 426 names (from 1543) of diseases, herbs, medicines and medical terms (such as 'Cordial: they call that cordial that comforteth the harte').

In addition to a dozen lists relating to medicine, there were some concerning animals – about shooting them, and about their diseases. On pages 32–6 of *The Boke of Husbandry* (probably published in 1523), John Fitzherbert gives thirty-eight words to do with 'The dysease and sorance of horses'. A typical entry is:

pursy Pursy is a dysease in a horse body and maketh hym to blowe short, and apereth at his nosethrylles and cometh of colde and may be well mended

Sorance was derived from adjective *sore* by suffix -*ance* (as in *grievance*) and referred to a sore or a state producing a sore. The first mention in the OED is from 1440 and the last from 1749. *Pursy* (or *pursive*) was an adjective 'short of breath', which is now retained only in some dialects from the north of England. *Thrylle* (or *thirl*) continued an Anglo-Saxon term *þȳrl* or *þȳrel* 'aperture, hole'; the compound *nose-thrylle* 'nose hole' shrank to become the modern noun *nostril*.

Some lists were intended as an aid to understanding the scriptures, such as the ninety-five entries in the 1569 publication *A Postill* [gloss] *or Exposition of the Gospels*. For example, a recent loan from Latin (attested from 1382) was explained in terms of familiar Anglo-Saxon words:

exclude to shutte out, put out, thruste out, or keepe out

Thirty or so of the lists covered cosmology, logic, rhetoric and geometry. There were forty-nine 'definitions' in *The Elements of Geometrie*, translated by Henry Billingsley (1570), including:

rhombus (or a diamonde)   is a figure having foure equall sydes, but it is not
                              rightangled

A dozen lists consisted of proper names, typically of places or gods. A 1561
book translated from Latin by Barnabe Googe was called *The Firste Syxe
Bokes of the Mooste Christian Poet Marcellus Palingenius, Called the Zodiake
of Life*. It explained 129 terms from classical antiquity, such as:

Alpes   exceading hie mountaines and rockes; separating Fraunce and
                   Germany from Italy
Calliope   the worthiest sister among the muses
Stygian lake   a river or lake in hel, by which the gods alwaies did sweare

Schoolmaster Richard Mulcaster longed for a full-scale monolingual English
dictionary, such as was then available for other languages. As a preliminary to
this he published, in 1582, a volume entitled *The First Part of the Elementarie
which entreateth chefelie of the right writing of our English tung*. This included
a 'general table', which was just a list of around 8,000 English words (of all
sorts, Germanic and Romance) – just a list, nothing more. Mulcaster commented on the wide variety of current spellings (as the reader will have noted
from the quotations in this chapter) and sought to standardise them. He insisted
that borrowed words should be divested of their alien shape and must be fully
assimilated into English.

Many of his spellings are those current today; for example, *rat, onion, hatch-
ing, shut, side*, and *swear* rather than *ratte, oynyon, hatchying, shutte, syde*,
and *sweare*. Others have been displaced, including *chefelie* and *tung* (rather
than *chiefly* and *tongue*) in the title of his volume. *Onely* 'only' in the quote
from Elyot became *onelie* for Mulcaster; we also find *morgage* 'mortgage' and
frindship 'friendship'.

Sometimes Mulcaster draws attention to homonyms by placing identical
words within a box, with different accents presumably intended to indicate
contrastive stress. For example:

desèrt   Distinct
desért

This undoubtedly relates to noun *desert* /'desət/ and verb *desert* /di'sə:t/.

Other boxes inveigled against a French spelling; for example, *reman-
ent* should be discarded in favour of *remnant*. A number of derivations are
included, such as:

    mercie
    mercifull
    mercifulnesse

Mulcaster writes suffix -*full* at the end of a word and -*ful* before a further suffix. In the sixteenth century, there had been variant spellings -*nes*, -*ness*, and -*nesse* for this Anglo-Saxon suffix, with Mulcaster opting for the last. And copious as Mulcaster's list might have been, it was by no means comprehensive, a fair number of common words not appearing; for instance, Germanic *always* and Romance loan (from 1425) *method*.

Monolingual Dictionaries

At last, monolingual dictionaries began to appear. The first three volumes which could be accorded this designation were:

- 1596. Edmund Coote [a school-teacher]. *The English Schoole-maister, teaching all his scholers, of what age soeuer, the most easie, short and perfect order of distinct reading and true writing our English tongue.* Includes texts, catechism, psalms and, on pages 74–93, a vocabulary of about 1,680 items with definitions (mostly of a single word) provided for about 90 per cent of them.
- 1604. Robert Cawdrey [a clergyman and school-teacher]. *A Table Alphabeticall, conteyning and teaching the true writing, and vnderstanding of hard vsual English wordes, borrowed from the Hebrew, Greeke, Latine, or French, etc.* ... Consists just of a vocabulary of about 2,540 items, all with definitions.
- 1616. John Bullokar [a physician]. *An English Expositor: teaching the interpretation of the hardest words used in our language. With sundry explications, descriptions, and discourses* ... Consists just of a vocabulary of about 4,250 items, all with definitions.

Coote's vocabulary was undoubtedly *the* pioneer monolingual dictionary of English. Cawdrey copied 87 per cent of Coote's entries, having an identical (generally single word) definition for about half of them, and expanding on it for the remainder. In turn, Bullokar's work was heavily dependent on Cawdrey's, sometimes having the same definition, sometimes expanding it. Each listing was, as would be expected, larger than its predecessor. However, it is interesting that some of the head words in Cawdrey do not appear in Bullokar; for instance, ***agglutinate***, ***artifice***, and ***discerne***.

In 1865, Henry B. Wheatley published a pioneering chronological account of English dictionaries in which he identified Bullokar's as 'the first English dictionary'. He was mistaken, Bullokar's being the third. It appears that Wheatley was not aware of the Coote and Cawdrey volumes.

Then, in 1933, Mitford M. Mathews published *A Survey of English Dictionaries.* and stated that 'Robert Cawdrey was the first to supply his countrymen with an English dictionary'. He was also mistaken, Cawdrey being the second. It appears that Mathews was not aware of the Coote volume.

Unfortunately, Mathews' uninformed statement has become the received dictum: *Cawdrey was the first.* Seminal volumes have included *The English Dictionary from Cawdrey to Johnson* (Starnes and Noyes 1946) and *The English Dictionary before Cawdrey* (Stein 1985), which describes bilingual dictionaries that involved English. There was a recent edition of Cawdrey's *A Table Alphabeticall* published as *The First English Dictionary, 1604* (Simpson 2007).

All of the early monolingual dictionaries were rather short and poor when compared, for instance, with the several thousand words in Thomas's Latin-English dictionary of 1587 or, indeed, with Mulcaster's listing (without definitions) of 1582. In fact, these early lexicographers had a specific and limited aim. This was to explain the meanings of 'hard words', by which was meant recent loans – almost all from French and Latin – which had not been fully assimilated into the language and which some people might need help in understanding.

In those days, books tended to have long titles. Added after Cawdrey's main title was: *With the interpretation thereof by plaine English words, gathered for the benefit and helpe of Ladies, Gentlewomen, or any other unskillful persons. Whereby they may the more easilie and better understand many hard English wordes, which they shall heare or read in Scriptures, Sermons, or elsewhere, and also be made able to use the same aptly themselves.*

There was thought no need to include common words which everyone knew. This covered all inherited forms from OE, and also some Romance loans into the early stages of ME. Words such as *gentle, faith, battle,* and *carry* were taken into English during the thirteenth century. No doubt they would have been recognised as recent foreign intrusions during the fourteenth century, but by the end of the sixteenth century such words were familiar. The 'dictionaries of hard words' dealt with some loans from the thirteenth and early fourteenth century but mostly with items taken into the language after about 1350. They 'defined' them in terms of well-known Germanic words.

Commencing a new endeavour is not an easy matter. Few enterprises start absolutely from scratch; people generally search for a foundation on which to build. So it was for Coote, Cawdrey and Bullokar – their monolingual dictionaries were, in large part, derived from the bilingual Latin-English dictionary of Thomas.

There are many examples of the following type:

	HEAD WORD IN LATIN	TRANSLATION INTO ENGLISH
Thomas	**angulus**	a corner or narrow place

	HEAD WORD IN ENGLISH	DEFINITION IN ENGLISH
Coote	**angle**	corner
Cawdrey	**angle,** fr[ench]	corner

	HEAD WORD IN LATIN	TRANSLATION INTO ENGLISH
Thomas	**dignitas**	worthinesse, manly maiestie or comelinesse

	HEAD WORD IN ENGLISH	DEFINITION IN ENGLISH
Coote	**dignitie**	worthinesse
Cawdrey	**dignitie**	worthinesse

A Latin form in the head word column is replaced by its cognate, a loan from Romance (*angle* is first attested in English from 1325, *dignity* from 1225) in the monolingual dictionary. And part of the translation equivalent from the bilingual dictionary is taken as the definition in the monolingual one. That is:

Diagram of the original methodology

BILINGUAL	head word in Latin	translation equivalent(s)
DICTIONARY		in English
	↓	↓
MONOLINGUAL	head word in English	definition in English
DICTIONARY	(cognate with Latin head word in bilingual dictionary)	

This is scarcely a satisfactory methodology. A bilingual dictionary considers words in the source language, one by one, and provides a range of translation equivalents in the target language. In contrast, a full monolingual dictionary should provide information on when to use one word rather than another, comparing each word with those of related meaning, explaining and illustrating their semantic and grammatical differences.

Note, though, that the compilations by Coote, Cawdrey, Bullokar – and their successors right through the seventeenth century – were *not* intended to be full dictionaries, but were instead just explications of a number of 'hard words', recent loans which were in the process of being assimilated into the language. For this purpose, the methodology set out in the diagram is not inappropriate.

When the eighteenth century came around, lexicographers extended their scope to cover all words in the language – both old and new, both Germanic and Romance. Unfortunately, the principles established by Coote and company were continued. Each word was considered on its own, and accorded a definition without reference to its role in the grand overall scheme of the language. This is when castigation is properly deserved.

For some entries, Thomas included the cognate English word among the translation equivalents for its Latin original, as in:

	HEAD WORD IN LATIN	TRANSLATION INTO ENGLISH
Thomas	**electio**	an election or choise
	HEAD WORD IN ENGLISH	DEFINITION IN ENGLISH
Coote	**election**	choise
Cawdrey	**election**	choise

	HEAD WORD IN LATIN	TRANSLATION INTO ENGLISH
Thomas	**oppōno**	to lay or set against, to oppose
	HEAD WORD IN ENGLISH	DEFINITION IN ENGLISH
Coote	**oppose**	set against
Cawdrey	**oppose**	set againe

Cawdrey's compilation was eight years later than Coote's, and often a little fuller as can be seen in:

	HEAD WORD IN LATIN	TRANSLATION INTO ENGLISH
Thomas	**castigātio**	a chastising, correcting or blaming
	HEAD WORD IN ENGLISH	DEFINITION IN ENGLISH
Coote	**castigation**	chastisment
Cawdrey	**castigation**	chaistisement, blaming, correction

Here, Coote simply took one of the three items from the Thomas entry while Cawdrey used all three. However, in the following examples, Cawdrey added an addition all of his own:

	HEAD WORD IN LATIN	TRANSLATION INTO ENGLISH
Thomas	**ponderitas**	weightinesse
	HEAD WORD IN ENGLISH	DEFINITION IN ENGLISH
Coote	**ponderous**	waightie
Cawdrey	**ponderous**	weightie, heavie

	HEAD WORD IN LATIN	TRANSLATION INTO ENGLISH
Thomas	**omnipotens**	almighty, omnipotent
	HEAD WORD IN ENGLISH	DEFINITION IN ENGLISH
Coote	**omnipotent**	almightie
Cawdrey	**omnipotent**	almightie, great, or high

Cawdrey included some words that were not in Coote and quite a few of them are taken almost verbatim from Thomas, including:

	HEAD WORD IN LATIN	TRANSLATION INTO ENGLISH
Thomas	**horizon**	a circle dividing the halfe sphere of the firmament from the other halfe which we doe not see

HEAD WORD IN ENGLISH DEFINITION IN ENGLISH

Cawdrey **horizon,** gr[eek]   a circle deviding the halfe of the firmament,
                                   from the other halfe which we see not

Bullokar followed a similar pattern. *Angle* was *a corner* and *election* was *choice*, identical to Coote and Cawdrey. For *omnipotent* he had simply *almighty*, the same as Coote and ignoring Cawdrey's addition. *Ponderous* was given as *heavy, of great weight*. Bullokar had the verb *castigate* defined as *to chastise, to correct* (using two of the three items from Cawdrey). *Oppose* was a little longer: *to object, to set one thing against another*. Bullokar did not include *dignity*. However, for *horizon*, he was fully original: *an imaginary Line compassing the lowest Part of the Heavens that we can see, so called, because it limiteth our Sight, dividing the Heavens, underneath us, from that which is above. The Sun rising and going down is ever in this Line.*

Besides the items he based on Thomas's bilingual dictionary and some taken from specialised vocabularies (mentioned in the last section), Coote had a fair number of original entries. He was no doubt familiar with Mulcaster's simple list of all kinds of English words, but was by no means confined to this. For instance, *method* (a loan attested from 1425) was omitted from Mulcaster but included by Coote. It is interesting to follow this word through:

	HEAD WORD IN LATIN	TRANSLATION INTO ENGLISH
Thomas	**methodus**	a ready way to teach or do any thing
	HEAD WORD IN ENGLISH	DEFINITION IN ENGLISH
Coote	**method,** g[reek[	order
Cawdrey	**method,** gr[eek]	an order, or readie way to teach, or doo any thing
Bullokar	**method**	a direct way to teach or do any thing

It appears that Coote provided his own definition, independently of Thomas. Cawdrey simply combined Coote and Thomas, while Bullokar modified Thomas/Cawdrey, omitting Coote's *order*.

One can gain an idea of how Cawdrey simply copied from Coote – or expanded some definitions, and added new items – by comparing entries commencing with *gen-*. These are given in the order in which they appear in the two dictionaries. Coote did gather together all words commencing with *gen-*, but within this set there was no strict alphabetical arrangement. Cawdrey simply copied Coote's idiosyncratic ordering.

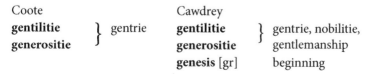

Coote
gentilitie } gentrie
generositie

Cawdrey
gentilitie } gentrie, nobilitie,
generositie gentlemanship
genesis [gr] beginning

Coote		Cawdrey	
gentile	a heathen	**gentile**	a heathen
generation	ofspring	**generation**	ofspring
gender			
geneologie, g	generation	**geneologie**	generation, or describing
		[gr]	of the stock or pedegree
		genitalles	privities
		genuine	peculiar, or naturall
		genius	the angell who waits on man, be it a good or evill angell
genitor	father	**genitor**	father

It can be seen that Cawdrey simply repeated Coote's definitions for *gentile*, *generation*, and *genitor*, and added to them for *genitilitie/generositie* and *geneologie*. And he added four new words: *genesis*, *genitalles*, *genuine*, and *genius*.

For about one-tenth of his entries, Coote provided no definition. In most instances Cawdrey simply ignored these, as here with *gender* (a loan from 1390).

Just occasionally, Cawdrey does include a word Coote only listed, and then adds a definition. (Note that in Cawdrey all words were defined, as in Bullokar and many – although not all – later dictionaries.) For example:

Coote		Cawdrey	
abhorre	<no definition>	**abhorre**	hate, despise or disdain
banquet	<no definition>	**banquet**	feast

Bullokar's dictionary does not include **banquet**, but does have **abhor**, with an original definition: *detest or loath*.

Bullokar included around 1,700 more entries than Cawdrey but, for those which were in both dictionaries, there was as much copying as we saw between Cawdrey and Coote. Compare:

Coote	**faction**	devision
Cawdrey	**faction**	devision of people into sundry parts and opinions
Bullokar	**faction**	a sect[ion] or division into sundry opinions

Bullokar's definitions were often more detailed than those of his predecessors. Sometimes this was achieved through referring back to Thomas's bilingual entry. For example:

	HEAD WORD IN LATIN	TRANSLATION INTO ENGLISH
Thomas	**anathema**	a gift or offering which is hanged up in the Church: a man which in times past was given to the devil; excommunication, execration
	HEAD WORD IN ENGLISH	DEFINITION IN ENGLISH
Coote	**anathema**	accursed
Cawdrey	**anathema** [gr]	accursed or given over to the devill
Bullokar	**anathema**	any thing hanged up in a church, as an offering to God; sometimes it signifieth excommunication; or a man excommunicated and delivered to the power of the divell

Bullokar also included a different kind of 'hard word' – ME terms which were no longer in general use (some surviving just in local dialects). For example, *yexing, sobbing.*

The first three monolingual dictionaries, repositories of 'hard words' – and the half-dozen which followed – were rudimentary affairs, especially when set against the opulence of Thomas's bilingual compilation. But each one did advance a little further along the path.

It is interesting that the earliest dictionaries often included nominalisations, but not the forms they are based on. Both Coote and Cawdrey feature nouns *communication* and *stipulation*, but not the verbs they are derived from, *communicate* and *stipulate*. Why should this be? The reason is that in many instances the nominalisations were borrowed into English at an earlier stage than the underlying verbs.

Both Coote and Cawdrey included *castigation* but not *castigate*. A handful of years later, Bullokar had verb *castigate*, but omitted *castigation*. In fact, *castigation* was first noted in Chaucer's writing, from 1397, while *castigate* only turned up 200 years later in Shakespeare's play *Timon of Athens*.

Bullokar did move ahead of his predecessors in including quite a few basic roots and derivations from them. For instance:

stipulate   to make a contract
stipulation   a solemn contract or bargain

depend   to hang upon another thing
dependence   a hanging or staying upon

One fascinating set of entries in Bullokar is:

historian	one well-read in history
historical	of or belonging to a history
historiographer	a writer of histories
historiology	the knowledge and telling of old histories

But why did Bullokar not also include the underlying root *history*? There is a straightforward explanation. *History* was one of the few Latin loans into Old English. By Bullokar's time, it had been in the language for more than 800 years and was a familiar word, not in need of explanation. There was a direct descendent of the Latin word *historia* in French where it spawned derivations, and these were borrowed into English, during the fifteenth and sixteenth centuries, as *historian*, *historical*, *historiographer*, and *historiology*.

Most of the time Bullokar simply juxtaposed related words without explicitly stating there was a link between them. Just occasionally, there was a semblance of grammatical insight. After the entry for **metaphysics** he added 'Adject[ive] *metaphysical*' and after that for **method** 'Adject[ive] *methodical*'.

This chapter has traced the evolution from textual glossaries, through bilingual dictionaries and specialised vocabularies, to general lists of 'hard words', the first compilations which could be termed monolingual dictionaries. Things continued much the same through the seventeenth century, and then expanded – but at first only with a whimper – during the first part of the eighteenth century. This is the topic of the next chapter.

5   Putting Everything In

The seventeenth century continued much as it had begun, with new volumes explaining difficult terms (of recent foreign origin) through familiar Anglo-Saxon words. Then the first half of the eighteenth century saw a fresh approach – include in the dictionary *all words*, of whatever type, exotic or common. And this included fully grammatical words such as *this*, *you*, and *but*.

It began, in 1702, with a rather feeble *New English Dictionary* by John Kersey. Then, in 1730, Nathan Bailey published his more compendious (and discursive) *Dictionarium Britannicum*, an uneven work. Things were moving forward, albeit unhurriedly.

More Hard Words

Seven years after Bullokar, a new and slightly novel compilation appeared, by Henry Cockeram. There were two publications in 1623, almost identical, from different publishers in London. The title page of that put out by Edmund Weaver read:

The English Dictionarie: or, an Interpreter of Hard English Words.

Enabling, as well, Ladies and Gentlewomen, young Schollers, Clarkes, Merchants; as also Strangers of any Nation, to the understanding of the more difficult Authors already printed in our Language, and the more speedy attaining of an elegant perfection of the English tongue, both in reading, speaking and writing.

Being a collection of the choicest words contained in the Table Alphabeticall and English Expositor, and of some thousands of words never published by any heretofore.

It is interesting that this printing freely acknowledges the use Cockeram made of materials in the Cawdrey (*Table Alphabetical*) and Bullokar (*English Expositor*) dictionaries, as people did at the time, and for a long time afterwards, although normally without such explicit acknowledgement. However, the other London printing of 1623, from Nathaniel Butter, differed in just one particular: the omission of the final short paragraph referring to the two earlier volumes. It is likely that Weaver insisted on this acknowledgement since he had been the publisher for all four editions of Cawdrey; Butter apparently felt no such obligation.

Cockeram's volume was divided into three 'book(e)s'. The first was a stand-ard dictionary of (almost 6,000) hard words, 'the choicest words themselves now in use ... to which the common sense is annexed'. 'The second Booke contains the vulgar words, which whensover any desirous of a more curious explanation by a more refined and elegant speech shall looke into, he shall there receive the exact and ample word to express the same.' In other words, the second book was more-or-less a reversal of the first. For example:

FIRST BOOK		SECOND BOOK	
applause	a clapping of hands for joy	**a clapping of hands for joy**	applause, aplaudity
exclude	to shut out	**to shut out**	exclude
gemme	a jewell	**a jewell**	gemme
incredulous	that will not beleeve	**which will not beleeve**	incredulous
information	an instruction	**an instruction from God**	inspiration
inspiration	a breathing into	<no entry for breathing into>	

Note that entries in Book Two are in (rough) alphabetical order by the letters underlined.

Basically, the head words for Book One and the 'definitions' for Book Two are Latinate 'hard words' whereas Anglo-Saxon forms make up the definitions for Book One and the 'vulgar' head words for Book Two. Many entries are simply reversed – *applause*, *exclude*, *gemme*, and (with slight adjustment) *incredulous*. Book Two added, after *applause*, *aplaudity*; this did not occur in Book One (the OED records only two instances, one from 1626 and the other in Cockeram). But *information* (first attested in 1387) is defined in terms of another recent loan, *instruction* (attested from about 1412). Book Two does not include a simple entry for *instruction*, only **instruction from God**, which is defined as *inspiration* (a loan first noted from 1303). Book One does include *inspiration* but treats a quite different sense of the word, *breathing into*.

Cockeram's work is somewhat haphazard. For instance, spellings vary. In Book One, *obesitie* is defined in terms of *fatnesse* but Book Two has *fatnes* given as *obesity*. However, his *Dictionarie* did sell well. The twelfth and last edition, in 1670, was revised and enlarged by Cockeram's son, with Book Two sensibly omitted.

Book Three (retained in all editions) was effectively an encyclopaedia, 'treat-ing of Gods and Goddesses, Men and Women, Boyes and Maids, Giants and Divils, Birds and Beasts, Monsters and Serpents, Wells and Rivers, Hearbes, Stones, Trees, Dogges, Fishes, and the like.'

For Book One, Cockeram made good use of his predecessors' work. For example:

Coote	**benigne**	favourable
Cawdrey	**benigne**	favourable, curteous, gentle
Bullokar	**benign**	friendly, gentle, favourable, courteous, kind
Cockeram	**benigne**	gentle, favourable

Coote	**centre**	middest
Cawdrey	**centre**, gr[eek]	middest of any round thing or circle
Bullokar	**center**	the point in the midst of a round circle or the inward middle point of a globe. Wherefore the Earth is called the Center of the World, because it is in the midst thereof
Cockeram	**center**	the point in the midst of a round circle and therefore the earth is called the center of the world because it is in the middst thereof

Bullokar's typically lengthy entry for *center* used *world* in a then prevalent sense for what we would now call 'the galaxy' or 'the universe'. This was copied into the 1623 edition of Cockeram. However, by the twelfth edition of Cockeram's volume, in 1670, the entry for *center* had been shortened to just *the point in the midst of a circle or globe*.

Many more of Cockeram's entries repeated material from Cawdrey and Bullokar, or just from Bullokar. And there were some from Cawdrey which Bullokar had not included; for example:

Cawdrey	**hallucinate**	to deceive or blind
Cockeram	**hallucinate**	to deceive

Cawdrey	**agglutinate**	to joyne together
Cockeram	**agglutinate**	to joyne or glue together

Cockeram's was the first monolingual compilation to include the word 'dictionary' in its title. Others soon followed. Bullokar's volume continued to be reissued until 1775 and from the tenth edition, in 1707, the title was amended to: *The English expositor improv'd, being a complete dictionary.*

From the 1640s, England underwent a turbulent period, with the Puritan revolution and a regal beheading. Once a measure of stability had been restored, there came the next major dictionary, in 1656, from Thomas Blount, a barrister and antiquary. It was entitled: *Glossographia, or a dictionary interpreting all such Hard Words, whether Hebrew, Greek, Latin, Italian, Spanish,*

French, Teutonick, Belgick, British or Saxon, as are now used in our refined
English tongue ... with etymologies, definitions, and historical observations
on the same.

Following tradition, Blount made full use of the entries in earlier dictionaries, often verbatim. He also added recent loans of a somewhat esoteric nature, basing his definitions on the translation equivalents in Thomas (using the 1632 edition) and other bilingual Latin-English dictionaries. For example:

	HEAD WORD IN LATIN	TRANSLATION INTO ENGLISH
Thomas	**adulatio**	properly the fawning of a dogge; flatterie
	HEAD WORD IN ENGLISH	DEFINITION IN ENGLISH
Blount	**adulation (adulatio)**	properly the fawning of a dog; flattery

Along similar lines were *adequate*, *adulation*, and *acrimony*. And Blount delved deeper, coming up with words that were as obscure as can be imagined, such as:

	HEAD WORD IN LATIN	TRANSLATION INTO ENGLISH
Thomas	**adoxia**	slander, ignominy, infamy
	HEAD WORD IN ENGLISH	DEFINITION IN ENGLISH
Blount	**adoxy (adoxia)**	ignominy, shame, slander, infamy

The OED reports just two instances of *adoxy*: in a political and moral treatise of 1595, and in Blount.

There was no copyright law in the seventeenth century so that plundering one's predecessors' works was an accepted practice. However, there were limits, and most authors did acknowledge their sources. Two years after Blount's meritorious dictionary, Edward Phillips – who was basically a hired hack – published *The New World of English Words: or, a General Dictionary...* which shamelessly reproduced much of Blount and with no acknowledgement. Blount responded angrily, calling Phillips 'a lexicographic mercenary'.

And so dictionaries of hard words rolled on. Elisha Coles, a schoolmaster, produced *An English dictionary...* in 1676, which was notable for sourcing specialised vocabularies for dialectal words and also 'cant', the patois of the underworld. "Tis no disparagement to understand the Canting Terms. It may chance to save your throat from being cut, or at least your Pocket from being pickt.'

The idea that a reader need to have only difficult words explained continued in a small way into the eighteenth century. A new book appeared in 1753 entitled *The Complete English Dictionary, explaining most of those hard words, which are found in the best English writers. By a lover of good English and common sense.* Although issued anonymously, this was in fact a minor work by John Wesley, whose main claim to fame was as the founder of a religious denomination:

a methodist   one that lives according to the method laid down in the bible

Wesley's compact volume appears like a throwback to the days of Bullokar. However, Wesley did not altogether rely on his predecessors. Many definitions were his own. And his religious bent was sometimes evident; for example:

purgatory   a place where the papists fancy departed souls are purged by fire
a rosary   a set of popish beads

On a rosary, each bead relates to a prayer, and this should have been stated.

Thomas, in his bilingual dictionary, had explained the Latin word *nectar* as *a pleasant liquor feigned to be the drinke of the Gods.* Cawdrey used this almost verbatim:

nectar   a pleasant drinke, which is feyned to be the drinke of the gods

And it was repeated, with minor variations by Bullokar, Blount, and Phillips. Also by Wesley, but with a necessary Christian adjustment:

nectar   the supposed drink of the heathen gods

A dictionary should provide scientific documentation. But it can also be made to serve a social role. It may be prescriptive, detailing how the dictionary-writer thinks the language should be used (irrespective of the way in which people actually do speak it). The lexicographer may relieve the daily grind by popping in a grain of wit, sometimes disparaging, as with Samuel Johnson's definition of the noun *canter* as: *a term of reproach for hypocrites, who talk formally of religion, without obeying it.* If an author has an agenda, as did Wesley, this may motivate the wording. But it would surely have been fairer – to both papist and non-papist readers – for Wesley to have mentioned that each bead on a rosary relates to a prayer (as earlier dictionaries by Blount, Kersey, and Bailey had done).

All Encompassing

In some nations, scholarly folk were concerned about the profile of their language. Members of the Academia della Crusca, founded in Florence in 1583 (and continuing until today), wished to maintain the purity of the Italian language, and in 1613 published the first edition of their dictionary, the *Vocabulario,* with generous quotations from Italian literature. In 1634, Cardinal Richelieu founded the Académie française, to be the official authority on the French language. Its extensive *Dictionnaire* was published in 1694.

England lagged far behind. There never has been a body similar to those in Italy and France, so that full documentation of the language has been largely left to individuals. John Kersey was an active lexicographer who prepared, among other things, new editions of Edward Phillips' volume. And in 1702 he produced *A New English Dictionary, or a compleat collation of the most proper and significant words, commonly used in the language.* Kersey attempted to cover words of every kind, both familiar Anglo-Saxon items and loans from Romance and other languages. He excluded esoteric words, such as those which he considered to be 'obsolete, barbarous, foreign or peculiar to the several counties of England' (that is, those found only in local dialects).

This must be acknowledged to be the first general monolingual dictionary of English. But in fact it is a pitiful document. This can be seen through examination of a couple of consecutive sets of entries.

easy to be done,	also generous or good-natur'd
to eat	
eatable,	or good to eat
an eat-bee,	a bird
eaten	
the eaves,	of a house
to eaves-drop,	or hearken at the windows, or doors
an eaves-dropper	
an ew,	or female sheep

No definition is offered for *to eat*. In the case of this and many further words (including *drink*, *kiss*, *give*, *house*, *girdle*, *rain*), just its inclusion in the alphabetical list appears to be regarded as sufficient. Perhaps Kersey simply wished to remind the readers that these words existed, assuming that they would know how to use them. Similarly with verb form *eaten*, although *eatable* is provided with an acceptable definition. An *eat-bee* (later called *bee-eater*) is a bird of the *Merops* genus. For *eaves* we are told that it relates to a house, but not in what way (is it a window, or a door, or a foundation, or a back wall, or a roof, or what?). For *eaves drop* and *ew(e)* the definitions are helpful. *Eaves dropper* is accorded no definitions (such as 'person who eaves drops'). Presumably, Kersey assumed his readers would know that suffix *-er* indicates an agentive nominalisation. *Easy to be done* is a trifle idiosyncratic; note that this is the only entry for *easy*.

Looking now at another consecutive series of entries:

a sirname, or surname,	the name of one's family
sirrah! (an injurious term),	denoting a rascal or vain person
a siskin,	or green finch
a sister	
a sister-in-law	
twin-sisters	
sisterhood,	the quality of a sister, or a society of spiritual sisters or nuns
to sit,	at table, at work &c
a site,	or situation
a sithe,	to mow with

No definition is given for *sister*. Nor for *sister-in-law* – which could have been 'sister of one's wife or husband' – nor for *twin sisters*. For *to sit* and *sithe*, Kersey simply provides contexts in which the words may be used. We are not told the material or shape of a scythe. This dictionary provides odd hints concerning most (but not all) of the words it lists, but is far from supplying adequate definitions, let alone sufficient information which will let the dictionary user know when to use one word rather than a related one.

Nathan Bailey was a schoolmaster and a prodigious lexicographer. In 1721 he issued an 'etymological dictionary', and then in 1730 his magnum opus, *Dictionarium Britannicum: Or a More Compleat Universal Etymological English Dictionary than any Extant....* This was a far more ambitious work than Kersey's – larger, and much better printed. In addition, it included more then 400 illustrations, relating to terms in heraldry, in architecture, and in geometry, plus implements such as a battering ram, a windlass, a back-quadrant, and a barometer, as well as a dove-tail joint, and a calumet or pipe of peace (used among the Virginian Indians).

Bailey's compilation, the second general monolingual dictionary, was a handsome volume. It included encyclopaedic entries for many proper names of people and places, and also lengthy definitions. Compare Kersey's (perhaps too) succinct entries with Bailey's (perhaps too) elaborate ones:

Kersey	**mittimus**	a warrant to send an offender to prison
Bailey	**mittimus**	precept directed by a Justice of the Peace to a Goaler, for the receiving and life-keeping of a Felon, or other Offender by him committed to the Goal. Also a Writ by which Records are transferred from one Court to another

Kersey	a ledger-book	or merchant's accounts
Bailey	ledger	the chief of a Merchants Books, in which every Man's particular Account, and also all the Goods bought and sold, are distinctly placed, each by themselves; as Debtor on the left Page and Creditor on the right

There are a good number of entries in Bailey which are lacking from Kersey, such as:

Bailey	euphemism	a figure where a foul harsh word or speech is changed into another which may give no offence

Following tradition (then and now), both Kersey and Bailey showed no hesitation in appropriating the entries of their 'hard words' predecessors. On page 50 we noted that Coote's definition of *castigation* was *chastisement*. Cawdrey added *blaming, correction* from Thomas's bilingual dictionary. Both Kersey and Bailey had simply *chastisement*, identical to Coote. For *omnipotent*, Kersey had *almighty*, the same as Coote (less than Cawdrey's '*almightie, great*, or *high*'), while Bailey added *all-powerful* to this.

These two dictionaries from the early eighteenth century aimed to cover the whole spectrum of English vocabulary. It is instructive to delve below the fancy frontage and see how well they handled this task. How about familiar words such as *mouse* and *onion* – mentioned on page 43 in connection with Elyot's bilingual compilation – which had not featured in any previous monolingual dictionary?

Kersey	an onion	a plant
Bailey	onion	an edible root

Kersey	a mouse	a little creature
Bailey	mouse	an animal well-known

For *onion*, Bailey is slightly more informative than Kersey but his definition is still pretty feeble. Kersey's *a little creature* for *mouse* could equally describe a cockroach or a small bird, or a sardine. (*Creature* is one of those words in Kersey's book which is just listed, with no definition at all.) And here Bailey has simply not bothered. In fact, we find *an animal well-known* also given as the definition for *dog* and *goat*, and *a beast well-known* for *cow*, *bull*, and *horse*. (*Cat* fares a little better: *a domestick creature that kills mice*.)

Just occasionally, Bailey fails to provide a definition; for example, nothing is given after head word *woman*. Definitions of the type *an animal well-known* are empty. Bailey plainly assumes that all his readers will know what a woman or a mouse or a goat is. Kersey apparently makes the same assumption for those words which are not accorded any definition: *to eat*, *sister*, *creature*, *to drink*, *to give*, *rain*, and many more.

We can examine how Bailey deals with some of the items in the sets of entries that were quoted from Kersey.

to eat	to feed
an eat-bee	a small insect which feeds on bees
eaves	the edges of the tiling of a house
eaves dropper	one who clandestinely listens under the eaves, at the windows, doors, &c. of a house, to hear the private affairs of a family, in order to cause animosity among neighbours; a tale-bearer; a pick-thank
sister	a female born of the same father and mother, or of one of them
scythe	an instrument for mowing grass

Since *to eat* is given as *to feed*, one naturally looks up the entry for *feed*:

to feed	to furnish or supply with food; also to eat

Back where we started: *to eat* is *to feed* and *to feed* is *to eat*.

Bailey's next entry is simply erroneous. An *eat-bee* is a bird which eats bees (as Kersey had it correctly), not an insect. *Eaves* is an improvement on Kersey's *of a house*. *Eaves dropper* is fine, although typically long-winded in Bailey's style. (*Pick-thank* is explained on pages 152 and 200.) The definition for *sister* is absolutely spot-on.

But Bailey's treatment of *scythe* is disappointing, just adding *an instrument* and *grass* to Kersey's *to mow with*. Surely the nature of the implement should be described, something like: 'an instrument with a curved metal blade, sharpened on the inside edge, attached at right-angles to a long wooden handle, used for cutting or mowing grass or corn'.

This shows up a blatant inconsistency in Bailey's work. Some instruments, like scythe, are treated in a perfunctory manner, while others are accorded encyclopaedic delineations. For example, *perambulator* merited a drawing accompanied by a 14-line description.

Bailey's volume was certainly better than anything which had gone before. It could be said to pave the way for the magnum opus, in 1755, of Samuel Johnson, when English-speakers would at last have a dictionary that could compare with those of other leading languages. Johnson's work is surveyed in chapter 7. Meanwhile, it is appropriate to cast a glance at the disregard of grammar, and also to consider the nature and role of a monolingual dictionary.

PERAMBULA'TION, a Walking through any Point of the Zodiack to the fame again, &c. L.

PERAMBULA'TION [*of the Foreft*] the Walking of Juftices, or other Officers, about a Foreft, in Order to furvey and fet the Bounds of it.

PERAMBULA'TIONE *facienda*, a Writ commanding the Sheriff to make a Perambulation, and to fet down the Bounds of 2 or more Manours, the Limits of which are not fo well known.

PERA'MBULATOR, an Inftrument or Rolling-Wheel for  meafuring Roads, &c. a furveying Wheel. It is made of Wood or Iron, commonly half a Pole in Circumference, with a Movement, and a Face divided like a Clock, with a long Rod of Iron or Steel that goes from the Center of the Wheel to the Work: There are alfo 2 Hands, which (as you drive the Wheel before you) count the Revolutions: and from the Compofition of the Movement and Divifion on the Face, fhew how many Yards, Poles, Furlongs, and Miles you go.

PERCA [*old Rec.*] a Perch of Land.

PERCAPTU'RE, a Wear or Place in a River, made up with Banks, Dams, &c. for preferving or catching Fifh.

PE'RCASE, if perchance, if it be fo.

To PERCEI'VE [*percipere*, L. *appercevoir*, F.] to begin to fee, to difcover, to fpy or find out, to apprehend or underftand.

PERCEI'VABLE ⎱ [*perceptibilis*, L.] that may be per-
PERCE'PTABLE ⎰ ceived.

PERCE'PTIBLENESS, Perceivablenefs.

PERCE'PTION, the Act of perceiving, comprehending, or knowing; the clear and diftinct Apprehenfion of any Object.

The Other Words

A typical response to the question 'what is a language made up of?' is that it consists of a large pool of words, as listed in the dictionary. By and large, speakers are not aware of grammar – the matrix of structures and constructions into which words must be inserted in order to make a sentence and communicate meaning. If pressed, a speaker may suggest that grammar is something which comes naturally. Indeed, Kersey's definition of **grammar** is instructive: *the Art of right reading, writing, and speaking*.

As explained in chapter 1, grammar is – in essence – prior to lexicon. Grammar describes the overall organisation of the language. The structural patterns and ways of marking these, by special affixes or just by the manner in which words are ordered. The ways in which one kind of word is derived from another; for example, nouns *special-ity*, *special-ism*, and *special-ist*, plus verb *special-ise*, from adjective *special*. And things like demonstratives and personal pronouns which constitute closed classes that are fully specified – as to both meaning and function – within the grammar.

Where grammar leaves off, the lexicon takes over. *Blue* and *green*, *big* and *large*, *run* and *walk*, *cat* and *dog* have essentially the same grammatical properties and it is the role of the dictionary to distinguish them.

There were many grammars of Latin, a language with complex morphology such that one had to master the intricate paradigms of case, gender, tense, voice, aspect, and the like in order to understand anything at all. There had been similar complexities in Old English but they had been mostly lost from the modern language.

The early lexicographers we have been discussing were concerned with words, pure and simple. Bailey, Kersey and the rest did not consider it relevant to state whether a word was a noun, adjective, or verb. And when the principle of a monolingual dictionary was extended from 'hard words' to 'all words', it really did mean *all words*. That is, anything which was written between two spaces was a word and needed to be defined, in the same way as every other word. This included fully grammatical words, belonging to closed grammatical systems (and also clitics, which were mostly written as separate words).

Basic noun phrase structure

SLOT	determiner	modifier(s)	head of noun phrase
	↑	↑	↑
FILLER	articles, nominal demonstratives, possessive pronouns (all are closed systems)	adjectives (open class)	noun (open class)

This diagram shows the three basic slots that make up a noun phrase in English (other slots can follow the head, including prepositional phrases such as *in the garden* or *of wood* and relative clauses such as *who was asleep*). Only one item can be chosen from the determiner slot. There can be an article, as in <u>*A*</u> *large quantity of sugar*, or a demonstrative, as in <u>*That*</u> *big tree*, or a possessive pronoun, as in <u>*My*</u> *little sister*. It is not permissible to combine items from two of these systems – not ♦*a this* or ♦*the my* or ♦*that your*.

The items filling the determiner slot are small grammatical systems with closed membership. Each term is defined with respect to the other term(s) in its system; for example, if an article is not indefinite, *a(n)*, then it must be definite, *the*.

The nominal demonstrative system involves the intersection of two grammatical contrasts: {near speaker; not near speaker}, and {singular, plural}:

	SINGULAR	PLURAL
NEAR SPEAKER	this	these
FAR FROM SPEAKER	that	those

There are homonymous forms *that*, which can introduce a relative clause, as in *I know [the dog [that ran away]$_{RELATIVE.CLAUSE}$]$_{OBJECT}$* or a complement clause, as in *I know [that the dog ran away]$_{COMPEMENT.CLAUSE:OBJECT}$.*

Kersey and Bailey included all four demonstrative words, with the following definitions:

	KERSEY	BAILEY
this	as in this place	a pronoun
these	the plural of this, as these persons	those
that	so that, lest that, etc.	a conjunction &c
those	as those women	these persons or things

Kersey just provided examples of use for *this*, *these*, and *those*. It appears that for him each word had a single meaning. The clause-introducing form *that* was illustrated, and the demonstrative *that* ignored. Kersey usefully commented that *these* is the plural of *this*, but it seems that *those* is not the plural of anything.

Bailey distinguished several senses for a multitude of lexemes. For example, there were three types of **buckler** – a piece of armour, and a cut of beef, and a herb. But he did not distinguish the *that* which is a (demonstrative) pronoun, parallel to *this*, from the *that* which is a conjunction. And Bailey's equating *these* and *those* is simply weird.

A number of grammars of English had been published during the seventeenth century. They were mostly on the Latinate model but still dealt adequately with demonstratives and the like. The most authoritative was the *Grammatica Linguae Anglicanae* (first edition 1653, fifth 1699) by John Wallis, Savilian Professor of Geometry at Oxford. This was written in Latin, a language which Kersey and Bailey must have known well.

Wallis had a clear description (translating this into English): 'Demonstratives *this*, *that*, hic [near speaker], ille [not near speaker], plural *these, those*.' In another chapter he mentioned *that* among a list of conjunctions, which included other clause-introducing forms (*and, or, but, though, therefore, yet, except, when*, and a score more).

Why did Kersey and Bailey not consult Wallis (or one of the other contemporary grammars), realise that there were homonymous forms *that*, and utilise Wallis's clear description of the four demonstratives? It appears that for these early lexicographers, grammar was a world apart. They saw their role as being to deal with words, treating them all in the same way.

As was his wont, Kersey simply gave examples of use for some conjunctions – *or*, *as friend, or foe*; Bailey did not include *or*. Kersey had **therefore**, *for that cause*, and Bailey copied this. Both gave **though**, *although*. Bailey had no entry for *although*; Kersey just gave the word with no definition.

Overall, the attempts to 'define' grammatical words were not only misguided but also meagre and uninformative.

Vocabulary and grammar are the two facets of a language, intricately linked together. A proper account of the nature of any language has to involve both a grammar and a dictionary, framed in compatible terms, with much cross-reference between them. A dictionary could mention *this*, with a link to the section of the grammar dealing with the demonstrative system, its composition, meaning, and function. It is only possible to appreciate the meaning of *this*, for example, through comparing it with the complementary term *that* (supported by well-chosen examples), and with the plurals *these* and *those*.

This point will be repeated in later chapters. It is a fundamental principle which lexicographers today are still far from properly engaged with.

Rationale

The inclusive dictionaries from the first half of the eighteenth century are recognisable as precursors to the dictionaries of today. Their aim was to include *every word* in the language, each considered separately and accorded a 'definition'. We can enquire what function a dictionary of this sort serves? Who uses such a compilation, what do they use it for, how do they use it, and what do they get out of it?

The first point is that the user must know *something* of the language to gain any benefit from a monolingual dictionary. Someone who was completely unaware of at least the rough meanings of common words – such as *man* and *woman*, *water* and *fire*, *big* and *large*, *come* and *go*, *walk* and *run* – could not sensibly be directed to a monolingual dictionary. They just wouldn't understand it. A dictionary user must begin with a fair basic knowledge of vocabulary (and grammar). Then the dictionary will assist them in learning more.

A fundamental question then arises: what is the point of including in a dictionary commonplace words which everyone knows? In 1765, a printer from Birmingham called John Baskerville (inventor of the typeface which bears his name) published *A Vocabulary, or Pocket Dictionary....* Bucking the 'put-everything-in' practice established by Kersey, Bailey, and (by that time) Johnson, he stated that his listing was 'not crowded with the common words of the language such as every person must be supposed to understand'. Baskerville was not reverting to the 'hard words' approach which just explained recent longish loans from Latin and French. He dealt with the whole vocabulary, simply omitting the most ordinary words (which would, in any case, be the hardest to define).

The first monolingual dictionaries – of Coote, Cawdrey, Bullokar, and their successors – explained hard Romance-origin words in terms of familiar Germanic terms. Once Kersey had opened the door to an 'everything in' policy, common Germanic words had to be defined as well – in terms of other common Germanic words. As we have seen, Kersey sometimes skirted this self-imposed responsibility by simply leaving a number of head words without definition. This included just about all basic kinship nouns. There was nothing against the head word for *sister*, *brother*, *father*, *mother*, *daughter*, *son*, *child*, *grand-child*, *grand-mother*, *grand-father*, *or grand-daughter* (there is not even a head-word entry for *grand-son*). However, Kersey does inform the reader that *an aunt* is *a father's or a mother's sister*, and *an uncle* is *the father's or mother's brother* (note difference in articles).

Bailey did not shirk definitions to the same extent. However, what he did provide was not always wonderfully informative. Consider:

a child	a son or daughter
a daughter	a female child
a son	a relative term apply'd to a male child, considered in the relation he bears to his parents

(Since OE times there had been two senses for *child*: (i) son or daughter, and (ii) young human being. Although Bailey described multiple senses for other words, he failed to do so for *child*.)

For *mother*, Bailey simply gives *of a child*, and does not specify what makes a woman the mother of a child (the act of giving birth).

Including uninformative definitions X = Y and Y = X has been a pervasive feature of dictionaries, both then and now. Alongside Bailey's *child/daughter/son* from 1730, can be placed the following circular entries from the 2214-page *Random House Unabridged Dictionary* of 1987:

parent	a father or a mother
father	a male parent
mother	a female parent

Basically, the fault lies with the system, with the basic methodology, and only secondarily with the implementation of it. We can recall how it all began, as set out in the diagram from page 49:

Diagram of the original methodology

| BILINGUAL DICTIONARY | head word in Latin | translation equivalent(s) in English |
| MONOLINGUAL DICTIONARY | ↓
head word in English (cognate with Latin head word in bilingual dictionary) | ↓
definition in English |

Monolingual and bilingual dictionaries are entirely different creatures. The purpose of a bilingual dictionary is to suggest translation equivalents, in the target language, for words from the source language, taken one by one. The translator should then consult a monolingual dictionary – of the type recommended here – for the target language, to decide which translation equivalent to employ in each particular context of use.

The early 'hard words' dictionaries – of Coote, Cawdrey, Bullokar, and the rest – had a limited purpose. They aimed to explain recent rather esoteric loans in terms of familiar, well-established words. It was when the 'transfer from bilingual to monolingual format' (in our diagram) became the basis for full monolingual dictionaries that the unsatisfactory nature of the endeavour becomes apparent.

Alphabetical ordering is a necessary device for locating a word but an inadequate one for explaining meanings. That is, for fulfilling the purpose of a dictionary – providing information to the user which will enable them to decide when to use a particular word rather than a similar one, and how each word fits into the overall semantic matrix of the language.

Entries for individual kin terms should all carry direction to an inclusive discussion of kin terms as a semantic set – diagrams and discussion showing the links between *mother, father, parent, son, daughter, child, sister, brother, sibling, husband, wife, spouse*, and the rest. There will also be links to *man* and *woman*. It is important that the defining criteria be clearly stated: a woman is a member of the sex which can bear children; a mother is a woman who has borne a child. (Not stating this essential criterion for mother – on the part of Bailey in 1730 and Random House two and a half centuries later – may have been due to not wanting to mention childbirth for reasons of delicacy, but it does vitiate the value of the endeavour.)

What came out of the diagram was (a) dealing with each word as an isolate, and (b) providing a 'definition' for it. It was often suggested that the definition could substitute for the head word, maintaining the overall meaning of the sentence. As was demonstrated in chapter 3, the roles of verbs *finish, cease*, and *stop* can be discussed and explained in relation to each other, in a way that they cannot be through separate (and unlinked) 'definitions'.

Baskerville saw no point in cluttering his dictionary with words that everyone would be familiar with, such as *big*, *large*, *little*, and *small*. This was fair enough within the conventional shape of a dictionary, which Baskerville followed. It is true that dictionary users would know roughly what *big* and *large* mean. What an ideal dictionary should do is indicate circumstances in which it is only appropriate to use *big*, not *large*. And vice versa. And when either would be appropriate. Dictionaries should aim not just to explain hard words in terms of simple ones (a relic of their beginnings), but should rather explain and illustrate how to use *all* words – when it is felicitous to employ a certain word, rather than another with similar meaning.

In terms of the traditional view of dictionaries – with isolated entries and separate definitions – Baskerville's position is sensible. It is a waste of time, space, and effort to include familiar words whose meanings are roughly known to everyone. An alternative vision – the theme of the present volume – is that the user of a dictionary needs to know what *exactly* the difference is between words, both high-flown and familiar, which have similar meanings.

Consider the definitions provided by Kersey and Bailey for *big*, *large*, *little*, and *small* (plus *great* and *ample*, words used in definitions of *big* and *large*):

	KERSEY	BAILEY
big	or great	great, large
large	great, or ample	broad, great, wide, extensive
little	small, or short in stature	small
small	or little	little in size or in number
great	big, large, huge, mighty, powerful, &c	large, big, huge, mighty, noble
ample	or large	of large extent, also abundant; also noble

Note that similar definitions – consisting just of one or more semi-synonyms – will be found in many present-day dictionaries.

A foreign learner, or a young person, or any dictionary user, will already have *some* idea of the meanings of these words. They look to the dictionary to help refine their initial ideas, to give them confidence about when it would be appropriate to use *little* and not *small*, for example.

The next chapter explores the semantic set based on *big* and *little*, *large* and *small*, as a tentative demonstration showing how users' needs may be met.

Discussion is extended to *ample* (together with its congeners *enough* and *sufficient*) and also *great*, in various guises.

6 Semantic Set: *Big* and *Little*, *Large* and *Small*

We can begin with an examination of the adjectives *big* /bɪg/, *large* /lɑːdʒ/, *little* /lɪtl/, and *small* /smɔːl/, each of which is of common occurrence. In terms of rough-and-ready meanings:

- *big* and *large* refer to considerable/substantial size or extent.
- *little* and *small* refer to limited/restricted size or extent.

There are the following **pairings**:

- *big* and *little* form one pair; e.g. *big sister* = elder, *little sister* = younger.
- *large* and *small* form another pair; e.g. *a large number of*, *a small number of*.

The adjectives in a pair generally (but not absolutely always) pattern together; exceptions will be pointed out.

Little and *a little* also function as quantifiers and as adverbs; these uses are described towards the end of the chapter.

These words have varied histories. Old English contrasted *micel* and *lȳtel*, two of the four adjectives to have suppletive comparative and superlative forms (the others were predecessors of *better/best* and *worse/worst*):

	COMPARATIVE	SUPERLATIVE
micel 'big'	māra	mǣst
lȳtel 'little'	lǣssa	lǣst

Micel survived into Middle English (spelled in various ways, including *mickle*) with the meaning 'of substantial size, numerous (people), powerful, great'.

Big came into Middle English, probably from a Scandinavian language, about 1300, meaning 'strong, sturdy'. By 1500, *big* had replaced *micel* in the standard dialect, taking over its range of meaning. (*Micel/mickle* survived only in Scots and northern English dialects.) *Big* thus paired up with *little*, as *micel* had before.

Big formed regular comparative and superlative, *bigger* and *biggest*. As described in chapter 1, the old forms from *micel* – now *more* and *most* – became the grammatical indexes of positive comparison and superlative for words not taking *-er* or *-est*.

The irregular comparative and superlative associated with *lȳtel* have become the negative indexes of comparison and superlative, *less* and *least*. This left adjective *little* with no comparative and superlative forms, something which persisted until late in the twentieth century. One had to use *smaller* and *smallest* in place of the inadmissible ♦*littler* and ♦*littlest*. However, regular forms *littler* and *littlest* are now coming into use (sooner in some dialects than in others).

The other two words have a more prosaic etymology:

- The Old English word *smale*, meaning 'narrow, slender, small, fine (powder)', has developed into modern *small*.
- *Large* was a twelfth-century loan into Middle English from French, originally meaning 'abundant, ample, roomy'. It developed a pairing with *small*.

Meanings and Use

We can now survey the occurrence of these adjectives:

- In some contexts only *big* or *little* may be used.
- In some contexts only *large* and *small* may be used; in others these are preferred.
- In some contexts either pair may be employed with little substantive difference in meaning.

Big has some of the characteristics of a superordinate term. In a number of contexts where *large* is preferred (and would be so used by a sophisticated language user), *big* can be substituted within a sort of unrefined speech style. For example, one generally says *The firm made a large profit last year* but *The firm made a big profit last year* is a possible alternative.

Note that the reverse does not apply. For example, one says *She gave a big shout* and *I see big trouble ahead*, not ♦*She gave a large shout* or ♦*I see large trouble ahead*.

I   Contexts for *large* and *small*.
Ia   Only *large* and *small* can be used (not *big* and *little*). This applies for some nouns referring to quantity. For example:

> They have a large/small number of horses
> The shed houses a large/small quantity/amount of oats
> A large/small part of the building remains unpainted
> They operate on a large/small scale
> Do you have a large/small size in shirts?

Garments are typically marked as *small, medium, large*, or *extra-large* (not as *big size* or *little size*). There are compounds *large-scale* and *small-scale*.

In printing, one distinguishes between LARGE CAPITALS and SMALL CAPITALS (not *big* and *little* ones).

Ib ***Large*** **and** ***small*** **are preferred, but** ***big*** **and** ***little*** **are also possible.**
(i) This applies for a fair number of nouns referring to a specific kind of quantity. For example:

> He ate a large/small portion of the pie
> This magazine has a large/small circulation
> The Duchess has a large/small fortune
> They're requesting a large/small subsidy

Other nouns in this category include *volume, majority, increase, income, profit, bet, audience, staff*. Plus *price rise, body of soldiers, post office, railway station*.

(ii) Nouns referring to distance and area, as in:

> The town is a large/small distance away
> We need a container with a large/small radius/circumference
> We bought a large/small area/expanse of forest

There are a fair number of idioms involving *large* and *small*. For instance, *The robbers came in the small hours of the morning* (early in the morning), *She is larger than life* (with an impressive, overwhelming personality), *By and large what he said is correct* (most of it is correct), and *The escaped tiger was at large for two hours* (roaming freely about).

II Contexts where only ***big*** **and** ***little*** **can be used** (not *large* and *small*). A number of semantic fields are involved here.
IIa Kinship seniority. *Big* is used for older and *little* for younger brother or sister. Their actual size may be quite different and (to avoid confusion) can be referred to through *large* and *small*:

> My little sister is larger (in size) than my big sister
> My little sister is large and my big sister is small

Alternatively, it is perfectly possible to say: *My little sister is bigger than my big sister*, using *big* in two senses (*bigger* here refers to size, as in III below).

IIb Importance. Both *big* and *little* may be acceptable, as in:

> I'm going to the big [senior] school next year; you will still be in the little [junior] school

Alongside *Mary has been promoted and now she's a big boss*, someone else may respond in echo-fashion, half-jokingly, *And I'm still only a little boss.*

Often, only *big* may be employed, when it would scarcely be cogent to refer (with *little*) to relative lack of importance:

We just had a big break	I see big trouble ahead
He's a big-name director	We're in the big money now
It's a big bargain	It was the big win of the season
It's a big headache	She has a big future in front of her

In a number of instances with *big* in the 'important' sense, either *little* or *small* can be used, showing an exception to the general principle of pairing:

Mary has landed a big role in the new film; John only a little/small one

Toes on opposite sides of the foot are *big toe* and *little toe* (never ♦*large toe* and ♦*small toe*). And there is *little finger*. (What would be *big finger* has a different name, *thumb*.) Like many common words, *big* enters into a number of idioms, including *get a big kick out of it* (really enjoy it). It is also used as an emphatic modifier, as in *He's a big fool* (very foolish) and *He's a big bore* (very boring).

This sense of *big* may be employed ironically – as *He's a big expert on it, I don't think* – or disparagingly – *He's too big for his boots* (he thinks he's more important than he is).

IIc Noise. For example:

There was a little click and then a big bang
She gave a big (loud) shout, and he replied in a little (tiny) whisper

IId Words and speech acts. Examples include:

He tends to use big (long erudite) words when little ones would be
more understandable
They had a big/little argument over it
She threw a coin into the fountain and made a big/little wish

With some nouns only *big* is appropriate:

The boss unveiled her big vision/plan/idea for the firm's expansion
Should we amalgamate or not, that's the big question
His one big regret was that his father had not lived to see him win the
scholarship

IIe Activities. For example:

They had a big/little accident/fight
There was one little mystery and three big ones

Also with *voyage, thrill,* and *fright. Big* may be used (but *little* is only marginally acceptable) with *deal, puzzle,* and *temptation.* With *effort* and *problem,* one may use *big* and – at the opposite pole – either *little* or *small,* further exceptions to the general principle of pairing.

III Contexts where *big/little* and *large/small* are substitutable, with no real difference in meaning. This relates to size (and covers a high proportion of the uses of all four adjectives). The nouns involved generally have concrete reference. For example:

> It's a big/large/little/small town/house/office/map/monkey/bunch of bananas/pile of manure
> They established a big/large/little/small committee to decide on it

Some speakers opine that *a large building* is more commodious than *a big building*; opinions vary. *Big,* but not *large,* may be modified by *great – a great big building* exceeds *a big building* in size. (*Great* is discussed later in this chapter.)

Little may sometimes imply a lesser size than *small.* Thus, *a small room* may be less cramped than *a little room.* Overlying this, *little* often indicates an endearing character; *a small dog* just describes size whereas *my little dog* carries affection. Compare:

> It's a small sensible compact house, easy to maintain
> It's a dear little house, covered with ivy and full of history

Some nouns accept *big, large,* and *small,* but scarcely *little.* For example:

> He has a big/large/small appetite
> She pointed out a big/large/small discrepancy in the forward estimates

This is probably due, at least in part, to interference from the modifying sense of *little,* as in *He has little appetite for it* and *There was little discrepancy in the forward estimates.* It is discussed at the end of the chapter.

There are idioms relating to size. One which dates from the early sixteenth century (and now sounds a trifle archaic) is *She is big with child,* referring to a woman at a late stage of pregnancy.

It is instructive to compare *large* and *big* with the same noun:

It's a large river	Of considerable size (sense III)
It's a big river	EITHER: It's an important, major tradeway, with many people living on its banks (sense IIb)
	OR: Of considerable size (sense III)

He's a large man   Of considerable size (sense III)

He's a big man   EITHER: He's important and powerful, with much
                     influence (sense IIb)

                     OR: Of considerable size (sense III)

Writers can play amusing games with words. In 1927, P. G. Wodehouse wrote about a man who lived in a

> small [bachelor apartment]

He manipulated the parsing to

> [small bachelor] apartment

calling its occupant (and the novel) *The small bachelor*. Normally, *small* would not be used to modify *bachelor*; Wodehouse thus created an unusual and distinctive effect.

Large is the only one of the four adjectives to have been borrowed from French. It was soon followed by derived forms – adverb *largely* as in *He was largely to blame* (a large part of the blame falls on him), and verb *enlarge* 'to make or to become of increased size', as in *He enlarged the hole* and *Over time, the hole enlarged*. There are no corresponding derivations for *big*, *little*, or *small*.

This draft discussion of *big* and *little*, *large*, and *small* requires cross-references to semantic sets involving *deep* and *shallow*; *wide* and *narrow*; *long*, *tall* and *short*; *huge*, *immense* and *tiny*; *many*, *much*, *few* and *less*; *old* and *young*; *loud* and *soft*; and probably more besides.

Definitions quoted at the end of the last chapter related *large* to *great* and *ample*. In fact, *ample* may be used in some of the examples of Ia, while *great* is possible for many in Ia, Ib, IIc–e, and III, plus a few in IIb. We now examine *ample*, and then turn to *great*.

Ample, Enough and Sufficient

Ample is in fact a minor member of a semantic set with *enough* and *sufficient*, words of diverse origin:

- *Enough* /e'nʌf/ functions as both adjective and adverb, just like its Old English progenitor *ge-nōg*, whose adjective sense was 'enough, abundant, much, many' and the adverb sense was 'enough, very'. (This goes back to Proto-Indo-European verb **nek-* 'reach, attain'.)
- Middle English borrowed verb *suffice* /sə'fais/ from French at the beginning of the fourteenth century, adjective *sufficient* /sə'fiʃənt/ following soon after. It immediately accepted the Germanic suffix *-ly*, forming adverb *sufficiently*. Noun *sufficiency* came during the fifteenth century.

- There was another Romance borrowing with the verb coming first – *amplify* /'ampli‿fai/ attested from about 1400 and adjective *ample* /ampl/ following a few decades later. This formed comparative *ampler*, superlative *amplest*, and adverb *amply*.

Their basic meanings are:

- *Sufficient* indicates that there is what is needed for some particular purpose.
- *Enough* indicates what is needed in general terms.
- *Ample* indicates that there is more than is needed.

We can compare:

> Ben Towers has sufficient money to buy a car
> Rockefeller has enough money

Adjective *sufficient* expects some specification of the reason for the money being appropriate. This is generally shown by a following clause (such as *to buy a car*) or phrase (*for a car*), or it can be inferable from the context of utterance. In contrast, *enough* may be used for a general statement – Rockefeller has so much money he couldn't possibly need any more. Note that *enough* can be followed by a *for* or *to* specification, but this is entirely optional. *Ample* is similar to *enough*:

> Adam Thomas has ample money

This indicates that he has more than enough money for all his normal needs. A reason clause may be added, as in *Adam Thomas has ample money to buy a car* – he can buy a car and have money left over.

The corresponding adverbs exhibit the same meaning distinction – *sufficiently*, which precedes the adjective it *modifies*, and *enough*, which follows:

> The river is sufficiently deep to allow a medium-draught vessel to pass
> The river is deep enough

A shorter sentence, *The river is sufficiently deep*, sounds incomplete, and invites the response *Sufficiently deep for what?* In contrast, *The river is deep enough* sounds fine – the depth is adequate for all normal purposes. (A *for/to* addition is possible, but it is not felt to be required, as it is with *sufficiently*.)

Adverb *amply* – which also precedes a modified adjective – is not used a great deal nowadays, but one could say:

> The river is amply deep

This indicates that the depth is quite a bit more than is likely to be needed. Optionally, *to allow a medium-draught vessel to pass* could be added.

Consider the following corpus example:

> As for Solomon, he knew that she was the mother because she loved
> the child sufficiently to give him up rather than see him killed

It would not be appropriate to employ *enough* here. *She loved the child enough*
implies that she loved the child as much as any mother should. But *sufficiently*,
followed by the *to* clause, indicates the degree of love needed for the mother
to act in this way.

We can now examine the contexts of use.

I   As adjectives.

**Ia   With the plural form of a count noun, or with a non-count noun, each
with concrete reference.** All three adjectives can be used:

> We have sufficient sugar/batteries for the camping trip
> We have enough/ample sugar/batteries

We encounter:

> The programme included enough Beethoven

This implies that a balanced programme really should not include more
Beethoven than this. For *sufficient* to be used, a reason clause needs to be
added, something like:

> The programme included sufficient Beethoven to satisfy the demands
> of the sponsor

Ib   Following indefinite article *a*. *Enough* may not be used, only *sufficient*
(and *ample*, if its meaning is compatible with that of the following noun).

(i) With a noun that has collective meaning:

> They have obtained a sufficient/ample supply/amount/quantity of bat-
> teries/sugar for the expedition
> She has secured a sufficient/ample number of votes to ensure election
> There was a sufficient body of outside opinion to bring to bear on
> the task
> Dr Wood has a sufficient library for his research needs

It is possible to use a comparative or superlative of *sufficient* or *ample* with a
noun showing collective meaning:

> They have assembled a more sufficient/ampler supply of batteries than
> any previous expedition
> They have assembled the most sufficient/amplest supply of batteries
> that I have ever seen

More/most sufficient and *ampler/amplest* are used only rarely, but they are permissible. In contrast, *enough* never takes a comparative or superlative; one

cannot say *more enough* or *most enough*. This is in large part due to *enough* not being used with collective nouns. It also implies that *enough* indicates 'exactly what is needed, neither more nor less'.

(ii) With other singular nouns. For example:

> She provided a sufficient answer to satisfy the committee
> The conditions were satisfied to a sufficient extent for work to proceed

Ic As copula complement. Here, *enough, sufficient* (and sometimes *ample*) can be used:

> The information already provided is enough/ample
> The information already provided is sufficient to ensure his conviction

A typical use of *enough* is:

> She started to sing and that was enough

It implies that no one wanted more; her singing was so bad that we couldn't stand it. As the saying goes, *Enough is enough*. If *sufficient* were to be used here, some addition would be expected: *She started to sing and that was sufficient for us to tell she had no musical ability.*

Id As a complete noun phrase. *Enough* is common in this function; *sufficient* is possible but less used (*ample* would be inappropriate):

> I think I have said enough
> They have enough to do

II As adverbs.

IIa Modifying a clause. The adverbs are used rather seldom in this function. One instance was the King Solomon sentence quoted above, with *she loved the child sufficiently.*

Sufficiently can follow the verb:

> Eric has improved sufficiently to be allowed to go home from the hospital

Alternatively, *sufficiently* could precede *improved* here. However, adverb *enough* must follow the verb, as in:

> I think I have talked enough

Sufficiently would not be too felicitous in this sentence. One might instead say something like: *I think I have explained things sufficiently to make the plan clear.*

IIb Modifying an adjective. Here, *sufficiently* must precede the adjective and *enough* follow the adjective:

> It was a sufficiently responsible body to be awarded a grant
> It was a responsible enough body
> The storage period will be sufficiently long for the fruit to ripen
> The storage period will be long enough

When *enough* is added after an adjective, it may convey the sense 'beyond doubt', as in:

> He was a nice enough young chap
> What she said was true enough

Enough is found in some idiom-like combinations, including *oddly enough*, *strangely enough* (it is indeed odd/strange that...) and *likely enough* (fairly likely).

Interestingly, the items in this semantic set can be combined. Adverb *amply* modifies *enough* as head of a noun phrase in:

> She carried a small purse containing amply enough for the evening

And adverbs *sufficiently* (before the adjective) and *enough* (after it) reinforce each other in:

> It is hoped that the rainy weather will stay away sufficiently long enough not to spoil the outdoors festival

The prototypical uses of these adjectives and adverbs have been outlined here. *Sufficient(ly)* normally occurs with a *to* or *for* reason specification, but sometimes this is just understood from what has been said before or from shared knowledge of speaker and addressee. *Enough* and *ample/amply* do not require a reason to be appended, but this can be included.

Ample and *amply* may be used in place of *sufficient* or *enough* to indicate 'more than is needed', if this is a plausible thing to say. And there is a further sense of adjective *ample*.

III Ample may also mean 'of considerable size', as in:

> Edwina married an ample Tongan chief
> She nurtured the baby at her ample breast

This indicates something which is of more substantial size than usual, more than is really necessary, but that this is quite agreeable.

Large (or *big*) could be used in place of this sense of *ample*, with a neutral tone. And *large* (but not *big*) may be used in place of *ample* in sense Ib above: *They have obtained a large supply/amount/quantity/number of batteries.* However, this does not relate to any need.

This draft discussion of *enough, sufficient,* and *ample* requires cross-reference to sets including adjectives *adequate* and *appropriate,* verbs *suffice* and *amplify,* and more.

Great

Great is descended from Old English *grēat* 'thick, stout, bulky, big; coarse (as in coarse flour)', going back to Proto-Indo-European verb **ghrēu-* 'rub, grind'. This adjective has a pervasive – and unique – role in the modern language, with varied senses and functions.

I   Indicating 'to a high degree'.

Ia   Modifying a noun referring to a state. *Great* with the noun is equivalent to *very* with the corresponding adjective. This sense of *great* can be used with a base noun and *very* with an adjective derived from it, as in:

> The nurse showed great care
> The nurse was very careful

Or *very* with a base adjective may correspond to *great* with a state noun derived from it, as in:

> The seer is very wise
> The seer has great wisdom

This is a very common use of *great*. There are many examples where it is the adjective which is derived. They include:

great beauty	very beauti-ful	great passion	very passion-ate
great value	very valu-able	great skill	very skill-ful
great fame	very fam-ous	great energy	very energ-etic
great anger	very angr-y	great comfort	very comfort-able
great prejudice	very prejudice-d	great greed	very greed-y
great danger	very danger-ous	great effect	very effect-ive

And those where the state noun is derived include:

great happi-ness	very happy	great ugli-ness	very ugly
great jealous-y	very jealous	great intelligen-ce	very intelligent
great stupid-ity	very stupid	great original-ity	very original

There are also a few irregular derivations:

| great pride | very proud | great poverty | very poor |

In some instances, adjective and noun have quite different forms:

| great age/antiquity | very old | great size | very big/large |
| great speed | very fast | great distance | very far |

Ib Modifying other nouns, for which there is a derived adjective:
(i) Nouns referring to humans:

| a great fool | very fool-ish | a great comic | very comi-cal |

(ii) Nouns with abstract reference, and nouns referring to noise:

| a great advantage | very advantage-ous | a great profit | very profit-able |
| a great success | very success-ful | a great noise | very nois-y |

Ic Modifying a noun, where both noun and adjective are derived from a verb:

| great vari-ation | very vari-able | a great talk-er | very talk-ative |

Id Modifying a noun for which there is no corresponding adjective:

> a great relief   a great enemy
> a great scoundrel

Ie Modifying a dimension adjective. Here, *great* has a similar meaning to *very* but indicates a higher degree of the property. Thus there are pairs:

> great big building   very big building
> great tall skyscraper   very tall skyscraper
> great fat king   very fat king

Great in this sense only applies to positive members of antonym pairs; to *big*, *tall*, *high*, *wide*, *deep*, and *fat*, but not to *little*, *short*, *narrow*, *shallow*, and *thin*. Note that it applies to *big* but not normally to *large*.

In British and Australian dialects there is idiomatic use of *dirty* with *big* and especially with *great big*. For example:

> They came in a dirty great big truck to take the furniture away
> There's a dirty great big oil slick in the gulf

In this meaning, *dirty* bears no reference to lack of cleanliness, but is simply a further emphatic modifier. In descending size there are *dirty great big*, then *great big*, then *very big*, then *big*.

A positive dimension adjective can relate to *great* in two ways. For example:

SENSE Ia   The hole has great depth
              It is a very deep hole
SENSE Ie   It is a great deep hole

Note that in sense I, *great* is neutral as to whether the property, or the high degree of it, is a good or bad thing. We get *great prejudice*, *great jealous-y*, and *great stupid-ity* alongside *great beauty*, *great charm*, and *great happi-ness*. This contrasts with sense II.

II **Indicating approbation.** *Great* here functions as an adjective, with similar meaning to *good* (the effect is more like *very good*). In this sense, *great* occurs modifying a different set of nouns from those involved in sense I, or it can be copula complement. For example:

> We had a great time at the circus
> She's a great girl
> It was a great result
> That's a great idea
> He has a great physique
> It's a great language
> She's great with children

It is interesting that the 'good' sense of *great* may combine with the endearing sense of *little*, as in:

> They live in a great little cottage on the edge of the moors

This sense of *great* may refer to something which is important, and generally it is also good:

> Jim has studied all the great literature
> I know that you will achieve great things in life
> America is a great nation
> The Queen is a great lady

Sense IIb for *big* refers to importance. However, this is neutral as to perceived value. Compare:

> Mary Jenkins is a big boss
>   (she is in the higher echelons of management)
> Mary Jenkins is a great boss
>   (she does her job well, and the workers like her)

Some of the examples given in IIb for *big* can have *great* instead; for example, *It's a big/great bargain*. For others, *great* is scarcely acceptable; these include *I see big trouble ahead*.

The adjective has a rather different sense when *Great Power* is used to describe a nation with considerable military and economic strength, and thus power (but is not necessarily good).

III **Indicating considerable/substantial size or extent, similar to *big* or *large* or both of these.** In each instance, *great* is likely to imply something more substantial than *big* or *large* (although sometimes *great* may be preferred just for stylistic effect).

(i) With nouns referring to quantity. This is sense Ia for *large*, where *big* is not permitted. For example:

> The evangelist has a great number of followers
> A great majority of the people desire change

(ii) With nouns referring to a specific kind of quantity, or to distance or area. This is sense Ib for *large*, where *big* is also possible (but generally less preferred). For instance:

> A great crowd of people attended the rally
> He played a great part in getting them to agree
> It's a great distance to travel in one day

(iii) Some of the contexts where *big* may be used, but scarcely *large*. This is sense II for *big*. *Great* may be used for many instances of senses IIc noise, IId speech acts, and IIe activities:

> She let out a great scream
> They had a great argument over it
> It's a great mystery which will never be solved
> John received a great fright

Great is not substitutable in sense IIa (*big sister*). As just mentioned, sense IIb, important, for *big* overlaps with sense II, good (and sometimes also important), for *great*. For instance, *She has a great future in front of her*.

(iv) Sense III for *big/large*, referring just to size, where either may be used. *Great* is also acceptable; for example:

> There's a great cathedral, dwarfing the rest of the town
> He has a great appetite

This has outlined the main meanings for *great*. Other senses include 'do a lot'. *She's a great talker* can mean either that she talks well, or that she talks a lot. There are specialised uses such as *great-grandparent*. And *great* is also used as an approbatory exclamation: *We're going to Paris next month. Great!* (an alternative could be *Good!* or *Fine!* or *Terrific!*).

A special use of *great* is in place names. For instance, *Great Britain*, *the Great Barrier Reef*, *the Great Dividing Range*, *the Great Sandy Desert*, *the*

Great Wall of China. One group of islands in the Caribbean is named the *Greater Antilles* and its neighbour *the Lesser Antilles.*

A Little, A Few, and A Great Many

Great and *little* fulfil a further role (together with *few*).

With a count noun, there is a fascinating contrast between modifiers *few* and *a few*:

(A)	He has few horses	Has literal meaning: a small number of horses (perhaps, fewer than we thought he might have)
(B)	He has a few horses	Indicates that, surprisingly, he does have some horses (we thought he may have had none)

With a non-count noun, there is a similar contrast between *little* and *a little*:

(A)	He has little sugar	Has literal meaning: a small quantity of sugar (perhaps, less than we thought he might have)
(B)	He has a little sugar	Indicates that, surprisingly, he does have some sugar (we thought he may have had none)

In the (A) sentences, *few* and *little* behave like normal adjectives. For example, they can be preceded by *very*. In the (B) sentences, *a few* and *a little* behave quite differently. For example, they can be preceded by *just* or *only*. *He has only a little sugar* indicates that, surprisingly, he has less sugar than we thought he might have had.

There is a further possiblity just for (B) with count nouns:

(B)   He has a good/fair few horses

This indicates that, surprisingly, he has more horses than we thought he had; *a good few* is likely to indicate a larger number than *a fair few*.

We can now examine the opposite end of the spectrum of size. There is nothing here for non-count nouns, but for count nouns we get:

(A)	He has many horses	Literal meaning: a large number of horses
(B)	He has a good many horses	Indicates that, surprisingly, he has a larger number of horses than we thought he had
	He has a great many horses	Indicates that, surprisingly, he has a greater number of horses than we thought he had

Note that with *few* we can have *a fair few* or *a good few* or just *a few*. In contrast, with *many* we can have *a good many*, or *a great many*, but not *a fair many*, and not just *a many*. Both *little* and *few* can be used just with *a*, but for *many* to take *a*, *good* or *great* must also be included.

Little and *a little* can also contrast when functioning as complete noun phrases:

| (A) | They achieved little | A small amount, less than required |
| (B) | They achieved a little | More than expected |

There is a similar contrast when used adverbially:

| (A) | It was little understood | Less that it should have been |
| (B) | It was understood a little | More than it might have been |

(In each of these, the adverb could precede or follow the verb. *It was understood little* and *It was a little understood* are also acceptable. However, the orderings first given are the most natural ones.)

This chapter has provided a broad outline of the meanings and functions for *enough*, *sufficient*, *ample*, *great*, *large*, *small*, *big*, and *little*. Of these, *little* is the most pervasive, and quite a little more could be added to the account here.

7   Spreading Wings

Monolingual dictionaries in the seventeenth and eighteenth centuries came to be organised in a similar pattern. A strict alphabetical order was gradually adopted, but with eccentric treatment of letters *i* and *j*, and of *u* and *v*. This reflects – indirectly – the habits of Latin, which continued to permeate many aspects of the treatment of English.

The Latin alphabet was economical. It used a single letter for both the vowel *i* (as in English *bin*) and the semi-vowel (consonant), which is written as *y* in English (as in *yard*). The letter used here was usually 'i'. For example, in Elyot's Latin-English dictionary, head words came in the following order:

Iam	[yam]	nowe
Idioma	[idioma]	a propre forme of speche
Iento	[yento]	to eate meate afore dyner
Ignio	[ignio]	to inflame
Iugo	[yugo]	to yoke or couple togither

Initial letter 'i' represented semi-vowel [y] when it preceded a vowel and vowel [i] when it preceded a consonant. Sometimes 'j' was used in place of 'i', and sometimes 'i' would be used for the vowel and 'j' for the semi-vowel, but *i* and *j* would still be mingled together as if they were the same letter.

(English people today typically pronounce the *i* consonant in Latin as an affricate [dʒ], just like in English words such as *jealous*. This has no basis in antiquity.)

Latin also used a single letter for both the vowel *u* (as in English *wood*) and the semi-vowel (consonant) which is written as *w* in English (also as in *wood*). The letter here was generally 'v', sometimes 'u'. A further example of the ordering of head words from Elyot's bilingual dictionary is:

Vanitas	[wanitas]	vanitie, lyghtnes, lesyng, foly
Vltra	[ultra]	beyonde, more, moreouer, sometyme shrewdely or frowardely
Vocabulum	[wocabulum]	the denomination of any thynge
Vrbs	[urbs]	a wallyd towne, also a citie
Vulpes	[wulpes]	a foxe

Where the *v* semi-vowel was followed by the *v* vowel, as in the word for 'fox', a sequence *vu* was employed.

Old English had a single labio-dental fricative phoneme, written as *f*. This had voiced pronunciation [v] between vowels, and voiceless [f] initially and finally. For example, *fæst* [fæst] 'fast' and *efen* [even] 'even'. In Middle English and early Modern English times there were many loans from French with initial [v], such as *vast* (contrasting with *fast*). Letter 'v' was added to the alphabet, both for these loans and for the inherited medial [v]. Note that this *v* was a fricative, quite different from the consonant *v* in Latin which was semi-vowel [w]. (English had the semi-vowel letter, written as *w*, which had been created by writing *vv* – or *uu* – and linking the two letters together.)

The influence of Latin was so strong that in Mulcaster's long list, and in the first bilingual dictionaries by Coote, Cawdrey, and others, the letter 'v' was used (before a vowel) for fricative [v] and also (before a consonant) for vowel [u]. For example, the sequence of head words in Coote's dictionary of 1596 included:

vanquish
vineyard
vnion   [union]
vocation
vsurpe   [usurpe]

(In some of the quotations in chapter 4, I have silently adjusted *v/u*, and also *i/ j*, to make them more understandable for modern readers.)

By the middle of the seventeenth century, the two letters *v* (for the fricative) and *u* (for the vowel) had come into use but were treated as identical for alphabetical ordering (continuing to reflect the Latin convention, although in Latin consonantal *v* had been a semi-vowel and in English it is a fricative). Johnson continued with this bizarre practice (he was keen on tradition), and his ordering was:

vanquish
vineyard
union
vocation
usurp

It is somewhat unnerving for a modern reader to be confronted with successive running heads: VET, UGL, VIB, and so on.

Only in the work of Johnson's successors were words commencing with *u* and *v* separated out.

Old English had a palatal affricate, [dʒ], in non-initial position. It was at first written *cg* – as in *ecg* 'edge' – and later adjusted to be 'dg'. The flood of loans from French into Middle English included many words which had initial [dʒ], written as *j*. In the thirteenth century, French [dʒ] was reduced to just [ʒ], still written as *j*. Since English had [dʒ] as a phoneme, but not [ʒ], later loans of French words commencing in [ʒ] were rendered in English with initial [dʒ]. For example, *jacket* ['dʒakit].

Similarly to *v* and *u*, letters *j* and *i* were treated as they had been in Latin. Mulcaster, Coote, Cawdrey, and other early lexicographers wrote both as *i*. Before a consonant this would be interpreted as vowel [i] and before a vowel as consonant [dʒ]. (The difference from Latin was that in English, consonantal *i* was an affricate whereas in Classical Latin it had been a semi-vowel, [y].) Dictionary-makers from the middle of the seventeenth century, up to Johnson, did use distinct letters, *j* and *i*, but treated them as the same when alphabetising. A selection of head words, in the order given, is:

COOTE	JOHNSON
idiot	**idiot**
ielous	**jealous**
illusion	**illusion**
iudiciall	**judicial**

As with *u* and *v*, it was only in post-Johnson times that *i* and *j* were accorded separate entries.

Despite the English system of spelling being out of step with how the language was (and is) spoken, early dictionaries paid no attention to pronunciation. Mulcaster, in his word list of 1582, had provided illustrations of pairs of words distinguished just by stress. This was taken up again by Bailey, who contrasted *to dese'rt* and *a de'sert*. Johnson improved on this by specifying word class: *to dese'rt*, v[erb] a[ctive], to forsake... and *de'sert*, n[oun] s[ubstantive], a wilderness.... Webster, in 1828, repeated this information, but placed the stress mark at the end of the syllable (rather than after the vowel): verb *desert'* and noun *des'ert*.

The earliest attempt to relate the written to the spoken word came from novelist and playwright William Kenrick. His 1773 volume, *A New Dictionary of the English Language*, was the first to indicate pronunciation by diacritical marks, and to divide words into syllables.

The first modern-day encyclopaedia appeared in 1728. This was *Cyclopædia, or a Universal Dictionary of Arts and Sciences*, in two volumes, by Ephraim

Chambers (not related to the dictionary-makers of the same name from the end of the nineteenth century). It was much drawn upon by Johnson.

In 1749 Benjamin Martin, a mathematician and instrument maker, published *Lingua Britannica Reformata: or a New English Dictionary*. This was an ambitious undertaking, beginning with a host of grammatical paradigms in Hebrew, Greek, and Latin (in their own scripts), comparisons with German, Dutch, and French, and so forth. In the dictionary itself, the meanings of a word were – for the first time – separated into numbered senses. A second edition came out in 1754 and then it fell by the wayside, usurped by Johnson's landmark work.

Samuel Johnson, Lexicographer

Samuel Johnson was without doubt the foremost practitioner of traditional English lexicography, setting out the principles which his successors have followed, up until today. He was also a polymath, and one of the great literary figures of his age (indeed, of any age). Poet, essayist, novelist, critic, Johnson was at the hub of intellectual activity in London. His dictionary was a work of application and industry. The compiler's erudition, style and wit provided its distinctive panache.

Yet Johnson's ideas concerning the nature of language – although typical of his time – were in a number of ways misguided. Since the evolution of humankind, 100,000 years or more ago, the languages spoken would have had a subtle and systematic grammar, coupled with copious vocabulary. Writing was developed no more than 5,000 years ago and, until recently, was confined to a small educated coterie. Johnson considered that, without the discipline of writing, language would have been a 'wild and barbarous jargon' and that only after it was 'reduced to an alphabet' did order begin to prevail. He does not stop to wonder how a small part of a population learning to write could affect the speech habits of the remainder. In fact, writing is an optional addition, basically extraneous to the overall organisation of a language.

A language is always changing, ever evolving. Awareness of this is enough to daunt anyone intent on documenting it. But one may pretend otherwise. In his 1747 *Plan*, Johnson expressed the intention to establish the true and immutable nature of the language: 'to preserve the purity and ascertain the meaning of our English idiom'. Eight years later, in the preface (written last of all) to the finished dictionary, Johnson showed greater awareness, deriding the idea that a lexicographer could 'preserve words and phrases from mutability' and 'imagine that his dictionary can embalm the language, and secure it from corruption and decay'. A linguist's role, as envisioned today, is to describe, not to prescribe. While Johnson had definite ideas on what was correct, on what should and should not be said, he had begun to understand the benefits of sensible evolution (and the decay attendant on immutability).

Scholars such as Addison and Pope had yearned for a comprehensive English dictionary, to match those of Italian and French. Johnson actually did it. This would not have been possible without a group of booksellers commissioning the volumes and paying for work as it proceeded. But the major factors were Johnson's own vision, his unparalleled understanding of the language, and above all his confidence in his own ability (absolutely justified by the results).

Johnson's first expectation was that he could complete the task in three years. Dr William Adams, an old friend, visited Johnson soon after he had started work, and wondered at this estimate:

DR ADAMS: But the French Academy, which consists of forty members, took forty years to compile their dictionary.

JOHNSON: Sir, thus it is. This is the proportion. Let me see: forty times forty is sixteen hundred. As three to sixteen hundred, so is the proportion of an Englishman to a Frenchman.

In fact, it took Johnson a little over eight years, but the achievement is still colossal. There were two large folio volumes (page size 25 × 40 cm, or 10 × 16 inches) consisting of about 2,300 (unnumbered) pages with around 40,000 entries.

However, the essence lies not in quantity, but in quality. Each head word was characterised as noun, verb, adjective, and so on. Johnson worked with a corpus, rather than just introspecting or copying from predecessors. He illustrated many definitions with quotations from 'the best writers'. For a considerable number of words, their range of meaning was systematised into numbered senses. And the definitions themselves were pert and sometimes provocative.

The Method

Johnson decided that he should deal with ideas rather than with things. There were to be no proper names or geographical information. No technical terms such as the vocabularies of geometry, heraldry and architecture which had so graced the pages of Bailey. And no illustrations.

The aim was to describe the English language in its most sophisticated and cogent form. To this end, it was to be based on usage of the best writers. Johnson would go through volume after volume, picking out significant words. He underlined each, drew attention to it by placing a mark in the margin, and indicated the scope of the needed quotation by a '/' at its beginning and end. Five or six assistants were at work, copying the entries onto paper slips, which then had to be sorted into alphabetical order, and filed.

Johnson's work involved at first marking-up volumes and supervising the assistants. Later, it consisted of formulating definitions on the basis of quotations and his own intimate knowledge of the language. For perhaps three-quarters of the entries, one or more illustrative quotations were attached (a selection from those which had been assembled).

Rather incredibly, Johnson combined this dictionary compilation with – at the same time – a range of other activities. For instance, between 1750 and 1752, he wrote more than 200 issues of *The Rambler*, a twice-weekly essay discussing morality, literature, society, politics, and religion.

Johnson explained that, in order for the size of his volumes not to 'fright away the student', he often edited quotations, missing out a middle portion, or simply recasting the whole. Examples 'thus mutilated' (Johnson's words) no longer represent exactly what the author said, but their sense was maintained, which was what the dictionary required.

For example, issue 429 of *The Spectator* (Saturday, 12 July 1712) included:

That he is conscious there is nothing more improper than such a Complaint in good Company, in that they must pity, whether they think the Lamenter ill or not.

Under the head word **lamenter**, Johnson amended this quotation to read:

Such a complaint good company must pity, whether they think the *lamenter* ill or not.   *Spectator Nº. 429.*

There are thousands of quotations from Shakespeare, and some appear unusual. For instance, Johnson's entry for the adjective **goodly** included the following from *King Lear*, Act IV, scene 3:

> Patience and sorrow strove
> Which should express her *goodliest*; you have seen
> Sunshine and rain at once. Her smiles and tears
> Were like a wetter May.   *Shakespeare's King Lear*

The quarto editions from the seventeenth century, and modern ones from the nineteenth and twentieth centuries, have a different last line: *Were like a better way.*

A little investigation reveals that Johnson must have been using the 1733 edition of Shakespeare's plays edited by Lewis Theobald, which does indeed have *Were like wetter May* (it is not known where Theobald got this from). Other oddities in Johnson's quotations from Shakespeare can also be traced to Theobald.

There are instances of what do appear to be errors in copying. For instance, under **stupid** Johnson included:

With wild surprise
A moment *stupid*, motionless he stood.   *Thomson*

This is from James Thomson's 1727 poem *The seasons*. The extract
actually reads:

With wild surprise
As if to marble struck, devoid of sense
A stupid moment motionless she stood.

Johnson had omitted the middle line as he often did, deliberately. There are
also two discrepancies. He has *A moment stupid* when it should be *A stupid
moment*, and *she* in the original becomes *he* in the dictionary quotation.

The general principle followed was not to quote from anyone still living 'that
I might not be misled by partiality, and that none of my contemporaries might
have reason to complain'. There were, however, some exceptions 'when my heart,
in the tenderness of friendship' led him to employ some contemporary source.

There was plainly a close friendship with feminist Charlotte Lennox.
Her novel, *The Female Quixote, or the Adventures of Arabella*, published
in 1752 (when she was just 22) refers, in the penultimate chapter, to 'the
greatest* genius of the present age', a footnote adding '*The Author of *The
Rambler*'. Johnson returned the compliment by praising Lennox's novel in *The
Gentleman's Magazine*.

In his second volume (the first had already been completed), Johnson used
twenty quotations from *The Female Quixote*, and from Lennox's *Shakespeare
Illustrated* (1753). For example, *The Female Quixote* included:

As her Romances had long familiariz'd her Thoughts to Objects of Grandeur
and Magnificence, she was not so much struck as might have been expected,
with those that now presented themselves to her view.

Johnson provided a succinct version of this for sense 4 of the noun **view**:

She was not so much struck with those objects that now presented themselves
to her *view*.   *Female Quixote.*

The Results

Johnson had fewer entries than Bailey and, by and large, they were words of a
different sort. For example, Johnson does not include *ledger* or *perambulator*
or (surprisingly) *euphemism*. His definition for *mittimus* is short and succinct,
when compared with Bailey's wordy effort (page 61):

mittimus   a warrant by which a justice commits an offender to prison.

A study of head words commencing in 'L', between Bailey and Johnson, reveals 732 items in common; Bailey had 909 not in Johnson (1,641 in all) and Johnson 394 lacking from Bailey (1,126 in all).

For example, we find just in Bailey:

la'barum   a Royal Standard which the Roman Emperors had born before them in the wars.
la'bes   a Spot, Blemish or Stain.
la'bis   any Forceps to suchlike instrument.

And just in Johnson:

la'biodental, *adj*   formed or pronounced by co-operation of the teeth and lips.

      The dental consonants are very easy; and first the *labio-dentals f, v*, also the linguadentals *th, dh.*   *Hld. El of Sp.*

la'bra, *n. s.*   [Spanish.] a lip

      Word of denial, in thy *labras* here
Word of denial, froth and scum thou liest. *Shakespeare.*

Both dictionaries included: ***label*** (accompanied by a diagram in Bailey; three senses with four quotations in Johnson), ***labial***, ***laboratory***, and so on.

It is interesting to see how Johnson dealt with the two common words which we have followed through the centuries:

mouse, *n. s.*   the smallest of all beasts; a little animal haunting houses and corn fields, destroyed by cats.
[plus four quotations]

onion, *n. s.*   it hath an orbicular, coated, bulbous root; the leaves are hollow or pip; the stalk also hollow and swells out in the middle; the flowers consisting of six leaves are collected into a spherical head; the style of the flowers becomes a roundish fruit divided into three cells, containing roundish seeds.   *Mill.*
[plus three quotations]

The entry for *mouse* is an original by Johnson. One naturally looks up critical words in it. Quoting just the first part of each:

beast, *n. s.*   an animal distinguished from birds, insects, fishes, and man.
animal, *n. s.*   a living creature corporeal, distinct, on the one side, from pure spirit, on the other, from mere matter.

That for **onion** was copied, word for word, from *The Gardener's Dictionary* by Phillip Miller, which first appeared in 1732. Johnson was content simply to quote Miller's account for *onion*, and also for *cabbage* (more than sixty lines long), *carrot*, *turnip*, *cedar*, *cherry*, and many others. Definitions of medical terms were similarly taken from John Hill's 1751 *A History of the Materia Medica*, and definitions of legal terms from a 1727 edition of *The Interpreter*, a law dictionary by John Cowell (first published in 1607). Johnson saw no value in trying to improve on such authorities.

He was, on the whole, an exception to the lexicographical habit – followed by his predecessors and his successors – of wholesale copying from earlier dictionaries. Of the 732 head words commencing with 'L' which were shared with Bailey, Johnson copied no more than about thirty straightforward definitions. For example:

linchpin, *n.s.*   an iron pin, which keeps the wheel on the axle-tree   *Dict.*

The final '*Dict*' acknowledges his debt to Bailey's dictionary.

Johnson's major focus was on terms for which many citations from 'the best authors' had been assembled. For instance, **hot**. He recognised seven senses and included sixteen quotations. This entry can fruitfully be condensed to just one quotation for each sense (save the last, for which Johnson gave none).

1. Having the power to excite the sense of heat; contrary to cold; fiery
        Hot and cold were in one body fixt;
        And soft with hard, and light with heavy mixt.   *Dryden*
2. Lustful, lewd
        Now the *hot* blooded gods assist me! remember, Jove, thou
        was't a bull for thy Europa.   *Shakesp.*
3. Strongly affected by sensible qualities; in allusion to dogs hunting
        Nor law, nor checks of confidence will he hear
        When in *hot* scent of gain and full career.   *Dryden*
4. Violent; furious; dangerous
                Our army
        Is now in *hot* engagement with the Moors.   *Dryden*
5. Ardent; vehement; precipitate
        Come, come, lord Mortimer, you are as slow
        As *hot* lord Percy is on fire to go.   *Shakesp. Henry IV*
6. Eager; keen in desire
            It is no wonder that men, either perplexed in the necessary
        affairs of life, or *hot* in the pursuit of pleasure, should not
        seriously examine their tenets.   *Locke*
7. Piquant; acrid

Johnson's reliance on literary sources means that the definition does not reflect the way in which *hot* is used across the language. More than 80 per cent of its occurrences – nowadays, and certainly also then – relate to 'having heat' (Johnson's sense 1), and no more than around 10 per sent to his senses 2–6 combined.

A more appropriate definition would be, in outline (the senses added since Johnson's time are marked with a •):

I.   Having heat, with a high temperature (antonym of *cold*)
    Ia.   Hot to touch: hot stone, hot coals, hot dinner, hot water, hot bath
    Ib.   Weather: hot day, hot summer, hot place
    Ic.   State of body: hot with fever
II.   Spicy, burning sensation in mouth (not caused by heat): hot chillies
III.   Strong emotions
    IIIa.   Lustful: He's hot for her, She has the hots for him
    IIIb.   Keen for something: hot to undertake the task, hot in pursuit, hot on the trail, hot with enthusiasm
    IIIc.   Hot temper: hot argument, hot fight
    IIId.• Flustered: hot and bothered
IV.•   Current and exciting or dangerous: hot news, hot off the press, a hot topic, too hot to write about it yet

A detailed account would include further recent sub-senses, as in *hot goods* (stolen items), *hot-headed* and *hot jazz*.

Johnson's choice of words, and the senses exemplified, reflected his pre-occupation with high-class literary style, rather than with general use of the language. His selectivity was, in a rather different sense, continuing the philosophy of the 'hard words' lexicographers.

Grammar

It is a feature of Modern English that many lexical words undertake 'double duty', effectively belonging to two (or sometimes more) word classes. Bailey partly dealt with this by having two entries, one commencing with *to*. For example:

stone   a hard mineral that may be broken or wrought into forms for building, &c.
to stone   to throw stones at.

Kersey and Martin included similar double entries.

Johnson was the first to specify a word class for each entry:

stone, *n. s.*	1. Stones are bodies insipid, hard, not ductile or malleable, not soluble in water. *Woodward's Meth. Foss.* [plus nine more senses and seventeen more quotations]
stone, *adj.*	made of stone. Present her at the leet Because she brought stone jugs, and no seal'd quartz *Shakesp.*
to stone, *v. a.*	[from the noun] 1. to pelt or beat or kill with stones. [plus one more sense and three quotations]

The difficulty is that Johnson nowhere explains the abbreviations used. Some can be easily inferred: *adj.* for adjective, *adv.* for adverb, *pron.* for pronoun, *prep.* for preposition. For others, a little background is required.

Early Latin grammars used the term 'noun' for all words which inflect for case. At a later stage, this class was divided into two: 'noun substantive' (for words referring to substance) and 'noun adjective' (for those relating to quality). Johnson had shortened the latter to just 'adjective' but retained 'noun substantive', hence his abbreviation *n. s.*

Verbs are marked as either *v. a.* or *v. n.*, these labels being clarified by a pithy sentence in the grammatical sketch preposed to volume 1:

English verbs are active as *I love*; or neuter, as *I languish.*

The term 'neuter verb' is a little elusive. It appears to have been first used by Classical Latin grammarians Donatus and Priscian for 'those verbs which end in -*o* but have no passive form'. The term then evolved in various directions, and it was employed in three or four different ways in the eighteenth century (before dropping out of use). Inspection of Johnson's entries shows that he used 'active' for a transitive and 'neuter' for an intransitive verb. He can thus show (as Bailey could not) how some verbs are ambitransitive; that is, they can function in both transitive and intransitive clauses. For example, Johnson's entry for *smell* is (in abbreviated form):

to smell, *v. a.*	1. to perceive by the nose ... smell the same perfumes.
to smell, *v. n.*	1. to strike the nostrils ... the violet smells to him.
smell, *n.s.* [from the verb]	1. Power of smelling; the sense of which the nose is the organ.

Johnson was providing just one piece of grammatical information. Nothing much changed over the following 250 years, the same practice being – by and large – followed today. However, as demonstrated in chapters 1 and 2 (and, indeed, throughout this book), a language user needs to be provided with much more grammatical information in order to know how to use words appropriately.

Realising that the dictionary is not all there is to a language, Johnson added a short grammatical sketch. This was written and printed last and appears like an afterthought, showing no integration with the dictionary. Latin influence is still very strong and the orthography accorded importance. For example, discussing vowels Johnson states that '*A* has three sounds', the 'slender', as in *face, mane*; the 'open', as in *father, glass*; and the 'broad', as in *wall*. (These are, respectively, diphthong /ei/, long vowel /a:/, and long vowel /ɔ:/. There is also short vowel /a/, as in *hat*.)

The Latin model was evident in the section labelled 'Of nouns substantives', which commences:

The relations of English nouns to words going before or following are not expressed by *cases*, or changes of termination, but as in most of the other European languages by prepositions, unless we may be said to have a genitive case.

	Singular	
Nom.	Magister, *a*	Master, *the* Master
Gen.	Magistri, *of a*	Master, *of the* Master, *or* Masters, *the* Masters
Dat.	Magistro, *to a*	Master, *to the* Master
Acc.	Magistrum, *a*	Master, *the* Master
Voc.	Magister,	Master, *O* Master
Abl.	Magistro, *from a*	Master, *from the* Master

There is then a similar paradigm for plural.

Johnson was taking the classical category of case as a universal framework, giving the Latin inflections of *magister* 'master' in nominative, genitive, dative, accusative, vocative, and ablative cases, and showing the translation equivalents in English. He was also implicitly drawing attention to the fact that English has a system of definite and indefinite articles (*the* and *a*), which is missing from Latin.

The account of verb forms was also Latin-oriented and is, as a consequence, rather torturous. English was said to have a 'preterpluperfect', *I had had*, two 'preterite potentials', *I might have* and *I could have*, and a 'double preterite potential', *I should have had*. And so on.

As described in chapter 5, when lexicographers opted to deal not just with 'hard words' but with all words, they included fully grammatical words such as pronouns and demonstratives. This was soon extended to derivational prefixes and suffixes. Kersey, in 1702, included *un-* 'a negative particle put for the Latin *in*'. Bailey added a handful more, such as *dis-*, *mis-*, and *-hood*. These dictionaries lacked an accompanying grammar, within which affixes should properly be dealt.

In his grammatical sketch, Johnson discussed a couple of dozen derivational affixes. He also included a fair number in the dictionary itself. Some were in both places, such as *-hood*, *-ish*, *-ness*, *-some*, and *un-*. A number were only in the grammar, including *-age*, *-dom*, *-er*, *-ment*, and *-th*. A few were just in the dictionary, not in the grammar: *ante-*, *anti-*, and *pre-* among others.

The place for structural elements is in the grammar, where their function and meaning can be detailed in terms of the overall system of the language. At most they could be mentioned in the dictionary with a cross-reference to the grammatical discussion. Although Johnson added a grammatical sketch to his dictionary, there appears to have been no attempt at integration, or even consistency.

Consider the treatment of termination *-ship* in the two places:

DICTIONARY **Ship** A termination noting quality or adjunct, as *lordship*, or office, as *stewardship*.

GRAMMAR Some [words] ending in *ship* imply an office, employment, or condition; as, *kingship*, *wardship*, *guardianship*, *partnership*, *stewardship*, *headship*, *lordship*.

The import of *-ship* has plainly been rethought for the grammar.

Dictionary entries were provided for prefixes *dis-* and *mis-*, each in its place in alphabetical order (and no doubt written a couple of years apart):

Dis An inseparable particle used in composition, implying commonly a privative or negative signification of the word to which it is joined; as in *to arm*, *to disarm*....

Mis An inseparable particle used in composition to mark an ill sense, or deprivation of the meaning: as *chance*, luck, *mischance*, ill luck, *computation*, reckoning; *miscomputation*, false reckoning...

Within the grammar, negative-type prefixes were dealt with together. First, a lengthy disquisition on *un-* and then:

The prepositive particles *dis* and *mis* ... signify almost the same as *un*; yet *dis* rather imports contrariety than privation ... *Mis* insinuates some error ... To like, *to dislike*, ... to use, *to misuse*.

This shows the benefit of contrastive treatment of forms from the same semantic set. In its dictionary entry, *dis-* was described as privative, but within the grammar this is disclaimed, privation now being associated with one sense of *un-* (as in 'pleasant, *unpleasant*').

(Note that the terms 'prefix' and 'suffix' did not come into general use until after Johnson's time; he called them 'inseparable particles' or 'prepositive particles', and 'terminations'.)

Meaning

Many common words show a range of senses. There will be a central or prototypical meaning, and a number of both literal and metaphorical extensions. It is instructive to survey how the adjective *sweet* was dealt with by three dictionaries from the first half of the eighteenth century:

KERSEY   **sweet,**   pleasant to the taste, or smell, charming, or agreeable. [and there were the following entries: **sweet-heart, sweet-scented, sweet-smelling, sweet-spoken,** etc.]

BAILEY   **sweet,**   pleasant in taste, also in disposition, etc. [plus **sweet-heart**, a lover]

MARTIN   **sweet,**   1 pleasant to the taste
2 sweetened with sugar
3 odiferous, pleasant to the smell
4 agreeable to the eye
5 kind, or good
6 pretty, or handsome
7 free, or easy
8 that does not stink, that has no ill smell
9 flattering

Although Martin's 1749 dictionary distinguished nine senses, he provided no quotations or examples of use. As a result, it is today unclear how sense 7 was used.

Johnson recognised ten senses, providing one or more quotations for the first nine, and an example sentence for the last. We can list the headings, with a quotation extract for each:

1.   pleasing to any sense [the pleasant perceptions of almost every sense]
2.   luscious to the taste [this honey tasted still is ever sweet]
3.   fragrant to the smell [burn sweet wood to make the lodging sweet]
4.   melodious to the ear [a sweeter musick than their own to hear]
5.   pleasing to the eye [thou hast the sweetest face I ever look'd on]

6. not salt[sweet waters mingle with the briny main]
7. not sour [the juices of fruits, from more sweet to more sour]
8. mild; soft; gentle [sweet influence]
9. grateful; pleasing [sweet interchange of hill and valley]
10. not stale; not stinking; as, that meat is sweet

Similarities to Martin's senses may or may not be coincidental.

Johnson covers the semantic range of *sweet* fairly well, but in a disorganised fashion. The ideal practice is to structure the catalogue of senses in something like the following manner:

I. Agreeable physical sensation
    Ia. Prototypically, a pleasant taste, as of honey or sugar; not sour, salty or bitter; fresh rather than stale, rancid, or decayed
      [A sweet-tooth is someone who likes to eat sweet-tasting things]
    Ib. Extended to other senses:
      Ib-i The smell of something which is sweet-tasting, and other agreeable smells: sweet-scented
      Ib-ii A pleasing sound: a sweet voice, sweet music
      Ib-iii A pleasing sight: a sweet face, a sweet view
      Ib-iv A pleasing experience: sweet dreams, a sweet sleep, a sweet kiss
II. Extended to human (or animal) nature that is agreeable and not unsettling
    IIa. A pleasant quality: a sweet disposition, sweet-tempered, sweet words, smile sweetly, it was sweet of them to invite us
    IIb. A person (or animal) with such a quality: a sweet friend, a sweet little puppy

Scholarship can only progress one step at a time. Johnson's catalogue of senses, with supporting quotations, was a considerable advancement. If he had been followed by a lexicographer with similar perspicacity, steps might have been taken towards rationalising the semantic presentation. However, the next major dictionary was by Noah Webster who – here and elsewhere – only slightly modified Johnson's entry, retaining some of his quotations, and adding little new. (There is more on this in chapter 11.)

For a full appreciation of the meaning – and possibilities of use – for *sweet*, it should be considered within the semantic set of taste terms: *salty*, *bitter* (*bitter words* as the antithesis of *sweet words*) and *sour* (an alternative for *sweet* with *face*, *smile*, *mood*, and *temper*). A *sweet friendship* can turn *sour*. Memories can be *bitter-sweet*. Similarly for *hot*, discussed earlier in this chapter. It belongs with *cold*, *warm*, and *cool*, and relates to *fiery*, *fervent*, and *spicy* among many more.

Johnson did occasionally – but inconsistently – refer a term to its semantic congeners. Consider some of his entries for kin terms (extracted from their places in alphabetical order):

mother *n. s.*	a woman that has born a child; correlative to son or daughter
father *n. s.*	he by whom the son or daughter is begotten
parent *n. s.*	a father or mother
son *n. s.*	a male born of one or begotten by one; correlative to father or mother
daughter *n. s.*	the female offspring of a man or woman
brother *n. s.*	one born of the same father and mother
sister *n. s.*	a woman born of the same parents; correlative to brother
aunt *n. s.*	a father or mother's sister; correlative to nephew or niece
uncle *n. s.*	the father's or mother's brother
nephew *n. s.*	the son of a brother or sister
niece *n. s.*	the daughter of a brother or sister

A 'correlative term' is given for *mother* and *son*, but not for *father* or *daughter*; for *sister* but not for *brother*; and for *aunt* but not for *uncle*, *nephew*, or *niece*.

(When one examines the same entries by Webster – copyist without peer – there are mentions of 'correlative term' just for *mother*, *sister*, and *aunt*, three of the four in Johnson.)

It is now time to focus on matters semantic. The following chapter surveys various approaches towards linking and contrasting semi-synonyms, before examining the nature of definitions – their nature, purpose, and limitations. A final section explains the new proposal for a computer-grounded dictionary consisting of interlinked semantic sets, each expounding lexical and grammatical distinctions.

8 Semantic Organisation

Meaning is what language is all about. Words carry meaning. Grammar integrates meanings. Sentences convey meaning. Any study of a language must establish a rationale for dealing with meaning. And it has to be something more than considering words as isolated entities, and placing them in alphabetical order.

We begin with a survey of works which link together semi-synonyms. Then we examine the nature of definitions and attempts to avoid circularity, going on to the tradition of how dictionaries have been constructed. The final section details the approach proposed throughout this volume, of establishing and describing interlinked semantic sets, consisting of words with related meanings and similar grammatical properties.

'Synonym' Lists

Just a few of the early glossaries and dictionaries paid attention to semantic associations between words. There was mention early in chapter 4 of two Latin-English compilations – the vocabulary attached to Aelfric's grammar (around 1000 CE) arranged words into eighteen semantic fields, including 'Weather, universe', 'Wild animals', and 'Human vices'; and in the late fifteenth century the *Hortus Vocabulorum* was organised by semantic fields.

The breakthrough came in 1736 when Abbé Gabriel Girard published *Synonymes françois, leurs significations et le choix qu'il en fait pour parler avec justesse*. ['French synonyms, their meanings and the choice one makes between them for speaking with aptness.'] This was an account of 295 sets of words with similar meanings. (These were not really synonyms – words having precisely the same meaning – and would be better called 'semi-synonyms'.) For example *franchise* ('frankness'), *sincerité*, *naïveté*, and *ingenuité*.

Girard's work was several times expanded and reissued (and even translated into English!). It provided the inspiration for similar works in France, and also in Italy, Spain, Portugal, the Netherlands, Denmark, and Germany. The first follow-up in England came in 1766 from cleric John Trusler. His title indicated scope and also debt: *The Difference, between Words, esteemed synonymous,*

in the English language; and the proper choice of them determined: Together
with, so much of Abbé Girard's treatise, on this subject, as would agree with
our mode of expression. Useful, to all, who would, either, write or speak, with
propriety, and elegance.

Trusler discussed 370 sets of between two and nine words. They can be
illustrated by set 4 (with the original punctuation):

4, To abhor, hate, to loathe, detest
    All these words imply aversion, but require to be differently used, upon different
occasions.
    To *abhor*, implys an aversion to that, to which, we have a natural antipathy; *hate*, an
aversion activated by revenge; *loath*, is more applicable to food; *detest*, implies aversion
actuated by disapprobation.
    We *abhor*, what we cannot endure. We are apt to *hate* the person, who injures us. We
loath the food, by which we have been surfeited. We *detest* the man, who is guilty of a
mean action.
    The spendthrift, naturally, *abhors* niggardliness, and the niggard, profligacy. The *hat-*
red of the revengeful man, is roused, whenever the object of his revenge approaches.
The stomach *loaths* the very sight of that meat, by which we have been satiated. Every,
thinking, man *detests* the least degree of meanness, more particularly that, which is sor-
did or base.

This is limited and rather repetitive. The meanings are in fact much wider
than indicated here. Also, *dislike* has a similar meaning, and should surely be
included in the set. If the reader is to learn how to use these words, they should
be made aware of their varied grammatical possibilities. As described on
pages 21–2 *desist* only takes an -ING complement clause, *abhor* and *loath(e)* –
and also *dislike* – take -ING and THAT varieties, while *hate* also accepts a (FOR)
TO complement clause. And an important point is that *hate* has a wide general
meaning, with *abhor*, *loath(e)*, and *detest* being hyponyms of it, with more
restricted senses (and stronger import). *Hate* can always be substituted for
abhor, *loath(e)*, or *detest*; the opposite does not hold.

The next person on the scene exhibited style and wit but also had little
linguistic acumen. Hester Thrale had been a friend and sounding-board for
Samuel Johnson. Following the death of her English brewer husband, she married an Italian musician. Johnson broke off relations (and soon died). Away
from his shadow, Hester Lynch Piozzi blossomed and in 1794 published *British*
synonymy; An attempt at regulating the choice of words in familiar conversa-
tion.... The two volumes consist of 310 little disquisitions on groups of from
two to twelve words. Occasionally they were short and pithy as with:

CRIME, SIN, and VICE are by no means strictly synonymous; for although there are many
actions which include them all, yet are the words still in their natures separate. The first
alluding to our human laws, expresses a breach made in social ties, and the necessary
compacts between man and man. The second implies offence against God; and the last

a depravation of the will increased by indulgence into gross enormity. Thus forgery is a CRIME, for example; infidelity a SIN; and gaming a VICE.

Most of Piozzi's entries were long and flowery, peppered with literary quotations (often unattributed). Another of the more useful essays commences:

TO PUZZLE, PERPLEX, CONFOUND, EMBARRASS, TO BEWILDER, ENTANGLE, or ENSNARE. These words are used synonymously every day, though of various derivations and, if we would be strict, perhaps should be appropriated thus, or nearly so: For a hard question PUZZLES a man, and a variety of choice PERPLEXES him; one is CONFOUNDED by a hard and sudden dissonance of sounds or voices in a still night; EMBARRASSED by a weight of clothes or valuables, if making escape from fire, thieves, or pursuit; likely to BEWILDER ourselves if we run into a wood for safety; ENTANGLED among the briars if 'tis too dark to pick the way, and possibly caught by accident in a trap laid by the near inhabitants to ENSNARE wolves or other creatures into a pit-fall....

The entry warbles on for a further three pages. Piozzi's discussions tend to be self-indulgent and unsystematic, although often entertaining. She pays no attention whatsoever to the grammatical functions of words.

A dozen further 'synonym' lists followed before the much-heralded 1852 volume by Peter Mark Roget, a physician, entitled: *Thesaurus of English Words and Phrases, classified and arranged so as to facilitate the expression of ideas and assist in literary composition.*

Roget adopted a hierarchical arrangement of concepts. First, there were six classes: Abstract Relations, Space, Matter, Intellect, Volition, and Affections. Each of these was further divided and subdivided. For instance, the Affections class split into Affections Generally, Personal, Sympathetic, Moral, and Religious. Personal Affections had five further divisions, one of which was Prospective, and this had twelve paragraphs including Hope, Courage, Rashness, and Desire. The reader was expected to master the scheme and through it locate any desired word. This was surely a daunting task.

What one did instead was use the alphabetical index (making up almost half the volume) to find the appropriate paragraph. For *enough*, the index gives '639 Sufficiency'. (This is actually in Class 5, Volition; Division 1, Individual Volition; Section 2, Prospective Volition; Heading 1, Actual Subservience – but do we care?). This paragraph begins, in a modern revision of Roget:

N, sufficiency, right amount; right qualities, qualification; right number, quorum; adequacy, enough, pass marks; competence, living wage; minimum, no less, least one can do; full measure, satisfaction, all that could be desired.

Note that *ample* is not included here. The index relates it to seven paragraphs, headed Great, Many, Spacious, Large, Broad, Plenteous, Liberal.

Roget's *Thesaurus* included a large number of lists of words and phrases, but none of them explained or contrasted in any way. No information is given concerning in what circumstances it would be appropriate to employ one word from a list in preference to another. The *Thesaurus* would only be of use to a fully competent native speaker who was familiar with these forms and merely wanted reminding of words with a similar meaning to some given item (but didn't need to be told about the actual similarities and differences of meaning). This was a quite different kind of enterprise from the works of Trusler, Piozzi, and others who had aimed at distinguishing the meanings of semi-synonyms, partly for the benefit of non-native learners.

Roget's *Thesaurus*, in its various editions and revisions, became a top best-seller. Every educated person felt that they should have a copy on their book-shelf, alongside a dictionary and (if so inclined) a Bible. But was it used much? I know that I purchased the Penguin edition about 1960 and referred to it per-haps three times over the next forty years (until it got mislaid). It felt good to have it, might well come in useful – but in fact it seldom did.

Many other thesaurus-type volumes have been published over the past century-and-a-half. Some just provide lists of words, like Roget; others dis-cuss groups of words, as did Trusler and Piozzi. Each of them includes a great deal of information but it is essentially ad hoc, without any regard for the interwoven semantic system of the language and its grammatical correlations. For instance, a 1969 compilation entitled *Use the Right Word* discusses *large* and *big*:

> These words refer to things of more than normal size or to things of unusual mass. *Large* and *big* are both very general and very vague; both are acceptable in contexts ranging from the most informal to the most formal, although *large* would tend to be substituted for *big* in extremely formal contexts. *Big* suggests something of more than normal size, but it is particularly relevant to material or bodily mass, whereas *large* might suggest even greater departure from a norm. In this case, the word's implications are less limited to the physical: a *big* stone; a *big* bully; a *large* house; trying on a *larger* size shoe; the *large* issues confronting us.

This is basically waffle, providing a few examples but telling little or nothing of the contrastive meanings of these words, as outlined in chapter 6. Note also that antonyms for *big* and *large* are given as *minute* and *small* (no mention of *little*).

Webster's New Dictionary of Synonyms, from 1973, is just as prolix, but a little more useful. For instance, it does mention '*small* (opposed to *large*) and *little* (opposed to *big, great*)'. Each group of words is accorded a lengthy and discursive essay.

One looks up *cuddle* and is directed to:

> *Caress, fondle, pet, cosset, cuddle, dandle* mean to show affection or love by touching or handling. *Caress* implies an expression of tender interest (as by soft stroking or patting) or of affection ordinarily without undue familiarity ... *Fondle* implies doting fondness

and frequently lack of dignity; it usually suggests attentions (as hugging or kissing) more obvious and less gentle than caressing ... *Pet*, sometimes, and *cosset* imply special attentions and indulgences including more or less fondling ... *Cuddle* chiefly suggests the action or a mother or nurse in drawing a child close to the breast to keep it warm, happy, and quiet ... *Dandle* suggests playful handling of a child (as by moving him up and down lightly on one's knee)...

The inclusion of words in this 909-page volume is highly selective. There is no entry for *hug* or *kiss*. None for *whisper, mutter,* or *murmur*. Nothing for *hot* (although *cool, warm,* and *cold* are there). And nothing at all for *enough* or *sufficient*. (*Ample* is included, grouped with *spacious, capacious,* and *commodious*.)

There are today a number of electronic 'thesauruses' but, by and large, they are even less useful than their hard-copy predecessors. For instance, the *Longman Dictionary of Contemporary English* (www.ldoceonline.com) has a thesaurus entry based on *big* which says 'large: a slightly more formal word than big, used to describe objects and amounts' while in the *Macmillan Dictionary Online* (www.macmillandictonary.com) we are told: 'large: bigger than usual in size'. (Compare with the discussion of these adjectives in chapter 6.)

A few conventional dictionaries include lists of synonyms (really, of course, semi-synonyms) – and sometimes also antonyms – after selected entries. Unfortunately, this appears always to be rather ad hoc and lacking system. For instance, the large 1987 edition of the *Random House Dictionary* gives *sweet* as an antonym for *sour*, but provides no antonym information for *sweet*. Under *large* there is a list of 'synonyms: *huge, enormous, immense, gigantic, colossal, massive, vast*'. Each of the entries for these words (except *massive*) features a list of 'synonyms', but none of them includes *large*.

The modern tool of convenience is Spell-check Thesaurus on a computer. This does provide useful suggestions for semi-synonyms but is unsystematic and unintegrated. It was plainly not implemented by anyone with an overview of the semantic system of the language. This can be neatly illustrated with antonym specifications (for the Microsoft Word 2003 program on my computer):

LOOK UP WORD:	ANTONYM GIVEN AS:
big	small
little	large
large	small
small	big

As pointed out in chapter 6, the pairings are in fact *big/little* and *large/small*.

Definitions

Definitions have been the pivot of traditional dictionary compilation. What is a definition? What is its function?

One prevalent notion is that a head word should be substitutable by its definition, maintaining the import of the sentence in which it occurs. This is sometimes possible, although rephrasing may be appropriate. One sense of *late* is *(recently) dead*. In place of *They are auctioning the goods of the late Mattia Pascal*, one could say *They are auctioning the goods of Mattia Pascal, who died recently* (which is more felicitous than ... *of the recently dead* (or *deceased*) *Mattia Pascal*). **Orphan** is defined as *someone whose parents have both died*. *Martin is an orphan* could be replaced by *Martin is someone whose parents have both died* (or, better, just *Both Martin's parents have died*).

But these are exceptions. Johnson gave for **cat**: *A domestick animal that catches mice, commonly reckoned by naturalists the lowest order of the leonine species*. This could hardly be used to replace *cat* in the observation *Samuel Johnson had a cat named Hodge*. However, Johnson apparently did think that substitutability was desirable, stating in the *Preface* (his italics):

> The rigour of interpretative lexicography requires that *the explanation, and the word explained, should always be reciprocal*; this I have always endeavoured, but could not always attain.

Had Johnson looked over his own volumes, he would have realised that the idea of reciprocability is a chimera (most especially for a dictionary as sophisticated as his). It is applicable in a few instances – for example, **chintz**, *cloath of cotton made in India, and printed with colours* – but only a few.

The idea that a dictionary entry and its definition should be 'reciprocal' (otherwise described as 'exchangeable' or just 'equivalent') is basically a red herring. Lexicographers should not aspire to a tenet which most of the time they do not – and in fact could not – fully follow.

Leaving this aside, established principles of defining have been enunciated:

I   Every word within a definition must itself receive a definition. (This should be 'every lexical word'; grammatical items are dealt with in the grammar.)

II   The definition should correspond to the word class of the word being defined. For example, **ugly** is an adjective and could be defined as *unpleasant to look at*. However, **beauty** is a noun and thus should not be defined as *pleasant to look at*. Rather, it could be something like: *a quality which is pleasant to look at*.

III   The definition should not include any words 'more difficult to understand' than the word being defined.

To these should be added: relevant grammatical information which tells the reader when and how to use the head word. Whether a noun is count (taking plural ending) or non-count. Whether an adjective forms its comparative by *-er* or *more* or either (or neither). What types of complement clause (if any) a verb may take. And so on.

Words may have essentially the same meaning but differ in degree of formality. Whereas shareholders would refer to Rex Jones as *the manager*, workers in the factory call him *the boss*. *Kids* is a more down-to-earth word than *children*. And a man might refer to *my wife* when talking to the social security people but *the missus* while chatting in the pub. This is information which a dictionary user needs to be told, if they are to function smoothly in society.

Many words have a range of meaning which good dictionaries encompass in a list of senses. In most instances, the senses are not all of equal consequence – there will be a **central meaning**, and other senses related to this in various ways. If an intelligent speaker is asked about a word, they will immediately volunteer the central meaning, and only maybe later follow this up with metaphorical extensions. For *hot* (pages 95–6) the central meaning is 'having heat, with a high temperature'. Other senses, such as 'spicy' and 'strong emotions', are secondary. The central meaning for *sweet* (pages 100–1) is 'pleasant taste, as of honey or sugar'. This then extends to smell, sound, sight, and touch, and to pleasing aspects of human (or animal) nature.

For *hot* and *sweet* the central meaning was the original one, with other senses developing out of it. This is not always the case. We saw in chapter 3 that the earliest sense of *stop* was 'close up a hole'; this is now a secondary sense, with the central meaning referring to interruption of an activity. *Want*, discussed in chapter 12, originally related to a lack. From this developed what is today the central meaning, referring to something which is both lacking or missing and desired.

Lexicographical principle I, that every lexical word within a definition should itself receive a definition, is of course essential. If a dictionary user does not know word X, and this is defined in terms of Y, which the user also does not know, then there is need for explication of Y. However, this does not always yield fruitful results.

Consider entries in *Collins Gem Dictionary and Thesaurus* (2009)

sorrow (feel) grief, sadness
grief deep sorrow
sad sorrowful

Suppose that a foreign learner knows English terms for everyday activities and for commerce but has not been much exposed to words relating to the emotions. They encounter *sorrow*, an unfamiliar word, look it up and are directed to *grief* and *sadness*, also words not yet within their ken. Look these up and it is right back to *sorrow*. A circle of definitions, of absolutely no pedagogic use. How can such circular trips be avoided? Indeed, *can* they be avoided, in terms of the established scheme of dictionary definitions?

We noted lexicographic principle **III**, that a definition should not include any words 'more difficult to understand' than the head word. This is sometimes rephrased in terms of frequency: a word should not be defined through items which are less common. Of the three words just mentioned, *sorrow* is the least and *sad* the most common, with *grief* falling between them. On this principle, *sorrow* could be defined in terms of *grief* or *sad*, and *grief* in terms of *sad*. *Sad* must then be explained without referring to *grief* and *sorrow*.

Consider the implications of this modified form of principle **III**. Each word should be defined in terms of more common words, forms which are easier to understand than the head word. This policy could be pursued to a limited extent. But what about the commonest words of all? These could, presumably, not be defined, but would have to be taken for granted.

A hesitant step in this direction came in 1935 with *The New Method English Dictionary* by Michael Philip West and James Gareth Endicott. They selected 1,490 words as basic and defined 24,000 other items in terms of them. This was the first dictionary 'written specially for the foreigner. It explains to him in [terms of] words which he knows' [presumably the basic 1,490], 'the meanings of words which he does not know' [the remaining 24,000 words and idioms].

One might think that the 1,490 words of the 'defining vocabulary' (which the learner is assumed to know already) might just be listed, not themselves accorded any definition but just used to define harder words. This was not so. The 1,490 words are not even identified in the dictionary itself (only in an accompanying *Teacher's Handbook*, which could at the time be purchased for sixpence but is now very hard to find). And the basic words were accorded traditional-style definitions such as:

big   large, great
large   taking up much space, able to contain a great amount, big
great   big, extending far and wide

It can be seen that circularity still prevailed among the defining vocabulary. But what about the 24,000 less common forms? We find:

enormous   very large
gigantic   very large; *giant*-like (*giant* = a person of more than ordinary size)
huge   very large
immense   very large
vast   very large

If the foreign learner were familiar with *large*, they would gain a vague idea of the meanings of these five words. But no assistance at all is given in deciding when to use one rather than another. (The fact that one may say *The clown has a huge nose*, but not ♦*The clown has a vast nose*, and *The vast majority of the people voted against him*, but not ♦*The enormous majority of the people voted against him*.)

The *New Method Dictionary* was an immense commercial success, being reprinted fifteen times within a dozen years, and also put out by German and French firms. Its publisher replaced it, in 1978, by the *Longman Dictionary of Contemporary English*, with editor-in-chief Paul Proctor. This was more ambitious and also more systematic. 55,000 entries were explained through a defining vocabulary of just over 2,100 items, which were actually listed in an appendix. (They included all grammatical items which can be written as words and also derivational suffixes, such as *-ish*, *-ment*, *-ness*, *-ous*, and *-th*.) If it was necessary – which didn't happen very often – to use a word from outside this basic stock in a definition, then it was printed in SMALL CAPITALS. For example:

loft   1 a room under the roof of a building; ATTIC
      2 a room over a STABLE, where HAY is kept
      3 a GALLERY in a church

It is interesting to compare the definitions of 'very large' adjectives in the Longman with those in the New Method dictionary:

enormous	very large indeed
gigantic	unusually large in amount or size
huge	very big in size
immense	very large
vast	very large and wide; great in size or amount; spreading a great distance

Looking up ***indeed***, we find sense 3: *used after* very + *adjective or adverb to make the meaning even stronger*. The definitions provided are slightly fuller than those in the New Method, but would only marginally assist a learner to understand when to use one of these adjectives rather than another.

The Longman editors boast that, by using a basic vocabulary, they fulfil 'one of the most basic lexicographic principles – *that is that the definitions are always written using simpler terms than the words they define*' (their italics).

That is, there should be no circularities. This will be true for the 53,000 or so words defined in terms of the basic 2,100. But how about the defining vocabulary itself? These words are provided with definitions and, as in New Method, circularity abounds. A sample instance of this is:

contentment	happiness; the state of being satisfied; satisfaction
happiness	the state of being happy
happy	feeling pleasure and contentment
pleasure	the state or feeling of happiness or satisfaction resulting from an experience that one likes
satisfaction	1 contentment, pleasure; 2 something that pleases

Over the last decades, a number of other dictionaries produced in England – many directed at foreign learners – have announced that only a small number of the most common words are used in their definitions. For instance, the *Collins COBUILD English Dictionary* states, somewhat vaguely:

Whenever possible, words are explained using simpler and more common words. This gives us a natural defining vocabulary with most words in the definitions being amongst the 2,500 commonest words of English.

The COBUILD dictionary is founded on a corpus of about 500 million words of English texts. On this basis, words are assigned to 'frequency bands' marked by a number of black diamonds:

◆◆◆◆◆ the most common 680 words   ◆◆ the next most common 3,200
◆◆◆◆ the next most common 1,040   ◆ the next most common 8,100
◆◆◆ the next most common 1,580   no diamonds, the remainder

(Note that about ninety of the five-diamond forms are actually grammatical words – pronouns, articles, demonstratives, prepositions, conjunctions, etc.) The most common 2,500 words are not specifically identified, but they should be among those with three diamonds or more.

Rather than the formal dictionary style, Cobuild's 'definitions' are often cast as explanatory sentences. For example:

hope (◆◆◆◆◆)   If you *hope* that something is true, or you *hope* for something, you want it to be true or to happen, and you usually believe that it is possible or likely.

This is more informative and user-friendly than regular dictionary definitions such as *expectation and desire combined*.

It is instructive to see how Cobuild deals with *sad*, *grief*, and *sorrow*:

sad (◆◆◆◆)   If you are *sad* you feel unhappy, usually because something has happened that you do not like.
grief (◆◆)   *Grief* is a feeling of extreme sadness.
sorrow (◆)   *Sorrow* is a feeling of deep sadness.

These are better definitions than those quoted from the *Collins Gem Dictionary and Thesaurus*, avoiding circularity and defining an uncommon word in terms of a more common one. However, their form is not really different from (only a little longer than) the traditional format, which would be:

sad   Feeling unhappy, usually because something has happened that you do not like
grief   A feeling of extreme sadness
sorrow   A feeling of deep sadness

In fact, the great majority of Cobuild definitions essentially have the traditional format expanded to make it into a sentence. More ambitious definitions, such as that for *hope*, are relatively rare.

And the overriding objection to alphabetically arranged dictionaries still holds. Each word is considered on its own, without reference to its contrast with semi-synonyms as regards meaning and use. For example, the distinction between 'extreme sadness', for *grief*, and 'deep sadness', for *sorrow*, would not be of much help to someone consulting the dictionary in order to learn how to *use* these words appropriately.

How about Cobuild's claim that most words used in definitions are among the 2,500 commonest? This is a laudable aim, although it is not always possible to implement. For example, there is no alternative to including words of lowish frequency in a definition such as:

brass band   A *brass band* is made up of brass (♦♦) and percussion (♦) instruments (♦♦♦).

However, generally uncommon words *are* defined in terms of more common ones. The critical question then recurs: how does Cobuild manage definitions for the most common words? We can pick at random an item, *choose*, from the high-frequency band (♦♦♦♦♦), and follow it through:

choose (♦♦♦♦♦)   If you *choose* someone or something from several persons or things which are available, you decide which person or thing you want to have.
decide (♦♦♦♦♦)   If you *decide* to do something you choose to do it, usually after you have thought carefully about the other possibilities.

Choose is defined in terms of *decide*, and vice versa. Would the dictionary user learn from these definitions when and how to use each word? (They might infer that deciding often involves careful thought, whereas choosing does not. This is correct, but would be more clearly shown if the two words were directly contrasted.)

We can now take stock. It all started off with bilingual dictionaries, which provide a selection of words, one of which should, in appropriate circumstances, translate a word from the source language into the target language. For example, a Swahili-English dictionary gives:

-**dogo**, a[djective]   little (in condition, quality, or quantity), small, slight, unimportant, young

In order to render into English a particular Swahili sentence involving -*dogo*, the translator should consult an English dictionary of the type recommended here, and study discussion of the semantic sets featuring *little* and *small* (as outlined in chapter 6) and also *slight*, *unimportant*, and *young*. That is, a bilingual dictionary is an *aid*, to be followed up in an informative monolingual thesaurus/dictionary. In each instance of use of -*dogo*, it can be rendered by one of the five alternatives given in the bilingual dictionary. Use of the English dictionary enables the translator to decide which one.

The first monolingual dictionaries grew out of Latin-English bilingual dictionaries. To repeat (and expand) an example from page 50:

BILINGUAL DICTIONARY	HEAD WORD IN LATIN	TRANSLATION INTO ENGLISH
Thomas (1587)	**electio**	an election or choise

MONOLINGUAL DICTIONARIES	HEAD WORD IN ENGLISH	DEFINITION IN ENGLISH
Coote (1596)	**election**	choise
Cawdrey (1604)	**election**	choise
Cockeram (1623)	**election**	a chusing, choice
Phillips (1658)	**election**	a choosing, or setting apart

Monolingual dictionaries developed from this basis. Following on from 'a Latin word could be replaced by a corresponding English word' came the notion of substitutability, as espoused by Johnson (as by his predecessors and successors): 'the explanation, and the word explained, should always be reciprocal'.

Each word has its own personality, as it were – a mingling of sound, sense, and effect. The meaning of verb *sip* is adequately rendered by the definition *drink a little at a time*. One could paraphrase *Lady Ermintrude delicately sipped the liqueur* by *Lady Ermintrude delicately drank the liqueur a little at a time*. However, the pragmatic flavour of the original has been lost, its elegance being replaced by something which sounds rather gross.

The tenet that – in a monolingual dictionary, as in a bilingual one – 'a definition should be able to substitute for the head word' is only sometimes viable and never really practical. It is a distraction, best discarded.

In the first monolingual dictionaries, unfamiliar words were explained in terms of commonplace ones, recent 'hard word' loans from Romance languages being defined through everyday Anglo-Saxon vocabulary. There could be no circularity here.

Then the eighteenth century brought with it the idea that every kind of word should be included. The dictionary was compiled in alphabetical order so that there was no check on two words with similar meanings – occurring some way apart – being defined in terms of each other. For instance, in Nathan Bailey's 1730 *Dictionarium Britannicum* we find:

likelihood   probability
probable   likely, or like to be

(There are no entries for *likely* or *probability*.)

Principle **III** suggests that a definition should not include any words more difficult to understand than the word being defined. Sensible, but hard to implement. It was replaced by 'the definition should not include words less common than the head word'. Frequency is easy to compute whereas 'how difficult to understand' is more elusive. Note that no attempt has been made to demonstrate that 'more common' does correlate with 'easier to understand', this being taken as obvious. (But is it always true? This is a topic which invites investigation.)

So a 'defining vocabulary' of 2,000 or so frequent words is established and all other words are defined in terms of these. So far, so good. But what of words in the defining vocabulary? Surely they should be left undefined? Not at all: the established expectations of dictionary buyers would not accept such a state of affairs. So the most frequent words are defined, necessarily in terms of each other. It has the inevitable consequence of circularity, as demonstrated a few pages back for *choose* and *decide* in Cobuild.

The established technique of definition really is left in something of a jumble. This triggers a further question: Does a dictionary user really need a traditional-type definition of every single lexical word? John Baskerville didn't think so (see pages 67–8). Well into the era of put-everything-in, he did not think it necessary to include, in his 1765 dictionary, the most basic words 'such as every person must be supposed to understand'.

No one could come to a monolingual dictionary knowing nothing whatsoever of the language. They must have a level of – at least sketchy – basic understanding in order to be able to use and benefit from it. (This could come, in part, from perusal of a bilingual dictionary linking their native tongue and English.) They must have at least a partial idea of the meanings attached to *stop* and *finish*, *big* and *large*, *fast* and *quick*, *want* and *wish*. What they require is not little stereotyped definitions, such as: *fast*, *capable of moving quickly*, and *quick*, *fast*.

One goes to a dictionary to find out when to use one word rather than some similar one. This need can be met through a careful, contrastive discussion of how each word within a set of semi-synonyms may be used, and an account of grammatical possibilities. (Among many other things, that one may say *Quickly, he ran to the bridge* but not ♦*Fast, he ran to the bridge*.)

This takes us to an exposition of the overarching motif for this volume, the abandonment of a definitional approach in favour of interlinked semantic sets within an electronic matrix. But first it will be useful to recapitulate on the tradition, which – the present volume suggests – should be replaced.

The Tradition

In the era of printed books, there have been three constraints on dictionary-makers – space, time, and money. A dictionary has to be of limited size; this will depend on its purpose and the targeted market. A 'pocket' dictionary will be of a few hundred small pages, a student's dictionary of a thousand or more medium-sized pages, and a comprehensive reference volume of several thousand large pages. Within the acceptable size, a balance must be sought between number of entries and average length of each entry. Succinctness is of prime value. If a word can be dealt with in three lines rather than six, this allows twice as many entries within a given number of pages, or half as many pages for a given number of entries. It will decrease the cost of producing the book, for the publisher, and the cost of buying it, for the user.

Ideally, the amount of time devoted to each word should be as long as is needed to assess all source materials, and then to craft an informative and felicitous entry. (It is invariably harder to write a shorter rather than a longer account, each with the same amount of information.) However, the time spent on compiling a dictionary must be limited. The lexicographers have to be paid, and this expense set against estimates of how much revenue the dictionary will generate. A publisher has only a finite sum of money to invest, and must expect a return on it within a reasonable period.

Dictionaries are published with entries in alphabetical order and are put together in the same manner. As Samuel Johnson completed each initial letter, this was sent to the printer, and set up in type while he was working on the next letter. It was thus not possible to look forward, and consider what might be said for *son* (*correlative to father or mother*) when dealing with *daughter* (no such addendum). He could of course have consulted what had been said earlier, but probably didn't (otherwise the comment *correlative to nephew and niece*, for *aunt*, should surely have also been included under *uncle*, which it wasn't).

James Murray's massive work, *A New English Dictionary, on Historical Principles* (later renamed the *Oxford English Dictionary*) was actually published bit-by-alphabetical-bit: *A–Ant* in January 1884, *Ant–Batten* in November 1885, *Batter–Boz* in March 1887, right up until *Wise-Wysen* in April 1928 (*X, Y, Z* had appeared, out of sequence, in October 1921). Oxford University Press required this piecemeal publication. Murray and his assistants were costing a lot of money and it was absolutely essential that some of it be recouped along the way.

The result was that words with related meanings were dealt with not only at different times but by different people. For example, *big* was done by Murray himself (published March 1887), *large* by Henry Bradley (January 1902), *little* also by Bradley (January 1903), and *small* by William Craigie (June 1912). There was, at the time, no other course available for such a mammoth work. But for a regular dictionary, published all-in-one, there is an alternative strategy. Suppose that a new dictionary is to be compiled, entirely from scratch. Nowadays, this is always done by a team. Typically, the work is assigned in something like the following way: Donald will be responsible for A and B, Ivan will do C, Vanessa D and E, and so on. However, the overall job would be easier and far more satisfactory if tasks were assigned by semantic areas: Donald could begin by dealing with verbs of speaking, Ivan with adjectives referring to physical properties, Vanessa with words relating to human emotions (adjectives such as *sad* and *happy*, nouns like *grief, sorrow*, and *despair*, verbs *worry, offend, grieve, delight*, and so on).

If a group of related words – such as *say, speak, talk, chat, converse, gossip*, and so on – were dealt with all by one person at one time, (a) this would take less time overall than if they were treated by different people at different times according to their places in alphabetical order, (b) the definitions would be harmonious, avoiding circularity or incompatibility. As a final step, head words would be placed in alphabetical order, producing a conventional dictionary.

This scenario was introduced by supposing that a new dictionary was to be compiled 'entirely from scratch'. In fact, this is *never* the case. Putting it politely, each dictionary builds on its predecessors. More bluntly, it plagiarises, consulting what earlier dictionaries have said about each head word, sifting and combining all this, perhaps adding a little fine-tuning. (This is discussed and exemplified in chapter 10 'No need to keep re-inventing the wheel'.) Working in this way, it is of course easiest to follow the same organisational scheme as all the other dictionaries.

Until recently, the only tools available were handwritten notes, then typed and printed materials. The world has now been revolutionised, by computers. These open up new dimensions for dealing with information – gathering, sorting, processing, and disseminating it. The amount of data that can be stored and accessed is almost unlimited. For a number of purposes, many people do still prefer books. But for most types of dictionary, computers are the ideal medium.

First of all, the constraint of space is gone. Rather than 'no more than 2,000 pages' (or whatever), there is now no limit save the sky. And cross-referencing becomes effortless. In traditional times, one might have to keep a finger in one page of a book while searching out an associated mention elsewhere. Now all it needs is a click, and a click back. Or, two (or more) pages can be opened at the same time.

From the beginning, lexicographers did embrace computers for gathering and accessing data. Replacing quotation slips, large chunks of written and spoken language were keyboarded. All examples of a word could then be extracted, together with the three words each side or, much better, with the whole sentence in which it occurred. If the computer program was sophisticated enough, a further click would retrieve the entire text, exposing the social situation in which the word was used.

This was as far as it went. Sure, you can find dictionaries online but these are more-or-less the same as printed dictionaries, just put on a screen.

My message here is that computers can be utilised for a new conception of a dictionary, one which will fulfil what should surely be its role – to assist a speaker in deciding when to use one word rather than another.

The Proposal: Semantic Sets

Underlying the new-look electronically based dictionary are an ASSUMPTION, a PURPOSE, a METHOD, a BASIS, and a scheme of OPERATION.

ASSUMPTION. Anyone who consults a monolingual dictionary will already have at least a superficial knowledge of core vocabulary, and of basic grammatical patterns.

They are likely to be familiar with lexical words such as *talk* and *speak*, *laugh* and *smile*, *look* and *see*. They will know that in English the subject precedes the verb and the object follows it, that an adjective comes before a noun it modifies, and that *give* and its hyponyms occur in a construction 'X *gave* Y to Z'.

PURPOSE. To provide detailed information on how to use a given word. This involves contrasting it, in sentential contexts, with words of similar meaning, thus revealing its semantic character and grammatical possibilities.

The dictionary user will have a general idea that *speak* and *talk* both refer to saying something in a language. *John is talking to the mailman* and *John is speaking to the mailman* are both acceptable and have more-or-less the same pragmatic effect. What the user seeks is more detailed information. For instance, that *speak* focuses on the fact that someone is using a language; one may ask *How many languages do you speak?* whereas ♦*How many languages do you talk?* is not felicitous. In contrast, *talk* relates to how a language is used, in what circumstances, and on what topics, as when saying *Don't talk in church!* and *What shall I talk about with your father? (speak* would be awkward here). This is just a sample of the sort of thing which will show someone how to use the two words in an acceptable manner.

The traditional dictionary definition has no role here. It treats each word as an isolated item, as if language consists of a set of word bricks which can simply be piled up. Language is rather like a collage of pieces, each with its own shape and colour, which must be joined and matched to produce a harmonious discourse.

METHOD. The new-style dictionary consists of an interrelated collection of 'semantic sets'. Each set adopts a 'conceptual template' in terms of which a number of semi-synonyms (and perhaps also antonyms) are investigated. By studying the contexts in which the words can appear – and contrast – insight is gained into the role they play in the close-knit lexico-grammatical matrix of the language. That is, how to use them in order to fully understand the language, and to speak it in an acceptable manner.

Example of semantic sets, in draft form, are in chapter 3 (*finish, cease*, and *stop*), chapter 6 (*big* and *little, large* and *small*, plus *ample, enough*, and *sufficient*, and also *great*), chapter 9 (*fast, quick, rapid, swift, slow*, and *speed*), and chapter 12 (*want, wish (for)*, and *desire*).

BASIS. Each semantic set works in terms of a 'conceptual template', involving notions that a dictionary user might be expected to be familiar with (in terms of the ASSUMPTION). If there does happen to be an unfamiliar notion, its import should be largely inferable from discussion regarding the semantic set. (Otherwise, it can be looked up in the dictionary.)

For example, exposition of the 'big' set, in chapter 6, relates to 'quantity', 'distance', 'area', 'noise', and 'importance'; that of the 'want' set in chapter 12, uses 'satisfaction', 'happy', 'feeling', and 'lack'; that of the 'finish' set in chapter 3 requires 'volition'; and that of the 'fast' set in chapter 9 employs 'time'. Another basic notion for chapter 9 is 'speed'. Note this is an abstract concept, something quite different from the lexeme *speed* (and its derivations, *speedy, speedily*, and *speediness*).

When a fairly sophisticated word is used, its meaning is immediately clarified by the co-text. For instance, one of the senses of *great* (page 83) employs *approbation*: 'II. Indicating approbation. *Great* here functions as an adjective, with similar meaning to *good* (the effect is more like *very good*)'. This explication, together with the dozen examples which follow, makes clear the meaning of *approbation*.

The new-style dictionary differs from most traditional ones in making appropriate reference to grammar. This is absolutely necessary for proper explication of what each word means and how it is used. For instance, it was explained in chapter 3 how *finish* has 'object orientation', contrasting with *cease* and *stop* which have 'subject orientation'. *John has finished writing his autobiography* states that the autobiography (the object of verb *finish*) is all done, whereas *John has ceased/stopped writing his autobiography* indicates that John (the subject of *stop* or *cease*) has lost the urge to write it and has – permanently or temporarily – given up on the task.

The idea of 'semantic sets', each with a 'conceptual template' is totally different from the conventional idea of a dictionary. Anyone who uses a dictionary must have some idea of the meaning of *large*. A dictionary entry: **large:** *big, great, ample* is of no use at all, and – as John Baskerville suggested – might as well not be included. What is needed is information on *when* to use *large*, rather than *big, great*, or *ample*, such as is given in chapter 6.

Since there are no definitions, there is no need to ensure that a word is not defined in terms of more difficult words, or less common words. Or to take care that circularity is avoided. No need for a 'defining vocabulary' of the most frequently occurring words, to be employed (to a greater or lesser extent) in explaining the remainder. Making definitions, within a monolingual dictionary (following on from how bilingual dictionaries are organised) was something of a game played by lexicographers. It was of only limited help to their audience.

Each treatment of a semantic set is a small essay, self-contained in one sense but open to connection with many other parts of the dictionary.

OPERATION. The new-style dictionary consists of a large number of semantic sets, such that every lexical word is featured in a set (sometimes in more than one, for polysemous items). Using it will be effortless. Open the 'dictionary file' on your computer, and enter a word, say *cease*. You will be directed to the semantic set 'finish', as outlined in chapter 3. Within this there will be connections to related semantic sets (involving *discontinue, leave off, quit*, and more), which can be accessed by a click.

The new-style dictionary is multi-dimensional, whereas traditional ones pursued a straight line from the first word in A to the last in Z. There is no need to employ alphabetical ordering (or any other kind of ordering) to locate a word. Just type it in, click, and you are directed into the appropriate milieu.

It would of course be possible to print out any semantic set, if that should be so desired. Printing out the complete dictionary would be possible but basically unhelpful. The semantic sets would not be ordered and there would be no index. The dictionary is a computer document, and is meant to be used as such.

Constraints on dictionary-making were summarised as space, time, and money. The space limitation is now gone, by virtue of using a computer as base. Time and money are still worries and there has to be added an important requirement: linguistic expertise. This is considered at the end of the book, in chapter 15, after all other issues have been ventilated.

Meanwhile, the next chapter provides further illustration of how words are best treated within the context of items with similar semantic content and grammatical habits (rather than in isolation).

9   Semantic Set: *Fast, Quick, Rapid, Swift, Slow*, and *Speed*

Of the six items in this set, five are of Anglo-Saxon origin, only *rapid* being a Romance loan.

- **Fast** /faːst/. Old English (OE) had adjective *fæst* 'firm, fixed, stiff' and adverb *fæste* 'firmly, vigorously' (going back to Proto-European **past-* 'solid, firm'). Within Middle English (ME), the adverb – now with the form *faste* or *fast* – expanded its meaning to include 'violently, eagerly' and then 'at a considerable speed'. This new meaning, which had gradually developed in the adverb *fast*, was then transferred to the adjective *fast* (the two now having the same form). In present-day English 'at a considerable speed' is the predominant meaning for both adjective and adverb. The original meaning in OE 'cannot move or cannot be moved' (overlapping with *firm* and *firmly*) is now a secondary sense and is discussed at the end of the chapter. (Verb *fast* 'abstain from food, etc.' – and related noun *fast* – is a homonym, with distinct etymology.)
- **Quick** /kwik/. In OE, adjective *cwic* meant 'alive' (emanating from Proto-Indo-European verb **gʷeia-* 'live'), this being extended during ME times to 'alive, lively' and thence (from the thirteenth century) to the central meaning today 'taking little time'. Along similar lines, OE verb *cwician* 'come to life, bring to life' developed into modern *quicken*. And adverb *quickly* followed suit.
- **Rapid** /'rapid/. Adjective *rapid* was a relatively late loan – entering early Modern English in the seventeenth century – based on French *rapide* and Latin *rapidus* 'hasty, snatching' (this came from Latin verb *rapere* 'seize', which developed from Proto-Indo-European **rep-* 'snatch'). Noun *rapidity* came at the same time, also from the two sources. Within a few decades, Germanic suffix *-ly* was used to create adverb *rapidly*.
- **Swift** /swift/. Adjective *swift* has basically retained its form and meaning from OE times until today. Derived adverb *swiftlice* and noun *swiftnes* are now *swiftly* and *swiftness*.

- **Slow** /slou/. OE had adjective *slāw* 'sluggish, lazy'; plus derived verb *slāwian* 'be or become sluggish' and adverb *slāwlīce* 'sluggishly, with delay'. Once again, modern meanings date from ME times, giving present-day adjective *slow* (which came to be also used as a verb during the sixteenth century) and adverb *slowly*.
- **Speed** /spi:d/. This goes back to the OE noun *spēd* 'success, prosperity, wealth, plenty', and verb *spēdan* 'succeed, prosper' (reflecting the Proto-Indo-European verb **spē-* 'thrive, prosper'). They developed their modern meanings in ME times. Derived adjective *speedy* and adverb *speedily* came into use in the late fourteenth century.

The central meanings of these words will be discussed and contrasted in terms of two basic concepts: '(length of) time' and 'speed'. (Note that 'speed' is here a basic concept, on a different level of abstraction from lexeme *speed*.) It is convenient to begin with the four adjective/adverb pairs:

ADJECTIVE	fast	quick	rapid	swift
ADVERB	fast	quick(ly)	rapid(ly)	swift(ly)

Fast has the same form as adjective and as adverb while the others add *-ly* to the adjective to derive an adverb. For all three this is optional. That is, the adjective form can also be used in adverbial function, as an alternative to the *-ly* form. This happens most frequently with *quick* (*You speak very quick, Get rich quick!*), less often with *rapid* (*Don't run too rapid!*) and seldom with s*wift* (*He ran as swift as he could*).

These words have overlapping meanings and in some contexts can be substituted one for the other with minor difference of effect. For example, all four can occur in:

(1) Diego is a fast/quick/rapid/swift walker
(2) The horse ran fast/quickly/rapidly/swiftly

However, there are significant differences in meaning and use. We first examine the four adjectives, then corresponding adverbs.

Adjectives *Fast, Quick, Rapid, Swift*

Focusing on the two most frequently occurring adjectives from this set, their core meanings appear to be:

- *quick*: takes little time
- *fast*: at a considerable speed

They contrast in:

(3q)	It was a quick race	Only run over a short distance and so took little time
(3f)	It was a fast race	The horses ran at considerable speed
(4q)	We had a quick lunch	Spent little time on it, perhaps didn't eat much
(4f)	We had a fast lunch	Ate the normal amount, but at considerable speed
(5q)	It was a quick journey	The distance was short, so it took little time (even though the train was by no means fast)
(5f)	It was a fast journey	The train went at considerable speed (although it did take a long time, the distance being great)

Only *quick*, not *fast*, is likely to be used in the following, which refer to time rather than speed:

(6)   They had a quick kiss
(7)   She asked a quick question
(8)   He told a quick joke
(9)   She offered a quick 'hello'
(10)   There was a quick shower of rain
(11)   Tom has a quick temper

In (6–10) the kiss, question, joke, greeting, and shower had a short time span. In (11) it is implied that it only takes a short while for Tom's temper to be aroused.

Only *fast*, and not *quick*, is likely to be used in the following, which refer to speed and not time:

(12)   Mario has a fast car
(13)   The 8.30 to Edinburgh is a fast train
(14)   She drove in the fast lane on the motorway

An important grammatical difference is that just *quick* may have added to it a purposive clause, introduced by *to*:

(15)   Kate was quick to volunteer
(16)   David was quick to understand the essence of the problem

These indicate that it only took a little time before the volunteering and understanding eventuated. One could not use adjectives relating just to speed – *fast*, and also *rapid* – in this context.

We can now add *rapid* to the mix. Its core meaning is similar to that of *fast* 'at a considerable speed'. Like *fast*, *rapid* would be unlikely to be substituted for *quick* in (6–11). A major difference is:

- *rapid* tends to be preferred over *fast* for something with a definite conclusion or which relates to definite items, as in:

(17)   She made a rapid inference
(18)   The war came to a rapid end
(19)   The queen made a rapid recovery
(20)   The manager noticed a rapid accumulation of errors
(21)   There has been a series of rapid social changes

It is possible to use *fast* in place of *rapid* in each of (17–21), but *rapid* is much more likely here. When the condition for *rapid* is not met, then *fast* is preferred, as in (12–14). *Rapid* is possible in these sentences but is scarcely felicitous.

Despite its ancient pedigree, *swift* is far less common that the other three. It is infrequent in written English, being predominantly employed in the spoken medium; it may offer a somewhat pretentious flavour. *Swift* effectively describes something which is rapid and/or quick but also crisp and concise. Typical instances include:

(22)   The government issued a swift denial
(23)   He delivered a swift, sharp blow
(24)   They were swift to repudiate the suggestion

Quick or *rapid* (but not *fast*) could be used in place of *swift* in (22) and (23), showing that here *swift* can relate to speed or to time (or both). However, only *quick* is possible for (24), since a *to* clause is not acceptable after *rapid* (nor after *fast*); the reference here is just to time. (*Swift* may also be used in (19), giving *The queen made a swift recovery*.)

A summary of the basic meanings of the four adjectives is:

- *quick*: takes little time
- *rapid*: action at a considerable speed towards a definite conclusion or relating to definite items
- *fast*: at a considerable speed, without the qualifications noted for *rapid*
- *swift*: action which takes little time and/or is at a considerable speed, and which is crisp and concise

These are the basic (or central) meanings of the adjectives. However, there is wide variation and casual usage involves considerable overlap (more than might be inferred from the account here).

An adjective may modify a noun – as it does in examples (1) and (3–24) – or it may function as copula complement, following the copula verb *be*. This applies to all four adjectives, where pragmatically suitable. For instance, *That race was fast/quick, The queen's recovery was rapid/swift*, and so on. In contrast, functional possibilities for adverbs show more variation.

Adverbs *Fast, Quickly, Rapidly, Swiftly*

Adverbs involve the addition of *-ly*, except for *fast*, which has the same form as the adjective. Before delving into meaning contrasts, we can look at the possible places in which adverbs may occur.

The positions in which an adverb may be placed within the sentence *They walked away* may be marked by $\boxed{W}$, $\boxed{X}$, $\boxed{Y}$, and $\boxed{Z}$:

(25) $\boxed{W}$, they $\boxed{X}$ walked $\boxed{Y}$ away $\boxed{Z}$

Three of the adverbs can be placed in any of the four positions. Thus: *Quickly, they walked away, They quickly walked away, They walked quickly away, They walked away quickly*. Similarly for *rapidly* and *swiftly*. However, *fast* is restricted to final position, $\boxed{Z}$. We may say *He walked away fast*, but not ♦*Fast, he walked away*, nor ♦*He fast walked away*, nor ♦*He walked fast away*. (Note that the same constraint applies to the secondary sense of *fast*, 'cannot be moved', discussed in the final section of the chapter.)

Whereas adjectives *rapid* and *fast* have similar possibilities for positioning, as has just been observed the adverbs differ significantly in terms of placement. Either of the following is acceptable:

(26)   A tendency to obesity increases rapidly in middle age
(27)   A tendency to obesity rapidly increases in middle age

Fast may be substituted for *rapidly* in (26), but not in (27).

The meaning difference between adverbs *rapidly* and *fast* parallels that between the adjectives. *Rapidly*, but not *fast*, is acceptable in:

(28)   Jane was rapidly promoted to be general manager

This is because the speed of her promotion related to a definite end-result.

The following sentence neatly exemplifies the contrast between adverbs *fast* and *rapidly*:

(29)   The thief ran fast but the policeman rapidly caught up with them

For the thief, we are just told that they ran at a considerable speed. For the policeman, their burst of speed was directed to a purpose – to apprehend the thief.

The meaning of *swift* is further elucidated by consideration of adverbs. Three of them may be used in:

(30) She spoke fast/rapidly/quickly
(31) He is eating fast/rapidly/quickly

In contrast, one cannot say ♦*She spoke swiftly* or ♦*He is eating swiftly*. We can infer that *swift(ly)* may be used of (a) motion, or (b) an activity with a definite ending, as in (1–2), (22–4), and (19). It is not used for an on-going activity – other than motion – such as speaking and eating.

Since *quick* has primary reference to time, rather than to speed, *quickly* has possibilities not open to the other three adverbs as in:

(32) Penelope and Leonard want to get married quickly

This does not mean that they wish the ceremony to be conducted at speed, rather that only a short time should elapse between their deciding to get married and actually doing so. The other three adverbs could not be used here, nor in:

(33) Sally's performance in the interview quickly convinced the committee that she was the ideal person for the job

Now consider the sentence *The caretaker opened the door*. There are two ways in which this activity can be described as *quick*:

(34) The caretaker was quick to open the door
   (That is, the caretaker took little time over getting to the door to open it)

(35) The caretaker was quick in opening the door
   (That is, the caretaker took little time over turning all the keys in the locks)

When adverb *quickly* is used, there are three possible positions for it:

(36) Quickly, the caretaker opened the door
(37) The caretaker quickly opened the door
(38) The caretaker opened the door quickly

Sentence (36) is most likely to be understood in terms of time getting to the door, as in (34), and (38) in terms of time taken undoing the locks, as in (35). For sentence (37) either interpretation is possible.

Slow, Slowly

Adjective *slow* and adverb *slowly* have a wide range of meaning – they can refer (a) to speed, then being antonyms of *fast/fast* and *rapid/rapidly*, or (b) to time, then being antonyms of *quick/quickly*.

(a) Speed sense. This is perhaps the default reading of *slow* and *slowly*. If *slow* were used with nouns *race, lunch,* and *journey* in (3–5), it would indicate a limited speed (the opposite of *fast*) rather than a short time (the opposite of *quick*). Corresponding to (12–14) there can be a slow car, a slow train, and a slow lane. Further examples include:

(39)   That clock is always slow/fast
(40)   The traffic is really fast-moving/slow-moving today

Slow can often replace *rapid*. We can have *The queen made a slow recovery,* relating to (19). *Slow* is also possible in (18) and (20–1) but scarcely in (17) – ♦*She made a slow inference* is just not plausible. Another example is:

(41)   Jacob's fortune increased at first slowly and then rapidly

(b) Time sense. There are many instances of *slow(ly)* referring to something which happens over a long period. For instance, one can say, corresponding to (6):

(6')   They had a slow kiss

Other examples include:

(42)   The president is quick/slow to take up new ideas
(43)   That pot plant was quick/slow to mature
(44)   Janice is quick/slow to anger
(45)   A quick/slow grin spread over his face
(46)   She quickly/slowly rose to her feet

Just as *quick* (but not *fast* or *rapid*) can be followed by a purposive *to* clause, so may *slow* be, in its time sense:

(15')   Kate was quick/slow to volunteer
(16')   David was quick/slow to understand the essence of the problem

All five adjectives and adverbs have comparatives (and corresponding superlatives) with the following forms (the principles for using *-er* or *more* were enunciated on pages 6–7):

ADJECTIVE	fast	quick	rapid	swift	slow
COMPARATIVE	faster	quicker	more rapid	swifter	slower
ADVERB	fast	quickly	rapidly	swiftly	slowly
COMPARATIVE	faster	more quickly	more rapidly	more swiftly	more slowly

Fast is one of the few adjectives in English which use the same form as adjective and as adverb, without the addition of *-ly* (others are *hard, early,* and *late*).

The comparative of the adjective then carries over to be the comparative of the adverb (without *more*, which all others use). Compare:

(47) John is a faster/slower runner than me
(48) John runs faster/more slowly than me

All the adjectives and adverbs may be modified by *too* and *enough*. For example, *They weren't fast enough to catch the thief* and *The apprentice worked (far) too slowly*.

Speed

Speed functions (a) as a noun, and also (b) as a verb. These are discussed in turn.

I **Noun *speed*** refers to 'rate of progress'. One can talk of *high speed* or *low speed*, of *fast speed* or *slow speed*. The following pairs have similar meaning:

(49) He was driving at a high speed/at a fast speed
(50) He was driving fast
(51) He was driving at a low speed/at a slow speed
(52) He was driving slowly

We also find *the speed of light, at full speed, a three-speed bicycle*.

If no modifier is included, the default sense is 'a high rate of progress', as in *a turn of speed* and:

(53) He was driving at speed when the accident happened
(54) That horse has speed

Noun *rapidity* relates to adjective *rapid*. This has a quite different meaning from *speed*, describing 'the fact of having a high rate of progress, towards a definite conclusion or relating to definite items' (the same qualifications as for adjective and adverb). For instance:

(55) They admired the rapidity with which he built the boat
(56) The rapidity of modern transport fosters short-term tourism
(57) They completed their tasks with equal rapidity

Unlike *speed*, *rapidity* cannot be modified by *high* or *low*, *fast* or *slow*. One can say *with great rapidity* alongside *at great speed* (note the difference of prepositions).

Derived noun *quickness* primarily indicates 'the fact of taking a short time'. It is often used of mental powers: *She has a quick wit, She is quick-witted, She shows quickness of wit*. Noun *swiftness* describes 'the fact of something happening swiftly', as in *The swiftness of the coup took the King by surprise*.

Noun *slowness* is used for 'the fact of having a slow rate of progress'.

(58)   He was appalled at the slowness of the building work

Derived adjective *speedy* and adverb *speedily* overlap in meaning with *fast*, *rapid*, and *rapidly*: *The queen made a speedy recovery* and *Jane was speedily promoted to general manager*. However, there can be a difference of degree. One might hear:

(59)   Tom's driving was a little bit speedy but Ursula's was downright fast

And there is the rather uncommon derived noun *speediness*, which has a similar meaning to *rapidity* (contrasting with that of *speed*).

II   Verb *speed* has two senses

(a) As simply *speed*, it can mean 'be going at a considerable rate, fast' and is then generally intransitive, as in:

(60)   Ruth was speeding along the highway
(61)   She was fined for speeding

(b) Adding *up*, *speed up* can mean 'increase the rate, go faster', and can be used intransitively, as in (62), or transitively, as in (63):

(62)   Andrea speeded up along the straight
(63)   The contractor speeded up work, since the project was behind schedule

Verb *quicken* (which evolved in ME) appears most often to relate to the predominant meaning of *quick* in an earlier stage of the language, 'alive, lively'. It can be used intransitively, as in *His heart-rate quickened at the tragic news*, and transitively, as in *She quickened her pace*, but has a low frequency in the present-day language. There was a verb *swiften* 'make swift or swifter' but this has now more-or-less dropped out of use. (*Fasten* relates only to the secondary meaning of adjective *fast* 'cannot move, cannot be moved' and is discussed at the end of the chapter.)

Corresponding to adjective *slow*, there is verb *slow*, which may be either *slow* or *slow down*. Its meaning corresponds to sense (b) of *speed* with the form *speed up*; that is 'decrease the rate, go slower'. Like *speed up*, it may be used intransitively, as in (64) or transitively, as in (65):

(64)   Andrea slowed (down) along the straight
(65)   The foreman slowed (down) the work, to make the job last longer

(*Up* cannot be omitted from *speed* sense (b), *speed up*, since it is needed to distinguish it from sense (a), plain *speed*. However, for *slow* there is only sense (b), *slow down*, and the *down* can thus be omitted without fear of confusion.) Interestingly, we also encounter *slow up*, as in *The generals slowed up the attack.* This has a very similar meaning to *slow down.* It is the sense of *up* meaning 'bring to a close', as in *Wind up proceedings!*, *Eat up the leftovers!* and *Tie up loose ends!*

Summary

The central meanings of items in this semantic set can now be recapitulated.

- Adjective *rapid* and adverb *rapidly* describe action at a considerable speed towards a definite conclusion or relating to definite items. Noun *rapidity* indicates the fact of an action being at a considerable speed, also with respect to a definite conclusion or definite items. Noun *rapids* is used for a section of a river where the water flows very rapidly, typically over shallow rocks.
- Adjective and adverb *fast* describe action at a considerable speed, without the qualifications noted for *rapid* and *rapidly.* It can be extended to *fast (way of) life*, where many things happen, often vicariously.
- Adjective *quick* and adverb *quickly* basically refer to something which takes little time (although they are sometimes used, like *rapid/rapidly* and *fast*, in relation to speed). The original meaning 'alive, living' persists in the archaic phrase *the quick and the dead.* An earlier sense 'lively' is reflected in verb *quicken* 'become more lively, increase in pace'. Noun *quickness* describes something taking only a short time (especially a mental faculty).
- Adjective *swift* and adverb *swiftly* are rather high-flown words which can refer to an activity which takes little time and/or is at considerable speed, and which is crisp and concise. They may be used of motion or of an activity with a definite ending. Noun *swiftness* describes the fact of something happening swiftly.
- Adjective *slow* and adverb *slowly* typically refer to a low speed (being then antonyms of *fast* and *rapid/rapidly*) but may also indicate taking a long time over something (and are then antonyms of *quick/quickly*). They can be extended to mental states: *slow-witted* is opposed to *quick-witted.* The associated verb *slow* or *slow down* (or *slow up*) indicates decreasing speed. Noun *slowness* is used for 'the fact of having a slow rate of progress'.
- Noun *speed* indicates 'rate of progress', which can be slow or fast or anything inbetween. There are verb forms *speed* 'be going at a considerable rate', and also *speed up* 'increase the rate'. Derived adjective *speedy* and *speedily* indicate 'high-ish speed', an attenuated version of *fast.* There is also noun *speediness* 'the fact of being speedy'.

Secondary Sense of *Fast*

The secondary sense of *fast* – as adjective and as adverb – refers to something which physically cannot move or cannot be moved. It overlaps in meaning with *firm(ly)*, *tight(ly)*, *secure(ly)*, and verb *fix.*

The same constraint applies to the secondary as to the primary sense of the adverb – it can only be placed at the end of a clause, position $\boxed{Z}$ in example (25). One may say *It was stuck firmly* or *It was firmly stuck*, but only *It was stuck fast*, not ♦*It was fast stuck*.

Example sentences are, with alternatives to *fast* added within brackets:

(66)   We were stuck <u>fast</u> between two great rocks [firmly, tight(ly)]
(67)   He held the prisoner <u>fast</u> [firm(ly), tight(ly)]
(68)   Clamp it down <u>fast</u>! [firmly, tight(ly)]
(69)   She bound his arms and legs <u>fast</u> [firmly, tight(ly), securely]
(70)   He made the knot <u>fast</u> [tight, secure]
(71)   They stood <u>fast</u> against the approaching foe [firm]

Fast can also be used of a state of mind which is not likely to change:

(72)   He held <u>fast</u> to his decision [firmly]

Derived verb *fasten* only relates to this secondary sense (not to the central sense of *fast* 'at considerable speed'). It indicates 'ensure that something cannot move', as in:

(73)   The shelf was <u>fastened</u> to the wall [fixed/secured]
(74)   We <u>fastened</u> the windows [secured]
(75)   The gate was <u>fastened</u> with a padlock [secured]

The verb *fasten* has an extension relating to something non-physical:

(76)   They <u>fastened</u> upon the fact that he had leaked details of the new design, and used it as a reason to fire him [fixed]

This could be said if he made many small indiscretions, none quite bad enough to justify dismissal. So they focused on the one really gross misdemeanour, leaking details of the new design, as sufficient reason for the sacking.

There is also the idiomatic expression *fast asleep*. Another, with related meaning, is *sleep tight*. One could say:

(77)   We told her to 'sleep tight!' and there she is fast asleep

Each of the alternatives given in brackets has a wide range of meaning which only shows minor overlap with this secondary sense of *fast*.

- **Firm** covers:
  (a)   A physical object which is unyielding (*firm ground, firm flesh, a firm platform, a firmly closed door*). It here belongs in a semantic set with *hard, rigid, solid, stiff*, etc. In this sense, adjective *firm* and/or adverb *firmly* have similar import to *fast* in (66–9, 71). This meaning of *firm*

is also extended to non-physical things, as in *a firm offer, the oil price has firmed*.

(b) A definite mode of action (*speak firmly, impose firm rule*) or a definite attitude (*firmly rejected the idea, took a firm stand against developers*). It here belongs in a semantic set with *resolute, forceful, definite, determined*, etc. Sense (b) shows just a little overlap with *fast*, as in (72); this may well be due to analogy to the physical sense of *hold fast* in (67).

- **Tight** relates to things being close together, with little (or no) gap between (*a tight squeeze, a tight curve on the motor-racing circuit, a tight schedule, packed tight, an air-tight joint*). It is in a semantic set with *taut, stretched, closed*, etc. *Fast*, in the sense 'cannot move or be moved' has similar import to adjective *tight* and/or adverb *tightly* 'be close together' in sentences (66–70).

- Adjective **secure** is used of something which is in a state such that it is unlikely to be affected by anything unwelcome (*a secure prison, the city was made secure against attack, a secure argument, he feels secure of her love, she feels secure in her job*). It belongs in one semantic set with *safe, locked, unimpeachable*, etc., and in another with *confident, sure, assured*.

Sentence (70) indicates that the knot could not come loose, with this being shown by adjective *fast* 'cannot move' or *secure* 'cannot be affected by anything unwelcome' (or *tight* 'parts being close together'). Similarly for adverbs *fast, securely* (and *tightly*) in (69). For sentences (73–5) a similar effect is used by employing either verb *secure* or derived verb *fasten* – the windows and gate are made so that they cannot be opened, and are thus free from criminal interference, and the shelf will not fall down (even if many books are placed on it).

(There is a further sense of *secure* which is in a semantic set with *get, obtain*, and *acquire*; for example, *She has secured the job/a loan/a firm promise*.)

- Verb *fix* describes something being 'arranged', in a wide sense of this term. One can *fix the time for the meeting, fix a place for the rendezvous, fix one's hair, fix a price of the vehicle, fix up accommodation, fix one's eyes on something*. It naturally extends to arranging something so that it is in proper order: *fix the radio, fix the problem in the finance department, I need to get my teeth fixed*. *Fix* belongs in one semantic set with *organise, arrange, establish*, and in another with *repair, mend*, etc. It can be employed as an alternative to *fasten* in (73) – the shelf was arranged securely on the wall so that it did not move.

Fix may be used for 'arranging' mental orientation, as in *fix your mind on the problem in hand*. In (76) *fasten* and *fix* have similar import, indicating focusing of attention.

Earlier chapters have mentioned many instances of what used to be called plagiary – now plagiarism – or copying (alternatively, 'building on earlier foundations'!) The next chapter examines this habit in some detail.

Early authors of monolingual dictionaries invariably 'used' the definitions of their predecessors. (Alternatively, one could say 'built on', or 'copied off', or 'purloined', or 'expropriated'.) To the examples given in previous chapters we can add a couple more, in each case tracing matters back to Thomas Thomas's bilingual compilation (an earlier treatment of *agilitas*, by Elyot, was on page 43).

	HEAD WORD IN LATIN	TRANSLATION INTO ENGLISH
Thomas (1587)	**agilitas**	nimbeleness, quickness, agilitie …
	HEAD WORD IN ENGLISH	DEFINITION IN ENGLISH
Coote (1596)	**agilitie**	nimblenes
Cawdrey (1604)	**agilitie**	nimblenes or quicknes
Bullokar (1616)	**agility**	nimbleness
Cockeram (1623)	**agility**	nimblenesse
Blount (1656)	<no entry>	
Phillips (1658)	**agility**	nimblenesse
Kersey (1702)	**agility**	nimbleness
Bailey (1730)	**agility**	nimbleness, activity

Blount did not include this word, but the tradition of copying continued, skipping this gap. However, this was not always so. Consider *dignity*, which was missing from Bullokar and Cockeram. In this instance the omission appears to have created a hiatus, with the process of copying being arrested, and then recommencing. (This is an extension of the table on page 49.)

	HEAD WORD IN LATIN	TRANSLATION INTO ENGLISH
Thomas (1587)	**dignitas**	worthinesse, manly maiestie or comelinesse...
	HEAD WORD IN ENGLISH	DEFINITION IN ENGLISH
Coote (1596)	**dignitie**	worthinesse
Cawdrey (1604)	**dignitie**	worthinesse
Bullokar (1616)	<no entry>	
Cockeram (1623)	<no entry>	
Blount (1656)	**dignity**	honor, reputation, advancement, some considerable preferment or employment
Phillips (1658)	**dignity**	honor, reputation, advancement, ...
Kersey (1702)	**dignity**	honor and worth
Bailey (1730)	**dignity**	advancement, honor, reputation; some considerable preferment, office or employment in church or state

Samuel Johnson came in as a fresh breeze. He did use materials from standard texts (for vegetables such as *onion*, and much more) and he took over some straightforward definitions from Bailey and others, always with due acknowledgement. But Johnson was his own man, crafting original definitions for most words. Sometimes there was some similarity to earlier work – for example: ***agility****: nimbleness; readiness to move; quickness; activity* (supported by a quote from Watts) – othertimes not. ***Dignity*** was accorded six numbered senses (each with its quotation), relating to the secular and religious norms of his time, plus a use in astrology (*the planet is in dignity when it is in any sign*).

The discontinuity between the sequence of definitions in earlier dictionaries and those in Johnson can be illustrated for the verb *annoy* (which was included for the first time in Phillips):

annoy:

Phillips (1658)	trouble, hurt
Kersey (1702)	hurt, or prejudice
Bailey (1730)	to endamage, hurt, prejudice, to be offensive in smell
Martin (1749)	to hurt, prejudice, molest, or endamage

Johnson (1755)	to incommode, to vex, to teaze, to molest (plus four quotations)

Johnson was a scholar, a professional, and not a thief (his definition of *pla-giarism* was: *theft; literary adoption of the thoughts or works of another*). Someone unfamiliar with modern practice might then surmise: ah, so did Johnson put a stop to the habit of copying which had so pervaded those early, rather primitive dictionaries? Not at all. Absolutely not! Later lexicographers vied in copying Johnson, and then each other.

How It Is Done

There are many dictionaries around nowadays, and this just means that there are many to copy from. In his seminal volume *Dictionaries: The Art and Craft of Lexicography*, Sidney L. Landau recounts how, when in 1961 he was taken on to the Funk and Wagnalls dictionary staff, 'we worked in a large open space at desks without partitions, a row of dictionaries propped before each of us.'

A row of dictionaries! Preparing an entry for a new word, the lexicographer would open each dictionary at that word. Maybe have them all open at once – but there might not be sufficient space? Take a large sheet of paper and copy down the definition from each dictionary in the row. At the bottom of the sheet, craft your own definition – blending, adjusting, fine-tuning bits from the entries copied above.

The dictionaries in the row are not independent documents. Each was compiled in the same way, on the basis of some of the other dictionaries in the row. Many modern dictionaries of English are, to a considerable extent, variants of a single document. This is rather like a vine, spreading from its root, branching, portions merging, some stalks being grafted together, this happening over and over again. Each final branch bears fruit, but these are fruits of a very similar nature.

However, not every dictionary-maker goes to the bother of constructing new entries on the basis of those in a selection of other dictionaries. There is a short-cut.

Consider two English dictionaries, published just a few years apart, which one might expect to be about as different as could be. From the USA there came, in 1987, the second edition of *The Random House Dictionary of the English Language, unabridged*. From Australia, in 1991, came the second edition of *The Macquarie Dictionary*, 'the National Dictionary' for Australian English. We can compare the beginnings of a few sample entries:

ENTRY	RANDOM HOUSE (1987)	MACQUARIE (1991)
desire	wish or long for, crave, want (often fol. by *after, for* or an infinitive)	wish or long for, crave, want (oft. fol. by *after, for* or an infinitive)

ENTRY	RANDOM HOUSE (1987)	MACQUARIE (1991)
wish	to want, desire, long for (usually fol. by an infinitive or a clause)	to want, desire, long for (oft. with an infinitive or a clause as object)
yearn	to have an earnest or strong desire; long	to have an earnest or strong desire; long
hanker	to have a restless or incessant longing	to have a restless or incessant longing
crave	to long for, want greatly, desire eagerly	long for, desire eagerly

There are thousands of other entries which are pretty-well identical (like *desire, wish, yearn, and hanker*) and many more where Macquarie has a shortened form of that in Random House (as for *crave*).

How can this be? Why didn't Random House sue Macquarie for blatant plagiarism (or should it be the other way round)? No answer to this puzzle can be found by perusing prefaces and suchlike in the two dictionaries themselves. But there is an explanation, albeit somewhat hidden.

It all emanated from *The Century Dictionary and Cyclopedia*, a multi-volumed work edited by William Dwight Whitney and published in New York between 1889 and 1891 (its origins are set out on page 156). A shorter version of this, *The New Century Dictionary*, edited by H. G. Emery and K. G. Brewster, was issued in 1927.

Our story properly begins in the 1940s, when Random House decided to enter the reference book market, and purchased rights to the Century dictionaries. Random House's *American College Dictionary* in 1947, edited by Clarence Barnhart, was a substantial revision (with sound etymologies) of *The New Century Dictionary*. There were then developments in two directions.

1.   Random House expanded on the *American College Dictionary* to produce, in 1966, a large volume – meant to compete with *Webster's Third* – which they called their 'unabridged dictionary'. (In fact it was not so much an original compilation which had not been abridged, as a smaller volume which had been augmented.) A great deal of new material was added but many of the definitions from the 1947 volume were retained. A second edition (the one just quoted from) followed in 1987.

2.   In 1971, the *Encyclopedic World Dictionary* was published by Paul Hamlyn in London. The editor, Paul Hanks, stated: 'we were fortunate in being able to secure the rights to the definitions and principles' of the *American College Dictionary*. A careful examination shows that the *Encyclopedic World Dictionary* actually *is* the *American College Dictionary*, anglicised in slight degree.

Over to Australia. *The Macquarie Dictionary*, published in 1981 and styling itself 'The National Dictionary' of Australian English, was in essence the English *Encyclopedic World Dictionary* (which was in essence the *American College Dictionary*), simplified and slightly Australianified. This genesis is vaguely acknowledged on page 13 of the first edition of the *Macquarie* by its editor Arthur Delbridge: 'Naturally, we could not prepare a book of this size without having access to another good dictionary for use as its base. We were fortunate in having access to the *Encyclopedic World Dictionary*, published by Hamlyn in England in 1971. This dictionary was itself based on the well-known *American College Dictionary*, first published in 1969.' (This date is erroneous; the *American College Dictionary* was first published in 1947.) However, from its second edition (1991) on, the *Macquarie* includes no mention of its antecedents.

Robert Burchfield (1982), editor-in-chief of the *Oxford English Dictionary*, closely examined and compared the three dictionaries. He found that around 93 per cent of entries in the *Macquarie Dictionary* were from the *American College Dictionary* and the *Encyclopedic World Dictionary*, with about 7 per cent being original, the addition of distinctively Australian words or meanings. He then wrote: 'What emerges with the utmost clarity is that the exact wording and ordering of senses has been carried over, and deemed appropriate, from an American dictionary of 1947 to a British one of 1971 and then to an Australian one of 1981.'

In summary, there are two standard methods of making a 'new' dictionary. A relatively easy way – buy the rights to an established work, and tinker with it. Or a much more time-consuming way – craft new definitions on the basis of those in a selection of existing dictionaries. Of course, there is a third possibility – start from scratch, making your own decisions and being little influenced by earlier work. That is what Samuel Johnson did, to a large extent. We return to this course of action at the end of the chapter, and again in chapter 15.

How Far Can One Go?

There are laws against plagiarism. Quite apart from these, people in most disciplines don't copy. They pride themselves on being original. Lexicographers, however, live in a different world. This is characterised by Sidney J. Landau in *Dictionaries: The Art and Craft of Lexicography*:

Dictionaries have always copied from one another, but no reputable dictionary today would take over entire sections of another work and print them verbatim.... If one makes a definition-by-definition comparison of a number of competing dictionaries one will find very few identical definitions ... On the other hand, one will find few sharp discontinuities. Although phrased differently, the definition of a given sense usually covers the same ground in all major dictionaries.

Facts and ideas cannot be copyrighted, only the way in which they are expressed – their actual statement. One dictionary may describe how some thing is constructed, what it is made from, what is looks like, and what it is used for. A second dictionary can replicate all this information just so long as it does not use exactly the same words. Landau continues: 'Dictionary editors look at each other's books, and though each editor may form his own opinion about what ground should be covered, he dare not depart too far from the area laid out by his competitors.'

Every aspect of a dictionary is likely to be copied – not just the information contained in definitions, but the whole organisation of the volume, the senses recognised for each word, how they are ordered, the kinds of (generally minimal) grammatical information provided, how pronunciation is represented, and indication of etymology.

In 1984, an invitation was extended to me to mount the lexicographic roundabout. For a couple of decades I had undertaken intensive fieldwork, working on grammars and linked dictionaries of a number of Australian Aboriginal languages. I had also assembled files on each of the 250 distinct indigenous languages of the continent, including all published and unpublished materials. James L. Rader, an etymology editor for the projected second edition of the *Random House Dictionary Unabridged*, wrote:

We need some expert assistance in reviewing the etymologies citing Native Australian languages. Most particularly, we would like to eliminate the label 'Native Australian' and replace it with the name of the language in question, when it is known, and then provide a separate entry in the dictionary defining that language/people. This would work to dispel, in a small way, any assumption of the reading public that 'Native Australian' was a single language which all Aboriginal Australians spoke.

More than 400 words have been taken into English from more than seventy distinct indigenous languages of Australia. Some are known all over the world and have been borrowed into other languages – most notably *kangaroo*, *boomerang*, *koala*, *dingo*, and *wombat*. In every dictionary they were labelled just as 'Native Australian' or 'Australian Aboriginal'. This is rather like tagging all loans into English from Finnish, Swedish, Welsh, Basque, Lappish, Greek, Hungarian, Italian, and so on, simply as 'European'. Even the first edition, in 1981, of the *Macquarie Dictionary*, which trumpeted its Australian authority, just said 'Aboriginal' for every indigenous loan.

It appeared that Random House wanted to include the eighty or ninety loans from Australian languages which were listed in the OED, and Rader sent along photocopies of the OED entries. Working with the files I had assembled, Research Assistant Clare Allridge and I provided etymologies for more than eighty words, which came from twenty-five different languages. For each loan, information was provided on which language it was taken from, and the original form and meaning in that language. For instance: **wallaby**, *small species of kangaroo* from *walaba* in Dharuk, the original language of the Sydney region, and **kylie**, *a boomerang*, from *karli* in Nyungar, the language of the Perth area.

On receipt of these etymologies, Rader wrote:

Since commercial dictionaries in the US seem to plagiarize each other shamelessly, I suspect that these etymologies, once they appear, will also turn up in other dictionaries, without any acknowledgement of their authorship. Perhaps you or Ms. Allridge should consider publishing them in a more scholarly format, so that your work will at least get a certain amount of recognition in terms of priority.

I replied that we were simply happy to make these etymologies available, and that anyone would be welcome to use them.

In the USA, two major competitors of Random House took note of etymologies provided for words from Australian languages (without any acknowledgement), and copied them absolutely correctly. The tenth edition of *The Merriam-Webster Collegiate Dictionary* (Mish 1993) only includes a few nouns of Australian origin, but for these the information is given exactly as in Random House – name of the language the word was taken from, its location, and the form of the word in that language. Similar comments apply for the third edition of *The American Heritage Dictionary of the English Language* (Soukhanov 1992). In the UK, the Oxford (and other) dictionaries appeared to be quite uninterested; there is more on this in chapter 14.

In Australia, the second edition of *The Macquarie Dictionary*, in 1991, used the new etymologies and did acknowledge this in the introduction. However, the etymologies weren't always copied accurately. To mention just one example, **pademelon**, *the name of a species of wallaby*, comes from *badimaliyan* in Dharuk; *Macquarie* gives the original form as *gadimalion*, writing *g* instead of *b* and *o* in place of *ya*. Okay, so copying is the modus operandi of lexicographers, but surely they should learn to copy correctly.

Every new edition of a dictionary – besides updating entries – aims to introduce new features. The second edition of the *Random House Dictionary Unabridged* had expanded coverage of words from American regional dialects and improved etymologies (including those from Australian languages). It also announced: 'This is the first unabridged American dictionary to list the dates of entry into the language of vocabulary items'. Note the 'unabridged'. Actually, the first American dictionary to add dates was Webster's Desk volume, the Ninth New Collegiate, four years earlier in 1983. (Random House only made the decision to include dates when it became known that the Ninth Collegiate was to feature them.)

It is interesting to compare the dates given in the OED and in these two American volumes:

	OED	Webster's Ninth Collegiate 1983	Random House Unabridged 1987
blame, verb	c1200	13c	1150–1200
bland, adjective	1596	1661	1590–1600
blank, adjective	1325	14c	1300–50
bleach, verb	1050	bef. 12c	bef. 1050
bleep, noun	1953	1953	1950–55
blight, noun	1611	1669	1605–15
blimey, interjection	1889	<no entry>	1885–90
blind, adjective	975	bef. 12c	bef. 1000
blond(e), adjective	1481	15c	1475–85
bollard, noun	1844	1795	1835–45
bounce, verb	c1225	13c	1175–1225

It can be seen – from *bland*, *blight*, and *bollard* – that the Collegiate dates were arrived at independently. Indeed, they were reassessed with each new edition; see pages 211–12.

In contrast, Random House appears to have taken its dates directly from the OED. The OED is organised on a historical basis, focusing on the earliest quotations for each word. Random House couldn't just reproduce the OED dates verbatim. That would definitely be transgressing the limits of 'fair play'. What they did was replace each OED date with a time span.

The strategy appears to have been as follows. For words inherited from Old English, put 'bef[ore] 900 or 1000 or 1050' (as for *bleach* and *blind*). For words introduced into Middle English, quote a fifty-year time span; which sometimes began or ended with a century (as for *blame* and *blank*) and othertimes with 25 or 75 (as for *bounce*). From the end of the fifteenth century, a ten-year span was adopted, beginning either with a ten (as for *bland*) or with a five (as for *blight*, *blond(e)*, and *bollard*). Finally, from the end of the nineteenth century, there was a five-year span (as for *bleep* and *blimey*). A little bit of the dating was original to Random House, but the vast majority was taken straight from the OED.

Wasn't this plagiarism? Well, as mentioned before, facts cannot be copyrighted, only the way in which they are expressed. The OED gave '1611' for *blight* but this was expressed differently by Random House as '1605–15'. The people at the OED told me that they had thought of suing Random House over this, but in the end decided not to.

There is a line which cannot be crossed, and Random House had just touched it.

Keep with the Familiar

For all of humankind, it is most comforting to go with what one knows. Life has a pattern – where we go, who we interact with, what we eat, which TV programmes we watch (or perhaps don't watch any). Anything out of the ordinary is likely to be strange, perhaps frightening, and really best avoided to maintain a relaxed peace of mind.

So it is, by and large, with lexicographers. In *A Handbook of Lexicography: The Theory and Practice of Dictionary-Making*, Bo Svensén explains:

Compilers of dictionaries have always utilized each other's work to a greater or lesser extent. Naturally, it would be absurd to 'invent the wheel' at the beginning of every new dictionary project and refrain from making use of the advances already made by lexicography. On the contrary, the survival instinct causes lexicographers to consult all dictionaries relevant to their own work in order to make sure that they have not overlooked anything important. However, as dictionaries are protected by copyright, great caution is required here.

The principle appears to be: we have many good dictionaries, each with first-class definitions. It's all there. No need to go back to first principles, to stand apart and start over again. Not only is there no need to do so, but who could want to undertake such a scary undertaking? As Landau confides, in his textbook of lexicography:

When one defines a new term one is truly on uncharted ground. The intellectual effort is analogous to that employed in deciphering a message in code, except that, unlike the cryptographer, the definer never knows whether he has the message right. Therefore, he seeks what aid and comfort he can get by comparing notes with whatever else is available.

But how can one know that everything necessary to characterise the meaning of a word is there in the similar, related, and mishmashed entries of current dictionaries? How can one know, unless one does take a step away and look at the word anew, without being befuddled by tradition? Oftentimes the established meaning may be perfectly satisfactory. But sometimes it may not be.

Let's take a look at how the verb *congratulate* has been dealt with in ten dictionaries, four older ones and six from the past few decades. (There are many further definitions, from both old and recent dictionaries; all are either identical or similar to those quoted.)

congratulate

(a)	1604	Cawdrey	to reioyce with another for some good fortune
(b)	1656	Blount	to rejoyce with one for some good fortune that has befaln him
(c)	1730	Bailey	to rejoice with one on account of his good fortune
(d)	1828	Webster	to profess one's pleasure or joy to another on account of an event deemed happy or fortunate ...
(e)	1951	Concise Oxford, 4th ed.	address (person) with expressions of sympathetic joy (on an event)
(f)	1961	Webster's Third	to express sympathetic pleasure to on account of success or good fortune
(g)	1987	Random House Unabridged, 2nd ed.	to express pleasure to (a person), as on a happy occasion
(h)	1990	Concise Oxford, 8th ed.	express pleasure at the happiness or good fortune or excellence of (a person)
(i)	1991	Macquarie, 2nd ed.	express sympathetic joy to (a person), as on a happy occasion ...
(j)	2001	Cobuild, New ed.	if you congratulate someone you say something to show you are pleased that something nice has happened to them ...

These are all re-statements of a single theme. *Rejoice* (or *reioyce* or *rejoyce*) is in (a–c) and then *joy* in (d–e) and (i). We find *pleasure* in (d) and (f–h), together with *pleased* in (j). Modifier *sympathetic* is attached to *joy* in (e) and (i) and to *pleasure* in (f). Note that for this entry, Macquarie, (i), does not simply copy Random House, (g). It keeps the same frame, *to express – to (a person), as on a happy occasion*, but instead of *pleasure* in the middle slot, Macquarie substitutes *sympathetic joy*, as in (e).

In many instances, *congratulate* does have the meaning of all these combined definitions. The congratulator does share the happiness/joy/pleasure of the congratulatee. For example: *Father congratulated his daughter on being accepted into music school.* But there is also a quite different sense: 'acknowledge to someone that they have a significant achievement or happening (without necessarily being at all pleased about it oneself)'.

For example, when a colleague got promoted – someone I don't care for and don't think much of – I wrote and congratulated them. This was perfectly sincere: I was acknowledging a significant achievement on their part and did it in order to be thought of as polite. In a different scenario, suppose that two people are competing for a prize, or to win a race. When the result is announced, the loser typically congratulates the winner. They don't experience any joy or pleasure or happiness at someone else having beaten them; they are just acting in a socially correct way in acknowledging the other person's triumph. In a presidential election, once sufficient votes have been counted for it to become clear who has been elected, the loser invariably makes a speech conceding defeat and congratulating their opponent. In fact, they probably feel angry and depressed, and are far from sharing the new president's joy.

A lexicographer, considering the entry for ***congratulate***, consults each of the row of dictionaries on their desk. They all say more-or-less the same thing (hardly surprising, since they will largely have been copied off each other). That must be right! The task is just to express this established sentiment in a slightly new way. No need to cast off the blinkers, and wonder whether there might be a further sense for this word beyond the oft-repeated one. In fact, there is a further meaning – *congratulate* can describe a social act, not necessarily accompanied by happiness for the congratulator.

When working on a certain word, shouldn't one look at what has been said about it by others? Of course one should, but at the *end* of the study, not at the beginning? If one starts out from what others have said (and find that they have all said more-or-less the same thing), one's mind is already programmed.

The scientific approach – which I have tried to follow in chapters 3, 6, 9, and 12 – is to start with a blank sheet. For the words in a semantic set, utilise your own knowledge and intuitions, and consult examples from appropriate corpuses to investigate contrastive sentences which demonstrate subtle differences of meaning. Work out the semantic system, plus its grammatical correlations. Then, at a late stage (and only then), consult what others have said, in order to perhaps expand and adjust your draft description.

We left the historical narrative in chapter 7, at Samuel Johnson. The following chapter takes up the story again, moving into the nineteenth century.

11   The Nineteenth Century

As time went by, the number of monolingual dictionaries of English mush-roomed. At least thirty-five new compilations were issued between Johnson in 1755 and the turn of the century, followed by more than fifty during the first half of the nineteenth century with an ever-expanding number after that.

All were useful, few memorable. An outstanding exception was *A New Dictionary of the English Language* by Charles Richardson, a London school-master, published in parts between 1835 and 1837. What was particularly noteworthy was that Richardson's work was entirely original; that is, he didn't copy. For each entry there was a definition – basically, a list of semi-synonyms – and then, like Johnson, supporting quotations. But Richardson had many quotations – far, far more than Johnson. Furthermore, he didn't use any from Johnson.

To illustrate these points, we can repeat Johnson's definition of *annoy* (from page 136), and compare it with Richardson's:

JOHNSON   to incommode, to vex, to teaze, to molest
RICHARDSON   to hurt, to harm or injure, to trouble or molest

Johnson included four quotations, including one from Spenser's *Fairy Queen*. Richardson had fifteen quotations, quite different. They went back to Chaucer, and included one from the *Fairy Queen* (but not the same one as Johnson).

As illustrated for *hot* and *sweet* on pages 95–6 and 100–1, Johnson typic-ally distinguished several senses for important words, and attached quotations to each. If a word functioned as both noun and verb, and if it had derivations, Johnson had a separate entry for each (for example, *dance* as verb, *dance* as noun, derivation *dancer*). Richardson had none of this, believing that each word had a single basic meaning. The rationale for this is explained on pages 150–1.

To accommodate all the quotations, Richardson's dictionary was an over-whelming document. Over 2,000 pages, each with three columns in very small print; not at all easy to use.

One issue on which Richardson was absolutely unsatisfactory concerned etymology. To explain how and why, an overview is needed.

Etymology

Some dictionaries confine themselves to describing how a word behaves in its accustomed habitat. Others also supply information about where it came from and what its form and meaning were in an earlier stage of the language, or in a language from which it was borrowed. A scholarly treatment – in a large dictionary – should surely trace each word back as far as can be.

Most languages of Europe and many from near parts of Asia belong to the Indo-European language family. That is, they have been shown to be genetically related, and to all descend from a single ancestor language which is called Proto-Indo-European (generally abbreviated to PIE). This was spoken some thousands of years ago, before the introduction of writing. A great deal of the phonology, grammar and vocabulary of PIE has been reconstructed, by means of a scientific technique of historical linguistics known as 'the comparative method'.

There are ten or so branches of the Indo-European family tree, and for a lexicographer of English three are of prime importance. English belongs to the Germanic branch, together with Dutch, German, Swedish, and so on. These go back to the reconstructed Proto-Germanic, which was a direct offspring of PIE. The Italic branch goes back to another offspring, Latin; its modern descendants include French, Spanish, Portuguese, Italian, and Rumanian. A third branch consisted just of Greek (Classical and now Modern).

In the light of modern scholarship, it is possible to trace many English words back along the path to their PIE origins. For example:

angle, noun. Central meaning: 'space between two lines or surfaces which intersect'
- borrowed into Middle English in the early fourteenth century from *angle* in Old French, meaning 'space between two intersecting lines; corner'
- this was a development from Latin *angulus*, with the same meaning
- and this came from the PIE root **ank-* 'to bend'

There are other words in present-day English which have the same progenitor as *angle* but progressed through different pathways. PIE form **ank-* developed into *ankura* 'hook, anchor' in Greek, which was borrowed into Latin as *ancora*, thence into Old English as *ancor*, giving modern *anchor*. Within the Germanic branch, PIE **ank-* gave rise to *angel* 'fishhook' in Old English and from this came the modern verb *angle* 'to catch fish with a hook and line'.

There are other words besides a*nchor* which came into English through two borrowings. For instance:

centre (or **center**), noun. Central meaning: 'midpoint of a circle'
- borrowed into Middle English, in the fourteenth century, from Old French *centre*
- this was a development from Latin *centrum* 'midpoint of a circle'

- and this came, in turn, from *kentron* 'midpoint of a circle' in Greek, which was derived from verb *kentein* 'to prick', since when a circle is drawn with a compass (a V-shaped geometrical instrument), the sharp point of one arm of the compass is pricked into the paper so that the pencil on the other arm may draw a circle around this centre
- the Greek verb came from PIE *kent-* 'to prick, jab'

Of course, many words in English came directly from PIE, via Proto-Germanic. These include:

sweet, adjective. Central meaning: 'agreeable physical sensation; prototypically, a pleasant taste, as of honey or sugar'
- this is a development from *swēte*, glossed in Sweet's Old English dictionary (Sweet 1896: 167) as 'sweet, pleasant to taste; fragrant; untainted; agreeable, pleasant'
- which came from Proto-Germanic *swōtja*
- which in turn came from PIE *swāde-* 'sweet, pleasant'

A Latin development from this PIE root was *suāvis* 'delightful, sweet', which became in French *suave* 'with a courteous and elegant manner', and this was borrowed into English during the sixteenth century.

We find words which have quite different meanings but go back to the same PIE root through diverse channels. For example, adjectives *merry* and *brief* both stem from PIE *mreghu-* 'short'. From this PIE root came:

PIE zero grade form *mregh*	PIE suffixed form *mregh-wi*
- giving Proto-Germanic *murgja* 'short, pleasant, joyful'	- giving Latin *brevis* 'short; of small extent'
- which became Old English *myrge* or *mirge* 'pleasant, delightful'	- which became Old French *bref* 'taking a short time'
- this developed into Middle English *merri*, and then modern *merry*	- this was borrowed into Middle English in the late thirteenth century, as *bref*, which has become present-day *brief*

There are other English words which go back to PIE *mreghu-*. Proto-Germanic derived the abstract noun *murgi-thō* 'pleasure, joy' from adjective *murgja-*, and this has developed into present-day noun *mirth*. Latin added prefix *ad-* to verb *breviāre*, creating verb *abbreviāre* 'shorten'; this descended into French and was then taken into English during the fifteenth century, giving verb *abbreviate*. (Note that the changes seen here – such as that from *mr* in PIE to *br* in Latin – are regular developments in these languages, with there being many examples of each.)

Scholarly work over the last couple of centuries has provided full etymological information for words from Indo-European sources, and also for those borrowed from other languages, such as Arabic and Hebrew of the Semitic family. However, only one modern dictionary includes such material in full – the American Heritage. (And they do not show it as clearly as has been done here, no doubt because of that bugbear of book-bound dictionaries – exigencies of space.)

How was etymology shown in the first monolingual dictionaries which were – it will be recalled – restricted to 'hard words', that is, recent loans? Coote (in 1596) marked a few words as coming from Greek; the remainder (with no marking) were assumed to be of Romance origin. Cawdrey (in 1604) added a few 'French' to Coote's 'Greek'; presumably the remainder were assumed to be from Latin. Bullokar (1616) and Cockeram (1623) paid no attention to origins, except for occasional remarks such as 'Canon, a Greek word'. Both Blount (1656) and Phillips (1658) identified some words as Greek, Latin, French, Dutch, Italian, and so on, but in a sporadic fashion. Kersey (in 1702) had nothing whatsoever on word origins.

Nathan Bailey (1721, 1730) and Samuel Johnson (1755) were the first to deal with the matter systematically, offering etymologies for just about every word, even going so far as the part-Arabic origin of *alchemy*. However, most often they only went one language back. Bailey and Johnson (as also Phillips) related *centre* just to *centrum* in Latin. It is interesting that – as quoted on page 57 – Cawdrey correctly had this as originally Greek (although with no details).

Serious work in comparative linguistics (at first called comparative philology) commenced soon after Johnson. In 1786, Sir William Jones, a British judge out in Bengal, suggested that Sanskrit, Greek, and Latin (and probably also the Germanic and Celtic languages) had 'sprung from some common source, which, perhaps, no longer exists'. These ideas were taken up by scholars firstly in Denmark and Germany (later in France, Poland, the United States, Italy, and elsewhere), reconstructing the nature of PIE and the systematic changes which had given rise to the profusion of modern languages.

England, meanwhile, was in what seems in retrospect to be akin to a time warp, where scholarship – and, indeed, common sense – were turned upside down. Two features characterised this period: one was a book by John Horne Tooke, and the other the reception it received.

Horne Tooke was a maverick politician, who supported the American colonists in their fight for independence (despite regarding Americans to be 'of a very inferior cast'). He was sent to prison, in 1777, for 'seditious libel', and spent the time there ruminating on the nature of language. In 1786 (the same year as Sir William Jones's insight, over in Calcutta) part I of Horne Tooke's *Epea Pteroenta or, the Diversions of Purley* was published.

He maintained that originally language consisted just of nouns and verbs with everything else (adjectives, prepositions, pronouns, articles, and so on) being abbreviations of underlying noun and verb sequences. He also believed that each word had a definite meaning which had remained constant from its origin. What makes the modern reader squirm most is the way in which Horne Tooke applied these principles, absolutely off the top of his head. For example, conjunction *through* was believed to be related to noun *door*, and conjunction *if* was said to have come from the imperative form of verb *give*. ('If' did have the form *gif* in Old English and verb 'give' was *giefan*, but these are not cognate, the similarity of form being coincidental.)

Sometimes there was vague similarity of form, other times not. 'I believe that *up* means the same as *top* or *head*, and is originally derived from a noun of the latter signification'. '*From* means merely *beginning*, and nothing else', so that in 'Lamp hangs from cieling (sic)', it is the case that 'Cieling (is) the place of beginning to hang.'

There are dozens more of such mental meanderings, lacking any basis in fact. *From* actually goes back to preposition *per in PIE and *up* to PIE preposition *upo. It is true that some prepositions have developed from lexical words, but none in the way Horne Tooke imagined. *Through* relates to the PIE verb **tere-* 'to cross over, pass through, overcome'. (As does the archaic noun *thrylle* 'aperture, hole' mentioned on page 45 in explanation of *nose-thrylle* as the earlier form of *nostril*.) *Door* is a development from *dhwer, which meant 'door, doorway' in PIE.

Horne Tooke's book was simply a raft of wild ideas. There may have been other books of this nature, but the scarcely believable fact is that *The Diversions of Purley* was accepted by the British public as an example of brilliant insight. Philosopher James Mill found Horne Tooke's work 'profound and satisfactory', 'to be ranked with the very highest discoveries which illustrate the names of speculative men'. The account of conjunctions 'instantly appeared to the learned so perfectly satisfactory as to entitle the author to some of the highest honours of literature'.

At a time when Rasmus Rask in Denmark and Jacob Grimm in Germany were commencing scientific study of comparative Indo-European – during the first decades of the nineteenth century – the British were still applauding Horne Tooke's nonsense. Charles Richardson was an enthusiastic admirer, and that is why in *A New Dictionary of the English Language* (in 1835–7) he gave a single 'definition' for each entry, eschewing Samuel Johnson's recognition of distinct senses, and also his separation of the varied functions of a word. For example, while Johnson had separate entries for *cool* as adjective, *cool* as noun, *cool* as active (transitive) verb, and *cool* as neuter (intransitive) verb, plus derived noun *cooler*, adverb *coolly*, and noun *coolness*, Richardson placed these within one box, with a single definition to cover all. Horne Tooke had maintained that each word has (and had always had) a single cohesive meaning, and this was the mantra Richardson followed. He also repeated many of Horne Tooke's ad hoc 'etymologies'.

Eventually, the people of Britain realised that they had been duped; the bubble burst, and with such a vengeance! A new edition of Horne Tooke's book in 1840 brought forth – for the first time – honest assessment. A review that year in *Blackwood's Edinburgh Magazine* attempted redress against past adoration:

> The *Diversions of Purley* is one of the most consummate compounds of ignorance and presumption that ever practiced with success on human credulity ... Tooke's discussions are gratuitous and incorrect ... almost every proposition is in error ... a fallacious and frivolous book.

So be it! Fifty years in stasis while serious scholarship on the continent of Europe established linguistics as a science. However, leaving frivolity in the past, there would – by the end of the century – be a ground-breaking new development in Britain. First though, let us cross to examine developments in the 'New World'.

Over in America

The first dictionary published in the USA – at New Haven, in 1798 – was *A School Dictionary: being a compendium of the latest and most improved dictionaries*. Only one full copy of this 198-page volume survives, in the library of Yale University. The author was Samuel Johnson, Junr. No relation – just an interesting coincidence.

Noah Webster served in the militia during the War of Independence and became a strong patriot. He had produced a spelling book for schools in 1783. Webster considered that:

> it is not only important, but, in a degree, necessary, that the people of this country, should have an *American dictionary* of the English Language; for, although the body of the language is the same as in England, and it is desirable to perpetuate that sameness, yet some differences must exist.

Webster worked towards this goal and in 1828 (at the age of seventy) published *An American Dictionary of the English Language*. This went into many later editions.

Joseph Emerson Worcester (twenty-six years younger than Webster) had edited a revision of a revision of Johnson and helped with an abridgement of Webster. Then, in 1830, his own volume – on which he had been working for many years – came into being, *A Comprehensive Pronouncing and Explanatory Dictionary of the English Language*.

These two volumes were of a very different nature. Webster's was modelled on Johnson's, with a list of senses for many words, supported by quotations, and copious etymologies. Worcester valued succinctness. For most entries, head word and short definition fitted on one line (in a double-column format). There was an occasional etymological note, such as '[L]' for 'Latin', and an occasional indication of pronunciation.

Both copied freely from Johnson. Bailey's definition of *eaves dropper*, given on page 63, included *pick-thank* (a word still in use, although rather rare today). Bailey and his three successors defined it as follows:

pickthank, noun

BAILEY	One who delights in finding and discovering the faults and weaknesses of others.
JOHNSON	An officious fellow, who does what he is not desired; a whispering parasite.
WEBSTER	An officious fellow who does what he is not desired to do, for the sake of getting favor; a whispering parasite.
WORCESTER	A talebearer, a parasite.

This is a typical progression. Johnson has an original definition, not relying on Bailey or other predecessors. Webster uses Johnson's entry, with minor amendment. Worcester is concise, and partly original.

It is fascinating to compare Webster's debt to Johnson with Johnson's to Bailey. Chapter 7 (page 94) quoted from an examination of the 732 words commencing with 'L' which occurred in both Johnson and Bailey; Johnson copied no more than about thirty straightforward definitions (and these were acknowledged). A study of the 2,014 words which begin with 'L' in Webster finds that 'Webster copied 333 of Johnson's definitions word for word', Johnson being cited as source in only sixteen instances. And 'Webster made very slight alterations (no more than three words changed, transposed, omitted, or added) in 987 definitions' (in eighty-six instances only one word was changed).

Webster did have a certain amount of new material – technical terms (which Johnson had generally eschewed) and a few specifically American words, such as *consociation* (of churches) and *skunk*. But in many instances he just copied Johnson. For instance:

counterbuff, noun

JOHNSON   A blow in a contrary direction; a stroke that produces a recoil.

> He at the second gave him such a *counterbuff*, that, because Phalantus was not to be driven from the saddle, the saddle with broken girths was driven from the horse.   *Sidney*

> Go, Captain Stub, lead on, and show
> What house you come of, by the blow
> You gave fir Quintin, and the cuff
> You 'scape o' th' sandbags *counterbuff*.   *Ben Jonson*

WEBSTER   A blow in an opposite direction; a stroke that stops motion and
causes a recoil.   *Sidney*

Johnson included two quotations. Webster used Johnson's definition, with
slight expansion, and just mentioned that the word occurred in Sidney, taken
from Johnson. This is typical of very many entries.

The earliest attestation of *counterbuff* was in 1575 and the latest in 1678; the
word was obsolete before 1800. Johnson included this word since it had been
used by two of the 'best (dead) authors', Sir Philip Sidney in 1590 and Ben
Johnson in 1633. Bailey did not see fit to include it, nor, sensibly, did Worcester
(nor Richardson). But Webster – for all his criticism of Johnson and insistence
on including vernacular terms in daily use rather than just items from the literary works – simply copied the master.

Where Johnson recognised several senses for a word, with quotations for
each, Webster typically followed suit, retaining just some of the quotations.
This is illustrated for the adjective *stupid*:

BAILEY
stu'pid [*stupidus*, L] Blockish, dull, senseless.

JOHNSON
stu'pid, adj [*stupide*, French; *stupidus*, Latin]
1. Dull; wanting sensibility; wanting apprehension; heavy; sluggish of
    understanding.
> O that men should be so *stupid* grown
> As to forsake the living God.   *Milton*
> Men, boys and women, *stupid* with surprise,
> Where e'er she passes, fix their wond'ring eyes.   *Dryden*
> If I by chance succeed,
> Know, I am not so *stupid*, or so hard,
> Not to feel praise, or fame's deferr'd reward.   *Dryden*
> With wild surprise
> A moment *stupid*, motionless he stood.   *Thomson*

2. Performed without skill or genius.
> Wit, as the chief of virtue's friends,
> Disdains to serve ignoble ends;
> Observe what loads of *stupid* rhimes
> Oppress us in corrupted times.   *Swift*

WEBSTER

stu'pid, a [Fr. *stupide*; L. *stupidus*, from *stupeo*, to be stupefied, properly to stop. *See Stop*.]

1. Very dull; insensible, senseless; wanting in understanding; heavy; sluggish.

    > O that men should be so *stupid* grown
    > > As to forsake the living God.   *Milton*
    > > With wild surprise
    > > A moment *stupid*, motionless he stood.   *Thomson*

2. Dull; heavy; formed without skill or genius.

    > > Observe what loads of *stupid* rhimes
    > > Oppress us in corrupted times.   *Swift*

WORCESTER

Stu'pid, a. Dull, insensible, sluggish.

Webster copied the two senses from Johnson and mildly modified the definitions. It is odd to have *dull* and *heavy* within both senses (and one wonders whether *formed* is an error for *performed*). Webster copied three of the five quotations in Johnson, using only the last half of that by Swift. In short, Webster added nothing of significance to the Johnson entry.

It was mentioned on page 93 that Johnson had incorrectly given the last line of the James Thomson quotation. The poet actually wrote:

A stupid moment, motionless she stood

Johnson had transposed *stupid* and *moment*, and replaced *she* by *he*; Webster perpetuated the error. It is clear that Webster did not check back to primary sources, but just copied Johnson, errors and all.

At the beginning of this chapter, we noted that Charles Richardson used many more quotations than Johnson, and they were all different. For entries that Webster copied off Johnson, he used fewer quotations, but they were invariably a selection of Johnson's. In the survey of entries in Webster commencing with 'L', it was found that 66 per cent of all quotations were taken from Johnson.

And the etymologies! Sadly, Webster was an admirer of John Horne Tooke and repeated many of the Englishman's eccentric – and incorrect – ideas, such as deriving *if* from the imperative of *give*, and *through* being related to *door*. Webster also pursued his own flights of unscholarly fancy; for example, *stupid* and *stupefy* do go back to the same proto-form but there is absolutely no etymological relation between them and *stop*. His dictionary abounds with false speculations of this kind.

Webster exulted that his *American Dictionary* should reflect the character of the proud new nation. What could be more American than words adopted from indigenous languages? Alongside the sometimes intricate etymologies for words of Indo-European and Semitic origin, surely it would be scholarly (not to say patriotic) to provide some indication of origin for words from American Indian sources? But there was not a whisper. Webster did have entries for *opossum*, *hickory*, *persimmon*, and *skunk* but with no indication that they came from a local language, let alone from which region. (In fact the first three were from Virginia, and *skunk* from Massachusetts.) We are told that **tomahawk** is *An Indian hatchet* but not that the name is of Indian origin. Other words – well-established in American (and other varieties of) English at that time – were omitted entirely. These included *pow-wow*, *squaw*, *hominy*, *pecan*, and *totem*.

It appears that *squaw* was beyond the purview of Webster, but not of Lord Byron, who in his lengthy poem *Don Juan*, in 1823, listed among 'the noble guests, assembled at the Abbey':

Mrs. Rabbi, the rich banker's squaw

Worcester was less nationalistic than Webster, often preferring British spellings over Webster's American ones, and looking to British English as the fountainhead. Yet Worcester, only two years after Webster, did include *pow-wow*, *squaw*, and *hominy* (with no etymology, but Worcester was most sparing over this). Neither of these lexicographers included *pecan* or *totem*, although each word had appeared in print half-a-dozen times before 1828.

Webster's and Worcester's works – each in successive new editions – were in competition for several decades in what has been called 'the dictionary war'. Besides competition in sales, this involved personal skirmishes, beginning when Webster accused Worcester of stealing some of his entries and definitions. What – Webster, who would surely win the prize for plagiarism if there were one – accusing someone else of copying from him! An angry exchange adorned the pages of the *Palladium* (a weekly newspaper published in Worcester, Massachusetts) between November 1834 and March 1835.

Webster listed 121 words which Worcester could have found in no 'other dictionary except mine'. It is true that none of them were in Johnson, but Worcester pointed out that around ninety were in some other earlier dictionary (a number in several). For instance, eighteen were in Nathan Bailey, from 1730. These included *slump*, *Ramadan*, *rhabdology*, and *raca* (which occurs in the *Gospel of St. Matthew*, 5.22). The entries for **raca** were:

	raca
BAILEY	<etymology in Hebrew> Word of contempt for a vain empty fellow.
WEBSTER	A Syriac word signifying empty, beggarly, foolish, a term of extreme contempt. *Matt v*
WORCESTER	[Syriac] A miscreant, a wretch.

There doesn't seem to be too much theft involved here.

Webster and Worcester both produced worthy volumes. Yet Webster is today placed upon a pedestal, with Worcester being scarcely remembered.

In 1883, C. Edwards Lester, in *Lester's History of the United States*, wrote the following paean:

Noah Webster is the all-shaping, all-controlling mind of this hemisphere. He grew up with his country, and he molded the intellectual character of her people ... His principles of Language have tinged every sentence that is now, or ever will be, uttered by an American tongue...

And so it went on. And so it continues today. How, why? Through a mix of political acumen and aggressive marketing.

The second edition of Webster's dictionary, in 1841, was self-published. After his death, in 1843, the go-ahead printing and bookselling firm of George and Charles Merriam purchased unsold copies and the rights to create new editions, the first of which came out in 1845 with many more to follow. Teams of lexicographers were hired to work on each revision, updating definitions and quotations, and making the etymologies more respectable. Merriam's energetic sales tactics involved sometimes securing an order, by decree of a state legislature, that their book was to be placed in every schoolroom.

Several new works were produced by Worcester, culminating in an 1860 revision which took a temporary lead in the sales war. Merriam-Webster responded with their own new edition in 1864. After Worcester's death the following year, his dictionaries ceased to be published, and his name was almost forgotten. The Merriam company did not shirk from hyperbole and their enterprising promotion established 'Webster' as an American icon. The beginnings have been reassessed; we now read: 'Noah Webster was instrumental in giving American English a dignity and vitality of its own'.

The Scottish publisher Blackie put out *The Imperial Dictionary of the English Language* in two large volumes (1847–1850); this was edited by John Ogilvie and was based on Webster's second edition of 1841. An expanded revision, now in four volumes, came out in 1882 under the editorship of Charles Annandale. Back in America, the *Imperial* was taken as foundation for *The Century Dictionary and Cyclopedia*, a multi-volume work edited by Sanskrit scholar and linguist William Dwight Whitney. As mentioned on pages 138–9, a slimmed-down version of this, *The New Century Dictionary* (1927), was revised to be Random House's *American College Dictionary* (1947). This in turn gave rise to Random House's larger 'unabridged' dictionary (1966, 1987) and also the *Encyclopedic World Dictionary* in England (1971), and thence *The Macquarie Dictionary* in Australia (1981). All had been begotten, albeit at several removes, by Webster.

In 1893–5 came another American initiative. *A Standard Dictionary of the English Language* by Isaac Kauffman Funk was notable for its innovation of placing the central sense of each word first. Many further editions followed, known as Funk and Wagnalls.

Meanwhile, over in England, things were astir.

The Oxford English Dictionary

Only a couple of centuries behind the Academia della Crusca, in Florence, and the Académie française, there was established in London – in 1842 – the Philological Society. One of its early ideas was the making of a dictionary. At first it was to be an addendum to Johnson, the words not included there. Then it became more ambitious – to document the history of form and meaning for every word in the language.

Work began in 1861 and the first editor, Herbert Coleridge, produced a specimen page (dealing with *Affect* to *Affection*). But Coleridge died of tuberculosis the following year (aged just 30). The editorship was then assumed by Frederick James Furnivall, who led an unconventional life and was hugely enthusiastic but rather disorganised. Appeals for assistance from the general public brought in oodles of quotation slips which Furnivall placed in stacks all over his house.

Finding a publisher was not plain sailing. On 22 February 1877, the project was declined by Cambridge University Press. Michael Black, the Press's historian, comments:

All publishers expect to make wrong decisions, and can only hope that they are small mistakes. This was possibly the largest wrong decision in publishing history.

The reason is said to have been the poor opinion which people at Cambridge had of Furnivall, and the casual letter he had written.

Henry Sweet, premier linguist in Britain, wasn't interested in taking on the editorship himself. However, he did write an irresistible – and absolutely misleading – submission to Oxford University Press, saying that they were being offered the result of nineteen years' work by members of the Philological Society, with half of it already sub-edited and ready for publication. Oxford accepted, in 1879, on condition that the editor should be James A. H. Murray, a meticulous and highly organised scholar.

In fact, it took fifty years for all of the great dictionary to be published. Cambridge would have been smirking as – at first – Oxford invested more and more into the project for limited returns. But in time, smiles and grimaces were exchanged. Today, the word *dictionary* is linked with *Oxford*. Besides the mammoth tome there came the *Shorter Oxford*, the *Concise Oxford*, the *Pocket Oxford*, the *Little Oxford*, the *Advanced Learner's*, and many more, bringing with them prestige and also rather significant income.

Murray essentially followed Johnson's scheme of organisation: head word, etymology, definition – divided, if appropriate, into senses, and Murray frequently added sub-senses – plus well-chosen quotations. Murray also provided the date for each quotation, and ranged them in chronological order under each sense or sub-sense.

Providing dates was a critical factor. Oxford University Press had signed a contract with the Philological Society for *A New English Dictionary on Historical Principles, Founded Mainly on the Materials Collected by the Philological Society*. This was the only title on the first published fascicle (*A to Ant*) in January 1884. However, from the eleventh fascicle (*deceit to deject*) in December 1894, it suited the publisher to add a further designation, *Oxford English Dictionary*. Gradually, this became the only title. Replacing *New* with *Oxford* was fair enough. Eliminating mention of the Philological Society made the title more succinct. But omitting *on Historical Principles* obscured the actual character of the OED. Its major focus is *not* on the central meaning of a word as it is used today, but on where it came from and how nuances of meaning shifted and expanded over time. The OED is 'on historical principles' and this should – as it was originally – be included in the title.

Basically, Johnson did all the important things himself. He chose those literary works which were to be the basis for his dictionary and marked them up, indicating which quotations the assistants should copy onto slips. Once the slips had been sorted it was Johnson who examined them, wrote the definition, and selected the quotations to be included. Johnson had estimated that the job would take three years, but in fact it extended over eight years and a bit. However, during this period, Johnson was not solely occupied with lexicography – he wrote more than 200 issues of *The Rambler*, a twice-weekly essay, and was a central figure in the intellectual life of London, providing a core of wit and vivacity.

Murray had wider vision, wanting to cover every word in the language (except the rude ones), extending back as far as could be. Every kind of written material was to be used as source, not just 'the best writers' (and dead ones at that). Murray chose the books and manuscripts and newspapers to be studied and issued them to a coterie of voluntary helpers, with instructions concerning the sort of thing to look for and how to enter quotations on slips. A group of assistants would collate the slips and prepare draft entries, but it was Murray himself who finalised the definition, etymology and pronunciation, and decided which quotations to use (a bit more than a third of those assembled).

Murray estimated that the complete job would take ten years. It soon became clear that such a time-frame was unrealistic. Commencing work in 1879, Murray had completed and published letters A and B by the end of 1888. He assured the worried publisher that he would get faster as the work progressed (in fact, this never happened). The Press insisted on the work being shared. In 1888 Henry Bradley, who had until then been assisting Murray, was put in charge for letters E, F, and G while Murray continued with C and D. Letter C was published, in 1893, and D and E in 1897. Completion still seemed over the horizon.

William Craigie became the third editor in 1901, tackling N, Q, and R. Charles Onions had been assisting Murray since 1895, and in 1914 he was made a full editor dealing at first with *Su–Sz*. The other editors followed Murray's plan to a certain extent (pages 209–11 discuss divergences). Murray died (aged 78) in 1915 having completed eleven letters in thirty-six years. Bradley followed in 1923 (he was 77) having done five letters in full and parts of two others in thirty-five years. It fell to Craigie, in 1928, to launch the full assemblage of twelve immense bound volumes, one set to be presented to King George V and another to President Calvin Coolidge, over in Washington.

Murray's first task had been to retrieve the million and more quotation slips which had been compiled under the aegis of Furnivall. Many could be extracted from the nooks and crannies in the Furnivall residence. Others were retrieved, often with difficulty, from the folk Furnivall had put in charge of miscellaneous parts of the alphabet (the 'sub-editing' referred to by Sweet). Their work was inconsistent and often poor, such that Murray resolved to start all over again.

There was a resounding response to a call for readers who would select and copy out quotations; they were of every age, sex, status, and nationality. A veritable industry evolved. Murray erected a metal shed in his garden, the Scriptorium, where he sat at a high desk, overseeing the work of assistants and crafting the entries. Soon, a thousand quotations slips were arriving each day, to be assessed and sorted into a myriad of pigeon-holes, awaiting the time when their alphabetical slot would come into focus. The dictionary would have many entries, and it is interesting to recount the criterion for a word to be included.

As described at the beginning of chapter 4, English naturally divides into three stages. These are Old English (OE) or Anglo-Saxon, spoken from the fifth to the twelfth century, Middle English (ME), from the twelfth to the end of the fifteenth century, and Modern English, commencing in about 1500. On the accepted criterion that languages are recognised as distinct if they are not mutually intelligible, each stage is to be regarded as a separate language. A speaker of modern English cannot understand ME or OE; nor could a speaker of ME fully comprehend OE, and vice versa.

Most dictionaries describe the language current at the time. Bailey followed this practice. Johnson, relying on usage from the 'best writers', did include words which had been current after 1500 even if they were no longer in use, such as *counterbuff*. Webster simply followed Johnson in this. But Worcester differed, being like Bailey in only dealing with words in current use. The same applied for Richardson. Whereas Johnson had only included quotations after about 1500, Richardson used more, utilising some going back to the earlier use in ME of a current word. However, he excluded words – like *counterbuff* – which had been used in Modern English but were by his time obsolete.

In contrast to all their predecessors, Murray and his co-editors put absolutely everything in (except for rude words). Not only words from an earlier
stage of Modern English which were no longer in use by the late nineteenth
century, but also all words in ME ('words now in use, or known to have been
in use since the middle of the twelfth century') including those which had not
made their way (in any form) into the modern language. For example, adjective
adel 'terrible, hideous, foul', which occurred in OE (in Beowulf) and in two
documents from the thirteenth century; noun *bombance* 'ostentation, pride',
attested just in one document from about 1325; and adjective *edmod* 'gentle,
humble, meek', for which eight quotations were provided, ranging from about
1000 to 1425. Including ME words in a current English dictionary is rather like
including in a dictionary of modern French words from Vulgar Latin which do
not have descendants in French.

Adding together the ME words and the Modern English words which were
by then obsolete, around one-third of the words in the OED were no longer in
use. But it was, after all, a dictionary 'on historical principles' even though the
publisher had decided to omit this necessary qualification from the title page.

Murray was absolutely meticulous, believing that if any errors were dis-
cerned, the work would lose all credibility, and perhaps be deserted by the
Press and by its readers. This was particularly important since it was being
published in instalments, over many years.

It will be useful to briefly comment on the sections of each entry.

(a) Head word. The standard spelling in the current stage of the language was
given, together with variant spellings, including – for words in Germanic origin – all spellings in ME and OE. To this the OED added the pronunciation,
according to a carefully worked-out scheme.

Grammatical information was minimal, confined to statement of word
class simply given as: *n.*, *v.*, *adj.*, *adv.*, *conj.*, *prep.*, and so on; the reader was
expected to understand these without explanation. Murray invented a new term
comb[ining] form but nowhere explained it. Indeed, the employment of this
term for *aero-* in his first fascicle is given as the first use in the dictionary's
entry for ***combining form***. (It appears to indicate something which can only be
used in combination with another form.)

(b) Etymology. This should indicate the history of the word. For a word borrowed from French, for example, the form (and meaning) in French should be
given, together with the form in Latin from which it was descended. Johnson
generally confined himself to this. However, the OED typically provided
cognate forms in some (but not all) other Romance languages (for example,
Italian, Catalan, Spanish, Portuguese). Giving forms in other languages
which descended from the same proto-form is tangential, and unnecessar-
ily expands the size of the dictionary. In similar fashion, Germanic forms

might be provided with cognates from Sanskrit and Sogdian, again unnecessary. What would be relevant is the Proto-Indo-European reconstructions which spawned the Latin or Germanic forms. However, at that time people in England were not attuned to the work on PIE which was progressing on the continent. (This did become easily accessible in the twentieth century; the minimal use that was made of it in revision of the OED is discussed on pages 212–13.)

(c) **Definition.** For words with a wide range of meaning, the OED followed Johnson in recognising several numbered senses, often adding sub-senses, and going into considerably more detail than Johnson.

This may be illustrated for the adjective *stupid*. Johnson's entry, given in full in the previous section, can be repeated, and compared with that in the OED.

JOHNSON, adjective **stupid**
1. Dull; wanting sensibility; wanting apprehension; heavy; sluggish of understanding. [four quotations]
2. Performed without skill or genius. [one quotation]

OED, adjective **stupid**
1a. Having one's faculties deadened or dulled; in a state of stupor, stupefied, stunned; esp. *hyperbolically*, stunned with surprise, grief, etc. *Obs. exc. arch (poet.).* Very common in Dryden. [seven quotations, 1611–1859]
†1b. Belonging to or characterized by stupor or insensibility. *Obs.* [four quotations, 1607–1818]
†1c. Of a part of the body: paralyzed. *Obs.* [one quotation, 1638]
1d. *Pathol.? Obs.* [one quotation, 1822–9]
†1e. Emotionally or morally dull or insensible; apathetic, indifferent. Const. *to* [compare French *stupide à.*] [six quotations, 1605–a1770]
†2. As the characteristic of inanimate beings. Destitute of sensation, consciousness, thought, or feeling. *Obs.* [eight quotations, 1626–1744]
3a. Wanting in or slow of mental perceptions; lacking ordinary activity of mind; slow-witted, dull. [fifteen quotations, 1541–1879]
3b. Of attributes, actions, ideas, etc.: Characterized by or indicating stupidity or dullness of comprehension. [eight quotations, 1621–1891]
†3c. Of the lower animals: Irrational. Also of individual animal: its propensities, etc.: Lacking intelligence or animation, senseless, dull. *Obs.* [four quotations, a1680–1867]
4. Void of interest, tiresome, boring, dull. [seven quotations, 1778–1901]
5. Obstinate, stubborn, *north dial.* [five quotations, 1788–1893]

6. *Comb.*, as *stupid-looking* adj.; adverbial with another adj., as *stupid-honest*, *stupid-sure* (nonce-wds.); **stupid-head**, a blockhead.

Note that sense 3b, which deals with *stupid* describing something other than a person, includes *Characterized by or indicating stupidity*. Six senses are given for ***stupidity***, three obsolete and one dialectal. Of the two current senses, that which relates to something other than a person is *A stupid idea, action etc.* The familiar circularity recurs – scarcely helpful.

One wonders whether so much detail is necessary (for some entries the sub-senses extend over dozens of pages), whether there could not be more generalisation. Consider two quotations assigned to different senses:

3a. No man who knows ought, can be so stupid to deny that all men naturally were borne free (Milton, 1649).
4.   If my letter is very stupid, forgive me (Creighton, 1884).

The first quotation refers to a person acting without intelligence. The second refers to a letter, but it clearly indicates that the person who wrote it was – in this instance – acting without intelligence. Surely, the meaning is essentially the same for the two quotations, and is the overarching modern meaning of the adjective.

Unlike most other dictionaries (really, all except for Johnson and Richardson), the OED's definitions were generally original and free of plagiarism. Sensibly, Johnson's work was made use of very occasionally, as appropriate. For example, in definition **3a** for ***enough***, Bradley gave 'also in weaker sense, implying "a slight augmentation of the sense of the positive" (J[ohnson])'. (However, he did not quote correctly; Johnson actually wrote: 'it notes a slight augmentation of the positive degree'.)

The OED was intended as a historical document. Senses are typically quoted chronologically, according to the date of their first quotation, or else in what the editor considers to be a logical manner. This often means that the first few senses quoted are obsolete (this applies to the first six for ***stupid***). In many instances, the prevalent current sense is buried a long way down, with no indication that this is the central meaning today. For example, the entry for verb ***want*** commences with what was the main sense in olden times, 'to be lacking or missing' (from 1225) and proceeds through a dozen obsolete and innumerable minor senses before eventually arriving at 'to desire, wish for', which is attested only since 1707 but accounts for three-quarters of the instances of *want* in a modern corpus.

(d) Quotations. For the OED, as for Johnson, quotations were critical for supporting and illustrating the definitions. Johnson had assembled about 240,000 quotation slips and utilised about 114,000 of them. Overall, the OED amassed around five million and included 1,827,306 in the volumes.

Murray and his co-editors took care to check each quotation back to its primary source before publication. Johnson did not do this and as a consequence a few errors crept in; see page 93. (In a large number of instances Webster just copied Johnson, errors and all.) For each entry the OED always included the earliest quotation and, for a word now obsolete, the last one also.

The two dictionaries made different selections from their stock of quotations. Where the same quotation was used by both, it is instructive to compare a few of them. First, a quotation for verb **desire**, taken from Dryden's translation of Virgil's *Ænid*:

JOHNSON
But since you take such interest in our woe,
And Troy's disastrous end *desire* to knew
I will restrain my tears, and briefly tell
What in our last fatal night befell.   *Dryden's Æn. b. ii*

OED
1697   DRYDEN *Ænid* ii, *init.*, Since ... Troy's disast'rous end [you] desire to know.

As often happens, the OED's entry is shorter. Their condensation is clearly shown, with '...' indicating the omission between *Since* and *Troy's*; and subject *you*, imported from the omitted line, is enclosed in brackets.

The OED always indicates the exact origin of a quotation; Johnson also does so in the example just given, but often he is vague. More quotations are taken from Shakespeare than from anywhere else; Johnson sometimes gives the name of the sonnet or play (although never details as to act and scene), but other times just *Shakesp.* is held to suffice. (Both feature in the entry for **hot** given on pages 95–6.)

The same quotation is used by both dictionaries to illustrate adjective **sweet**:

JOHNSON
Balm his foul head with warm distilled water,
And burn *sweet* wood to make the lodging *sweet*.   *Shakesp.*

OED
1596   SHAKES. *Tam. Shr.* Induct i. 49 Burne sweet Wood to make the Lodging sweete.

The OED gives full attestation, from *The Taming of the Shrew*, but omits the initial line of the quotation, which provides the context for why sweet wood was being burnt.

OED quotations are mostly shorter than Johnson's, but not always. Before seeing how the two dictionaries use an extract from Milton's *Paradise Lost* (book XII) to illustrate adjective *stupid*, we can read the original.

> Bred up in idol-worship: Oh, that men
> (Cans't thou believe?) should be so stupid grown,
> While yet the patriark liv'd, who 'scaped the flood,
> As to forsake the living God, and fall
> To worship their own work in wood and stone.

Now the two quotations:

JOHNSON

> O that men should be so *stupid* grown
> As to forsake the living God.   *Milton*

OED

1667   MILTON, *P. L* XII. 116 O that men ... should be so stupid grown,
While yet the Patriark liv'd, who scap'd the Flood, As to forsake the
living God.

Johnson just says *Milton*, whereas the OED provides exact attestation from
P[aradise] L[ost]. Johnson edits Milton's verse by putting together parts from
the first two lines, omitting the third line and including the fourth one. There
is no indication of the omissions. The OED, in contrast, shows the omission
of *(Cans't thou believe?)* by '...'. And note that Johnson always preserves the
separate lines within a poem, while the OED runs them on.

With 414,825 entries spread over 15,490 large pages, the OED was indeed
a magisterial compilation, taking the Johnsonian framework to its limit. It was
the product of careful organisation and unlimited perseverance. But how does
it measure up as a linguistic document?

It is useful to distinguish between synchronic study, the description of a language system at some point in time, and diachronic investigation, looking at
how a language system changes and evolves over time.

As emphasised in chapter 1, each language is an integrated system, with
grammar and lexicon interweaving and each supporting the other. The lexicon consists of an interconnected framework of semantic sets. Each word has
a range of meaning, complementary to – and defined by – the meanings of
other words in its set, and each set only has import through its relation to other
lexical sets and to their grammatical potentialities. Every part of the overall
system of a language (at some point in time) only exists – and has significance – with respect to the language system as a whole.

Language systems shift over time. One could describe the system of English
in Shakespeare's time, and that in the present day, and make a diachronic study
of the re-arrangements and adjustments which have eventuated between these
two synchronic stages.

Most dictionaries confine themselves to synchronic study of a language as currently spoken. The OED's coverage extends in time but in a manner which could be described as 'panchronic'. Every example, from the twelfth to late nineteenth century, is accorded equal weight, as if the language had remained stationary and operated with a single immutable system. More than that, the OED does not conceive of language as a system, but rather as a collection of individual words, separate and self-sufficient.

The OED's whole approach is fragmentary. In actual fact, a lexeme has a range of meanings, each section being linked to the rest. (If this were not so, it should be recognised as two homonymous lexemes.) The OED assigns to a word distinct senses, with only a small attempt to recognise an overarching meaning and to show how each segment of the word's semantic range is a specific realisation of this. Matters are obscured by 700 years being regarded as a single synchronic stage.

What one misses is characterisation of the range of meaning – central sense and extensions from this – in 1600, then how this altered by, say, 1700, then again by 1800. What had been a peripheral sense may have become the focal meaning (as happened with *fast*, described in chapter 9, and with *want*, in chapter 12).

The OED is first and foremost an outstanding historical resource, for giving examples over time of the uses of every imaginable word. There are, as has been pointed out, too many entries. Words which occurred only in Middle English – which was a different language – should be dealt with in a dictionary of ME (as indeed they are). Editors of the OED paid little attention to semantic generalisation, or to the fascinating question of how meanings shift over time (this is only possible through comparing synchronic descriptions at different points in time). There was no awareness or description of grammatical properties.

This was, then, the state of the art at the end of the nineteenth century. Despite its magnificence (and royal approbation) the OED scarcely engaged with what should surely be the main function of a dictionary – to explain to its readers when to use a particular word rather than another of similar meaning.

With publication of the final volume of the OED, in 1928, it was time to move on – a matter which will be taken up in chapter 14. Before that, the next chapter discusses a further semantic set, and then chapter 13 examines the role of grammar.

12   Semantic Set: *Want, Wish (For)*, and *Desire*

The three words *want, wish (for)*, and *desire* have – to some extent – overlapping senses (and are defined in terms of each other in many dictionaries). But, as will be shown, there are fundamental differences in meaning and in use. For example, all can be used in the frame *Grandfather – us to share the food around*. However, the three sentences have distinct implications.

(1)   Grandfather wished us to share the food around
           (he said that it was the appropriate thing to do)
(2)   Grandfather desired us to share the food around
           (he said that if we did this it would make him happy)
(3)   Grandfather wanted us to share the food around
           (we found out later that this was what would have made him happy; however, he didn't say anything at the time and we kept all the food for ourselves)

In (1–3) the three verbs take a TO complement clause (see pages 7–9). They can also take, as object, just a noun phrase such as *a baby*. It is acceptable to say *She wishes for/wants/desires a baby*. However, more felicitous expressions are:

(4)   Mary wishes so much for a baby
           (she wishes she could have a baby, but is barren)
(5)   The newly-weds want a baby without delay
           (they intend to start trying to have one at once)
(6)   Stella has always desired a real baby
           (ever since she got her first doll, as an infant)

There are contexts in which only two, or else just one, of the words may be used. *I want you* and *I desire you* have similar meanings, as an invitation to sexual activity. (There is a difference. *I want you* is more urgent and lustful, whereas in a more restrained courtship one might hear *Oh, how I desire you*.) However, one cannot say *I wish for you* (at least not with anything like this meaning). And there is no paraphrase involving *want* or *desire* corresponding to:

(7)   I wish (that) I could have met Charles Darwin

Wish and *desire* can also be used as nouns, with a similar meaning to when they are verbs. Thus:

(8)   He expressed a desire to do better next time
(9)   He expressed a wish to do better next time

Want could not be used in this frame. There is a noun *want* but the meaning is, roughly, 'lack', quite different from the sense illustrated above.

We can now provide a characterisation of the central meaning for each of the words.

The Three Words

1.   ***Wish*** /wiʃ/ is a development from the Old English verb *wȳscan*, with the same meaning (going back to **wen-* 'desire, strive for' in Proto-Indo-European). It came to be used also as a noun in the fourteenth century.

Verb *wish (for)* relates to a potentiality which, if it were realised, would provide satisfaction for the referent of the subject of the verb.

(10)   Mario wishes for an opportunity to clear his name
(11)   The club wishes to retain Bickman for next season

Wish generally requires *for* when directly followed by a single noun phrase, as in (4) and (10), but the *for* is omitted when a complement clause follows, as in (1), (7), and (11).

The potentiality may be something which is feasible, as in (1), (10), and (11). Or something which might have been, but just isn't, as in (4) and:

(12)   I wish (that) I could swim

It can describe an opportunity which has passed by:

(13)   I wish (that) I could have been the person to ask that question, not Jules
(14)   The boss now wishes (that) he had never agreed

Or just a wistful dream, not realisable because of the matter of time, as in (7), or actuality, as in:

(15)   Hannah wished (that) she had been born a man

Noun *wish* has more limited meaning; it may only be used if the potentiality is realisable, as in (9). Sentence (1) and (11) can be roughly paraphrased by:

(1')   Grandfather expressed the wish that we should share the food around
(11')   The club has a wish to retain Bickman for next season

Sentences such as (7) and (13–15) refer to something which could not (now) happen, and they cannot be restated with noun *wish*.

2.   **Desire** /diˈzaiə(r)/ is a Romance loan. Noun *desire* is based on French *désir*, and verb *desire* on French *désirer* (a development from Latin verb *dēsiderāre* 'long for some person or thing that is absent or lost; wish for'). Both were borrowed into English in the thirteenth century.

Today, the noun is more frequent than the verb. It describes a state of mind, a feeling concerning something which, if it happens, will make happy whoever has the desire. For example:

(16)   They recognised the desire for self-determination among the colonies
(17)   Maybe you feel the desire to be a good dancer?
(18)   He had a stubborn desire to get at the truth

Each of these could be revamped with *desire* as a verb. The essence remains, but the message comes through in a less effective manner:

(16')   They recognised that the colonies desire self-determination
(17')   Maybe you desire to be a good dancer?
(18')   He stubbornly desired to get at the truth

Desire being expressed by a noun in (16) conveys an intensity which is missing from (16'). Sentence (17) has *feel the desire*, and *feel* could not be included in (17') with verb *desire*. In (18), noun *desire* is modified by adjective *stubborn*. It is possible to include adverb *stubbornly* with verb *desire* in (18') but this sounds awkward and without the flavour of (18).

Desire is unlike *wish* in that it can only refer to something which has the potential to eventuate, not to anything which has happened already or could not happen.

3.   **Want** /wɔnt/ has two senses, one old and the other newish.
• The first sense, *want₁*, refers to a lack, to something being missing (that is, it is not where it could or should be). The word, with this meaning, was a borrowing from Old Norse about 1200 CE (emanating from Proto-Indo-European **eu-* 'lacking, empty'). It can be a noun, as in:

(19)   The explorers were daily becoming weaker from want of food
(20)   The battle was lost for want of a nail
(21)   She showed want of respect for her elders

Want₁ also functions as a verb, with a similar meaning to *need*; for example:

(22)   All the contract wants is your signature
(23)   She did not want for money, but she lacked serenity

(*Want₁* is in a semantic set that includes *lack*, which can also be both noun and verb, and noun *absence*. And there will be cross-reference to the set including *need* and *require*.)

- The predominate sense today, *want₂*, developed from *want₁* around 1700 CE and functions only as a verb; this is what belongs in the semantic set with *wish (for)* and *desire*. It was, historically, an extension of the meaning of *want₁*, referring to something which is both (a) lacking or missing and (b) desired. That is, it describes something which will make happy the referent of the subject of the verb.

(24)   I want to put my point of view
(25)   Jasmine wants (to get) a bicycle
(26)   I want (to have) your honest opinion on the matter
(27)   I want someone to read to me
(28)   Maria wants her daughter to marry the man she loves

Like *desire*, and unlike *wish*, *want₂* implies a potential for something to be realised, and cannot relate to the past.

Functions

Having outlined the basic meanings of the three words, we can survey the grammatical contexts in which they may occur. First, functioning as a verb taking a complement clause. All three verbs can take a (FOR) TO complement clause – as exemplified in (1–3) – while just *wish* and *desire*, but not *want₂*, may occur with a THAT clause. None of the three verbs may take an -ING complement clause (which describes an on-going activity).

I   **With a (FOR) TO complement clause.** As outlined in chapter 1, this refers to a potential activity. It is used with *wish (for)*, *desire*, and *want₂* although, as already mentioned, *desire* is used rather sparingly as a verb.

There are several subtypes.

Ia   **Main clause and complement clause have the same subject.** Complementiser *for* and the repeated subject are omitted from the complement clause. (Note that the *for* of *wish for* is dropped before complementisers *to* and *that*.) This is exemplified in (11) and:

(29)   Rebecca wants to get married in church
          (this will make her happy)
(30)   Rebecca wishes to get married in church

(although she herself lacks belief, all her ancestors have been married in that church and she wishes to continue the tradition)

(31) Rebecca desires to get married in church
(she has set her heart on it, despite doubts from her fiancé)

Sentence (31) is alright, but sounds a little awkward. It would be more felicitous to employ the noun *desire*:

(31') Rebecca has a (deep) desire to get married in church

Now consider

(32) John had wanted to win
(33) John had wished to win

The different attitudes of the subject are brought out when the sentences are expanded:

(32') John had wanted so much to win, and was devastated at the loss
(33') John had, of course, wished to win, but wasn't at all surprised when he missed out

In (32), the use of *want* confers an aura of intensity and of hope (John would be happy if he won), whereas *wish* in (33) is more formal and a little detached (John would be satisfied if he won). (The verb *desire* is scarcely acceptable in the frame of (32–3), the noun being preferred: *John evinced a strong desire to win*.)

If the verb of the complement clause is *have* or *get* (immediately followed by a noun phrase), it is typically omitted together with the preceding complementiser *to*, and the object of the complement clause effectively becomes object of *wish for, want*, or *desire*. This is illustrated for *want* in (25) and (26).

Any time that *want, wish for*, or *desire* is directly followed by a noun phrase, the sentence has an underlying structure with *to have* or *to get*. For instance, the underlying structures for (4–6) are *Mary wishes so much to have a baby, The newly-weds want to have a baby without delay*, and *Stella has always desired to have a real baby*. Sentence (10) is, underlyingly:

(10') Mario wishes to get [an opportunity to clear his name]

Wish and *desire* may omit *to have* or *to get* when this is just followed by a noun phrase. However, *want*$_2$ allows the omission of whatever follows. For instance, there are alternatives:

(33) Mary didn't want to have Bert as a lodger OR Mary didn't want Bert as a lodger

(34)   John wanted to get the deposit back OR John wanted the deposit back

But *Mary didn't wish to have Bert as a lodger* and *John wished to get the deposit back* could not normally be abbreviated to ♦*Mary didn't wish (for) Bert as a lodger* or ♦*John wished (for) the deposit back*. (The same would apply for *desire*.)

Ib   Main clause and complement clause have different subjects. This is exemplified by (1–3) and (27–8). When the complement clause subject immediately follows *wish*, or *desire*, the complementiser *for* (a different item from the *for* of *wish for*) is generally omitted. It can be included – for instance, in place of (1) we could have *Grandfather wished for us to share the food around* – but this is unusual. After *want* the *for* is invariably omitted.

However, when an adverb follows *want* or *wish* (or *desire*), complementiser *for* has to be included. Compare:

(35)   I want/wish Mary to go
(36)   I want/wish very much for Mary to go

Desire can be used in this construction and is most appropriately employed in somewhat formal circumstances, carrying as it does a degree of hauteur. For example:

(37)   The Queen desires (for) you to bring her the documents

There is one further kind of reduction. Complementiser *to* and copula verb *be* may be omitted when followed by an adjective or the past participle of a verb. For instance:

(38)   I want the pig (to be) cooked
(39)   I want the book (to be) finished before Christmas
(40)   John didn't want/wish Mary (to be) hurt

If the complement clause subject is the same as main clause subject, it can be included in this construction, in reflexive form:

(41)   I don't want myself (to be) killed

This *to be* omission is found after a rather small set of verbs; besides *want*, *wish*, and *desire*, it includes *need*, *require*, and *order*.

II   With a THAT complement clause. This occurs a lot after *wish*, a little bit after *desire*, and not at all after *want*.

As described in chapter 1, a THAT clause refers to an event or a state. The introductory complementiser *that* is optionally included (it is in fact omitted most of the time).

A THAT complement clause after *wish* has a range of meanings.

(a) Referring to the future. The complement clause then includes *will* or *would*, as in:

(42)   We are all wishing (that) the typhoon will not come our way
(43)   Faye wished (that) the kettle would hurry up and boil

These could – at a pinch – be paraphrased with (FOR) TO complement clauses: *We are all wishing for the typhoon not to come our way* and *Faye wished for the kettle to boil*. Similarly, the (FOR) TO examples already given could be rephrased with *that ... would*; for example, (1) would then be *Grandfather wished that we would share the food around*, and (35) as *I wish that Mary would go*. A THAT clause relates to a state of affairs, and a (FOR) TO clause to a potential happening. Because of this, the (FOR) TO construction is preferred when the complement clause subject is animate, and can control what it does – as in (1) and (35), and a THAT clause is more suitable when the subject is non-animate and the event just happens, as in (42) and (43).

(b) Referring to an unachieved potential. The complement clause then includes *could*, as in (12) *I wish (that) I could swim*, and:

(44)   We wish (that) Fido could come with us (but he isn't allowed to)

Compare this with *We want Fido to come with us* – involving a (FOR) TO complement clause with *want* – which could only be said if there were a good chance that Fido could come.

(c) Referring to something that is not the case. The complement clause then includes *were* or *was*, as in:

(45)   I do wish (that) the negotiators were not so stubborn
(46)   He wishes (that) his operation was over

(d) Referring to something which didn't happen in the past. The complement clause then includes *had*, as in (14) *The boss now wishes (that) he had never agreed*, and:

(47)   Alexandra wishes (that) she had learned Yiddish from her grandfather

It may describe something which could not have happened and is just a day-dream, such as (15) *Hannah wished (that) she had been born a man*.

Senses **(b)** and **(d)** can be combined, referring to an unachieved potential in the past, then including *could have*. It may be something which might have been possible, as in (13) *I wish (that) I could have been the person to ask that question, not Jules*. Or else something like (7) *I wish (that) I could have met Charles Darwin* – this is impossible since Darwin died many years before I was born; it also belongs in the daydream category.

Whereas *wish* occurs with a THAT clause about as often as with a (FOR) TO complement, *want₂* is, by its meaning, restricted to the (FOR) TO construction. *Want₂* has a directly pragmatic import, relating to something which has the potential to be brought about.

Desire falls between the other two verbs. It can take a THAT clause, but only one referring to a realisable event, and the complement clause is then likely to include *may* or *should*:

(48)   Mother desires that Caroline may have an adequate income

The use of *wish* as a verb may imply a statement of the wish, as in (1). The same applies for *desire*, and it can then involve a THAT clause:

(49)   The Prime Minister desires that you should cease imitating him on your
         radio programme

Desire may not be used in any of senses (b–d) for *wish* – referring to unachieved potential, anything which is not the case, or the past.

III   **Wish plus a state noun.** There are constructions where *wish* is followed by
        a noun phrase with human reference, and then one describing a state. For
        example:

(50)   Father wished us success/better health/joy

This indicates that father said something like *I hope (that) you have success*, and so on. In similar fashion, one may hear:

(51)   Father wished us hello/good morning/good luck

Here one infers that what father said was precisely *Hello* or *Good morning* or *Good luck!*

IV   **Omission of repeated element after the verb.** Consider:

(52)   You can sing if you want to sing
(52')   You can sing if you want to
(52")   You can sing if you want

When *want* is followed by repetition of what was in the previous clause, this can be omitted, and the complementiser *to* may either be omitted or retained. The same applies for *wish*. For *desire*, a slightly different construction is preferred, with *so* before *desire*:

(53)   You can sing if you so desire

Wish may also be used in this construction, but not *want*.
   An idiomatic sense just of *wish* is shown in:

(54)   Touch the stone and wish!

   It is interesting to note that although *wish* has the widest grammatical possibilities, *want* has a higher frequency of occurrence. In keeping with its direct pragmatic sense, *want$_2$* occurs more often than *wish* with a 1st person singular subject, *I*.

V **As a noun**. As mentioned earlier, *desire* is used most often as a noun. It may be followed by *to* or *that*, rather like two kinds of complement clause which the verb may take, as in:

(55)   The junkie had an overwhelmingly strong desire to take the drug
(56)   I had an intense desire that others should know what had become of me

These could be rephrased with verb *desire*, but the emphasis on what would make the subject happy is weakened, and modifiers *overwhelming* and *intense* could scarcely be accommodated.
   Related to (16), one could say:

(57)   The colonies desired (to have) self-determination

When this is recast with *desire* as a noun, the erstwhile object noun phrase, *self-determination*, is introduced by *for*:

(57') The colonies had a (strong) desire for self-determination

Whereas a desire relates to the activity of desiring, a wish describes what is wished for. A typical collocation is *make a wish*; sentence (53) could be restated as *Touch the stone and make a wish!* (One could not say ♦*make a desire*.)
   Want$_2$ is never expressed by a noun. *Wish* can be but – with the exception noted in the last paragraph – relatively seldom is; the meaning is more suited to use as a verb.

VI **Derived adjectives.** There is considerable variety in the meanings of adjectives derived from the three verbs. If one hears *John wishes to buy an antique Ford*, then John is **desirous** of making the purchase and he considers the antique Ford to be a **desirable** acquisition. If Mary desires to frighten Tim by creeping up on him, and she does this, and he is frightened, then her action has the **desired** effect. That is, *desirous* relates to the subject of verb *desire* while *desirable* relates to the object, and participle *desired* to the result. **Wishful** is typically followed by *thinking*, and refers to something that is unlikely to eventuate, as in *I keep wishing that May might return my love, but do realise that this is just wishful thinking*. **Wanting** is a rather archaic adjective relating to *want₁*, meaning 'lacking'. In contrast, **unwanted** is based on *want₂ – Nobody wants that dog, the poor little unwanted cur*.

Some Related Verbs

There are a number of less frequent verbs that are (in their main meanings), effectively, more detailed specifications of *want₂*.

4. Verb *long (for)*/lɒŋ (fə)/ comes from Old English *langian* '(days) grow long, feel tedium or discontent, long for' (which goes back to Proto-Indo-European **del-* 'long'). It indicates wanting something rather badly over a fair period of time. The verb can occur with a (FOR) TO complement clause, as in *She longs to see her grandfather again*, and *I long for Penelope to write*. Alternatively, with a noun phrase: *The pain-ridden cripple longed for death*. The derived noun, *longing (for)* is generally used after *have*, as in *She has a longing to see her grandfather again* and *He had a longing for death*.

5. Verb *crave* /kreiv/ – and noun *craving (for)* – go back to Old English *craftian* 'demand by right'. The meaning has shifted to give the predominant modern sense: want something to assuage a physical or mental need. For example: *The neglected child craves affection, The pregnant woman craves oysters at every meal*. Crave can be used for a speech act, as in *I crave forgiveness*; it is then similar to *wish for*.

6. Verb *covet* /'kʌvit/ was borrowed in the early thirteenth century from French *couvietier*, this coming from Latin *cupidītās* 'eager, desirous'. It indicates wanting something to which one has no right, typically something belonging to another person. For example, *Penelope covets Martha's job* and *No one would covet a constantly nagging wife*. Adjective *covetous (of)* relates to the subject of the verb – *Larry is covetous of Sam's new car*.

7. Verb *pine (for)* /pain (fə)/ developed out of Old English *pīnian* 'cause to suffer'. Modern senses include wanting something so badly that it leads to sickness, or wanting something which is really unattainable. For instance, *Lady Lucas sits in the same chair all day, pining for her dead husband*. Like *crave* and *covet*, *pine* does not take a complement clause.

8. Verb **hanker** /ˈhaŋkə/ was probably a loan from Dutch in about 1600 (going back to Proto-Indo-European **konk-* 'to hang'). It is followed by *for* or *after*, plus a noun phrase, or a (FOR) TO complement clause, and indicates constantly wanting something, generally something which is inappropriate or impossible to achieve. For example, *The prostitute hankered for/after respectability* and *Poor people hanker to be rich, while the rich hanker for freedom from responsibility.*

9. Verb **yearn** /jəːn/ goes back to Old English *georn* 'eager, desirous, zealous'. Its primary meaning indicates profoundly wanting something which should be obtainable but is in fact difficult to come by. It is used in a range of grammatical contexts. The verb can be followed by *for* or *after* plus a noun phrase, as in *She yearned for a simple life, not bombarded all day by e-mails* and *The soldier yearned after glory.* Or it may take a THAT or a (FOR) TO complement clause; for example, *He yearned that his new book should become a best-seller, so that he could retire from the post office* and *I yearn to be chosen to compete in the Olympics.* Noun *yearning (for)* follows a similar pattern.

    There is a rather different secondary sense, describing a feeling of compassion, as in *They yearned over the poor child's affliction* (wishing it could be otherwise).

These verbs (just the primary sense of *crave* and *yearn*) are hyponyms of *want₂*; their meanings are included within that of *want₂*. That is, *want₂* could be substituted for *long (for)*, *crave*, *covet*, *pine (for)*, *hanker (for/after)*, and *yearn (for/after)*, maintaining the same meaning but at a more general level. The reverse is not the case. (Since *want* does not take a THAT complement clause *wish that* would replace *yearn that*.)

The relevance of grammatical properties has been evident throughout this chapter. The meaning of a word correlates with the meanings of syntactic constructions it can occur in. Each determines, and is determined by, the other.

The next chapter expounds on the relevance of detailed grammatical study for dictionary-making.

13   The Role of Grammar

Lexicographers and grammarians of English – ne'er the twain doth meet. Each coterie inhabits its own world, assuredly self-contained. But lexicon and grammar are intertwined in the assemblage of language; lexicographers and grammarians *need* to fully appreciate each other's endeavours, and to integrate these.

Think of language as like a feast. Lexical words are the ingredients – fruits and vegetables, fish and meat. They are dissected, blended, shaped, baked, garnished, and daintily served; these processes are akin to grammar. Most of the ingredients are of little use on their own. And the bakery whisks, dishes, stove and plates require an input. Taken as a whole they create a meal; separated, each is simply a curiosity.

The short grammar which Samuel Johnson attached to his 1755 dictionary was a kind-of afterthought, something he considered should be there but attached only minor importance to. As shown on pages 99–100, there was no cohesion between grammar and lexicon. In 1828, Noah Webster included a fuller prefatory grammar, with a number of astute insights, but it was still on a Latinate model and essentially a thing apart. Subsequent dictionaries have generally left grammar alone, contenting themselves with stating the word class for each entry and a little morphological information, such as whether an adjective takes *-er* and *-est*, and the forms of irregular verbs.

Grammar deals with types of constructions – frames whose slots are filled by phrases and words – and with grammatical words and affixes which mark function (like possessive *'s*) and derive one type of word from another (as in *de-class-ify*). Modern dictionaries try to do too much, in one direction, and fail to specify information which is needed, in another.

Lexical words belong to large open classes – nouns, verbs, adjectives. In contrast, grammatical elements constitute small closed systems – articles, demonstratives, pronouns, and affixes such as *un-*, *in-*, *dis-*, *mis-*, *-ify*, and *-ise*. Dictionaries list these as if they were a deviant type of lexeme, treating each as a singleton, and attempting (typically without success) a 'definition'. Here they try to do too much, in a misguided and non-useful way.

Information which the user of a dictionary does need supplied – if they are to learn how to speak the language effectively – concerns which syntactic slots a given word may relate to. In chapter 9 we saw that adverb *fast* may only occur at the end of a clause while *rapidly*, with similar meaning, may be at the end or beginning or in the middle. And so on.

The next section examines grammatical information which should be included, and then the following one looks at what is not needed (and, when given, is incomplete and inappropriate).

Not Enough

Anyone who chooses to consult a dictionary will be familiar with the outlines of English grammar. That a subject noun phrase precedes the verb and an object one follows it. That an adjective comes before the noun it modifies and that a demonstrative or possessive pronoun must precede this (one says *my black cat* and *this little monkey* rather then ◆*black my cat* or ◆*little this monkey*).

When looking up a word in a dictionary, the user needs to find its meaning and also instructions on how to use it, in terms of variation on the basic format. We can draw attention to a sample of such issues.

1. **Plural or no plural.** There is a general rule that nouns form the plural by adding *-(e)s*. Many dictionaries do not think it necessary to state this, although they do give irregular plurals such as *children* and *women*. But only 'count' nouns form a plural. Dictionaries seldom indicate – as they should – that plural *-(e)s* cannot normally be added to 'non-count' nouns such as *mud* and *luggage*. A visitor tramps along a rain-sodden path and wishes to say (translating literally from their native tongue) ◆*There were many muds along the way*. They need to be told – and if not by the dictionary then by whom? – that *mud* does not take plural *-(e)s* and one has to say *There were many patches of mud along the way*. Similarly, ◆*three luggages* is not acceptable in Standard English; it has to be *three pieces of luggage*.

2. **Adjective functions.** Most adjectives have two major roles – (a) modifying a noun, as in *That clever girl* – and (b) in 'copula complement' function following the copula verb *be*, as in *That girl is clever*. But, as pointed out on pages 1–2, a minority of adjectives only have one of these functions not both. For example, *lone*, *future*, and *main* can only be used as modifier, while *content*, *glad*, and *rife* are normally confined to copula complement function. One can say *the main issue* but not ◆*This issue is main*, only *This issue is the main one*, and so on. This is essential information which should be included in a dictionary but seldom is.

3. **Comparative and superlative.** Most adjectives may form a comparative by either adding suffix *-er* or preposing *more* (superlatives follow a similar pattern, with *-est* and *most*). There are in fact four basic sets of adjectives with respect to comparative constructions:

(a) Just take *-er*. These include *kind, cheap, new, easy*.
(b) May take *-er* or *more*. These include *tender, simple, obscure, hungry*.
(c) Generally just take *more*. These include *difficult, peculiar, familiar*.
(d) Those which take neither; by their meaning they cannot occur in a comparative (or superlative) construction. For example, *first, opposite, right*.

(The basic phonological and grammatical principles underlying allocation of adjectives to the sets were outlined on pages 21–3, quoting additional examples.)

Dictionaries typically pay attention to morphological properties (*-er* and *-est*) but not to syntactic ones (*more* and *most*). They will thus either say that an adjective takes *-er/-est* or not say this. In the former case, one can't tell whether the adjective belongs to set (a) or set (b), and in the latter case whether it is in set (c) or set (d). The dictionary just does not provide sufficient information to enable its user to learn the full possibilities of use for a given adjective.

4. Transitivity. There are two basic types of clause:

- **intransitive** (intr), with an intransitive subject (abbreviated to S)
- **transitive** (tr), with a transitive subject (A) and a transitive object (O)

To these may be added peripheral elements indicating time, place, instrument, beneficiary, and so on.

Some verbs, such as *arrive*, may only be used in an intransitive clause. Others, including *recognise*, are confined to a transitive clause. For example:

[The guests]$_S$ have arrived   Jim$_A$ recognised [Pat's car]$_O$

Many verbs may be used in both intransitive and transitive clauses; they are termed 'ambitransitive'; for example *break, melt, eat*, and *preach*.

Samuel Johnson was the first to record the word class (or 'part of speech') for every entry. If a word had several functions, Johnson would have an entry for each – for example, *cool* as adjective, as substantive (noun), as transitive verb, and as intransitive verb (Johnson used the older terms 'a[ctive]' and 'n[euter]' verb). Noah Webster followed suit – as he typically did – but using designations 't[ransitive]' and 'i[ntransitive]'. The OED had separate entries for *cool* adjective, *cool* substantive, and *cool* verb, identifying transitive and intransitive senses within the latter. Most modern dictionaries have a single entry for each lexical word, listing word class and transitivity values within it. But they never attempt to link up the two transitivity values.

An important grammatical point is that ambitransitive verbs fall into two classes. For *break, melt*, and many others the referent of the S argument in intransitive use corresponds to that of the O argument when used transitively.

For another set, which includes *eat* and *preach*, S corresponds to A. This can be illustrated:

intr	[The branch]$_S$ broke	We$_S$ have eaten
tr	[The storm]$_A$ broke [the branch]$_O$	We$_A$ have eaten [lunch]$_O$
intr	[The ice]$_S$ melted	[Rev. Fred]$_S$ preached
tr	John$_A$ melted [the ice]$_O$	[Rev. Fred]$_A$ preached [the sermon]$_O$
	S = O AMBITRANSITIVE VERBS	S = A AMBITRANSITIVE VERBS

The grammar will describe these patterns. It is then up to the dictionary to specify which type each ambitransitive verb belongs to. None do.

A simple transitive verb should have an object stated. And there is a subtype, called 'ditransitive', which requires two kinds of object. For example, *give* – the Donor is always placed in A function, but there are two ways of coding Gift and Recipient:

Mary$_{DONOR}$ gave [a book]$_{GIFT}$ to John$_{RECIPIENT}$
Mary$_{DONOR}$ gave John$_{RECIPIENT}$ [a book]$_{GIFT}$

A dictionary should identify ditransitive verbs, and include a reference to the place in the grammar where their syntactic frames are described. (Others include *lend*, *sell*, *show*, and *tell*.)

5. **Complement clauses.** Some transitive verbs may only take a noun phrase as object (for example, *throw*, *surround*, and *eat*). Others may take either a noun phrase or a complement clause. The three main kinds of complement clause were outlined on pages 7–9.

- a THAT clause describes a fact
- an ING clause describes an activity
- a (FOR) TO clause described a potentiality (purpose or intention)

All three can be illustrated with the verb *remember*:

THAT type	Dr. Susan remembers that she examined Jim Jones (she knows for a fact they she did so but can't recall the details of the examination)
ING type	Dr. Susan remembers examining Jim Jones (she recalls all the tests she applied, and how Jim Jones reacted)
(FOR) TO type	Dr. Susan remembered to examine Jim Jones (she only remembered rather late and, by the time she looked in the waiting room, Jim Jones had got fed up and gone home)

Verbs take varying combinations of complement clause types. For example:

THAT type	ING type	(FOR) TO type	
√	√	√	like, hate, forget
√	√	–	dislike, enjoy, witness
√	–	√	wish, desire, seem
–	√	√	cease, begin, try
√	–	–	ensure, suggest, doubt
–	√	–	finish, detest, discuss
–	–	√	want, fail, cause

What is needed is access to a sound grammatical description which will specify the complement clause constructions available for each verb. This is by no means obvious. For example, a native speaker of German who taught linguistics for half-a-dozen years in Australia always erroneously used a (FOR) TO complement clause with *suggest*, saying ◆*I suggested her to go* (presumably by analogy with *I told/advised/persuaded her to go*). In fact, one can only say *I suggested that she (should) go*. The teaching aids which would have avoided this error were not available. (There is discussion of the meaning and grammatical possibilities for *suggest* on pages 220–6.)

A number of dictionaries (by no means all) do include some relevant information, dished up in an odd way. For example, one sense of the Latin category 'infinitive' (used in Latin to describe a nominalised verb) is employed to label *to* plus verb (such as *to go*). And a (FOR) TO complement clause is frequently designated as 'infinitive'. The definitions for *desire* and *wish* quoted on page 138 (identical between Random House and Macquarie) indicated that these verbs could be followed by 'an infinitive'. Even this is unusual. Many modern desk dictionaries have no indication that these verbs may take a clausal object. A whole dimension of meaning and function is missing.

6. **Adverbs.** The functions of adverbs, and their placement within a clause, show considerable variation. There is no topic on which speakers make more errors and need more special guidance. And there is no area in which dictionaries are more deficient.

Five basic functions of adverbs may be recognised. (Adverbs are underlined.)

(a) **Modifying a sentence**. There are here three possible positions, illustrated by *recently* in:

A   Sylvia has <u>recently</u> been writing poetry
I   <u>Recently</u> Sylvia has been writing poetry
F   Sylvia has been writing poetry <u>recently</u>

The most common position is 'A' in the middle of the sentence. The adverb follows the first auxiliary element if there is one (here *has*); otherwise it just precedes the verb, as in *Sylvia recently wrote some poems*. Alternative placements are in initial, 'I', or final, 'F', position.

Other sentential adverbs which may occur in all three positions include *now*, *truly*, *quickly*, *possibly*, *usually*, and *sensibly*. Some are more restricted – *certainly* and *indeed* are generally only found as A or I, *politically* as I or F, while *almost* is just in A slot.

(b) **Modification of verb (plus object if there is one).** Here, the adverb indicates the manner of the activity. It can be placed either immediately before the verb, position 'V', or after the verb (plus object), position 'O'. For example:

V   Cynthia easily completed the crossword puzzle
O   Cynthia completed the crossword puzzle easily

Most manner adverbs may occur in both positions, but a number are more restricted – for example, *really* can only be in position V, and *well* and *badly* only in O.

Some adverbs can be in either sentential or manner function, with appropriate meanings and positionings. Suppose that when an officer is inspecting a parade he asks a question of a soldier. The officer gets angry. There could be two reasons for this. The first can be shown by using adverb *stupidly* in sentential function. One could say any of:

A   The soldier must stupidly have answered the officer's question
I   Stupidly, the soldier must have answered the officer's question
F   The soldier must have answered the officer's question, stupidly

In this circumstance the question was rhetorical, and the officer got annoyed at being 'answered back'. Here the adverb indicates that the soldier was stupid to provide an answer.

There could be another reason for the officer's anger – the answer did expect a response and the soldier did provide one, but it was a stupid answer. To describe this, adverb *stupidly* would be used in manner function:

V   The soldier must have [stupidly answered the officer's question]
O   The soldier must have [answered the officer's question stupidly]

If there were no auxiliary verbs *must* and *have*, then A (sentential) and V (manner function) would coincide; that is, *The soldier stupidly answered the officer's question* would be ambiguous. Sentences F and O have words in the same order but they are likely to receive different intonation and pausing (as shown by the comma in F).

(c) **Modifying a noun phrase.** For example:

> [Even the oldest professor] couldn't convince Mosley
> [The oldest professor even] couldn't convince Mosley

Whereas *even* can either precede or follow the noun phrase, most adverbs in this function may only precede it; they include *just*, *almost*, *hardly*, *also*, *simply*, and *exactly*.

(d) **Modifying an adjective.** The adverb always precedes the adjective, as in *simply delicious*, *rather clever*, *really beautiful*, *stupidly obstinate*, and *exactly specified*.

(e) **Modifying another adverb.** This is a subset of those which may modify an adjective. Examples include *rather quickly*, *almost correctly*, *slightly stupidly*, and *atrociously jealously*.

Most adverbs have several of the five functions. A tentative sample of just some of the possibilities is:

sentence	adverb modifying verb (plus object)	noun phrase	adjective	adverb	
√	√	√	√	√	really
√	√	–	√	√	similarly
√	√	–	√	–	stupidly
√	√	–	–	–	rapidly
√	–	√	√	√	simply
√	–	–	√	–	recently
–	√	√	√	√	rather
–	√	–	√	√,	slightly
–	√	–	√	–	sweetly

A dictionary should be keyed to a good grammar which includes full description of adverb functions and placement (of which only a brief outline has been given here). Employing the same terminology as the grammar, for each adverb entry the dictionary should indicate its range of functions and – for functions (a–c) – the placement possibilities.

Grammar describes frames and provides examples of words which can occur in each slot for a given frame. The role of a grammar is not to give an exhaustive list of the perhaps hundreds or thousands of lexemes which may correspond to a given slot. Each lexical word will have an entry in the dictionary and it is here that full information concerning grammatical functions should be provided. (In fact, it almost never is.) Dictionary and grammar must go hand-in-hand.

Many lexicographers adopt a cavalier attitude towards grammar, considering it a minor matter. At the end of chapter 1 (page 15), we noted that, in *A Handbook of Lexicography*, Bo Svensén asserts: 'Grammar can be regarded as a set of rules. The grammatical information given in a dictionary can be taken as a description of how the [head word] functions in relation to these rules.' In fact, the grammatical information provided is pitiful, and has changed little since Samuel Johnson introduced it in 1755. By consulting a standard dictionary, one would not know which nouns always mark plural, how each adjective functions, or which adjectives taking *-er* may alternatively form a comparative with *more* and which may not. And so on.

A similar opinion is presented by Sidney J. Landau in *Dictionaries: The Art and Craft of Lexicography*: 'Grammatical information is more essential for the person who is trying to speak or understand a foreign language than for the native speaker'. The assumption is that the native speaker has an inherent (and complete) knowledge concerning the grammar of their language and needs help only with the meanings of words. For example, they are presumed to be aware that *lend* and *show* are ditransitive verbs, requiring two noun phrases to follow them, but don't know the meanings of these verbs. It is thought that they need to consult the dictionary for the meanings of *like* and *dislike* but already know that *like* takes a (FOR) TO complement clause whereas *dislike* does not. And it is supposed that they don't know the meanings of adverbs *really*, *simply*, and *slightly* (needing to look these up) but have inherent insight concerning which of the five adverb functions each may fill.

A successsion of 'advanced' dictionaries aimed at foreign learners were produced during the twentieth century and did provide some grammatical information (although little about adverbs, for instance), albeit in a rather cryptic fashion. For instance, the *Oxford Advanced Learner's Dictionary* summarises thirty-one 'verb patterns' in a single page on the inside back cover. We do find, tucked away within the entry for verb *like* (but missing from *dislike*), the code 'Ti', which is identified on the inside back cover as 'Intransitive verb plus to-infinitive'. The Cobuild dictionary includes grammatical notes down the margin in small and hard-to-read type, using codes which are generally (but not always) briefly explained in an alphabetical list at the beginning of the dictionary, often so obscurely that it would take a cryptographer to comprehend them. For instance, Cobuild places alongside *rife* 'v-link ADj' and 'oft ADj *with* n' which – one can only assume – is meant as an indication that this adjective may function as copula complement but scarcely as modifier to a noun.

These dictionaries do provide some grammatical information, although far less than is needed. But it is presented as a sort-of aside, in such a manner that it would indeed require an 'advanced' and dedicated student to assimilate and use it.

In truth, dictionary and grammar are equally important. Each complements the other and they should be prepared and published in conjunction. The grammar (of several hundred pages, not a listing on an inside back cover) will provide full information on grammatical constructions, marking of functions, derivations, and so on. The dictionary will include clear and explicit cross-reference to grammatical properties, which may vary from sense to sense for a given lexical word.

Too Much (and Also Not Enough)

A New Fijian Dictionary, by A. Capell, and *A New Fijian Grammar*, by C. Maxwell Churchward, were published in the same year, 1941. The authors cooperated; each was familiar with the other's work, and made use of it. Churchward needed information about lexical words when crafting his grammatical matrix. Capell provided definitions for lexical words. He did include grammatical forms within the alphabetical listing but had the sense not to attempt a lexical-type definition, instead giving cross-reference to the relevant section in Churchward's grammar (abbreviated as 'Gr'). For example:

iko cardinal pronoun 2nd person singular. Gr I.19.6 and 20.2.
na the common article ... Gr I.3-1-4.
ni prep, sign of possession. Gr 1.22.

Many accounts of languages which have been documented for the first time within the last couple of hundred years pursue a similar strategy. Systems of grammatical forms are fully explained – and related together – in the grammar, rather than being forced into the dictionary as if they were aberrant lexical words.

Why isn't this done for English (and other familiar languages of Europe and nearby)? There is, in part, a historical reason. Monolingual dictionaries, from 1596, defined English words in terms of other English words. Early grammars (commencing at about the same time) were, to a greater or lesser extent, on the Latin model. And the people who wrote grammars were quite separate from those who did lexicography. When dictionaries of 'hard words' were succeeded by volumes aiming to include every word, no distinction was made between lexical words and grammatical items. All were to be included – pronouns, articles, prepositions, and soon every kind of affix, inflectional as well as derivational. The stage was set, and each new dictionary followed its predecessors.

A dictionary is one-dimensional, whereas grammatical systems are multi-faceted. For example, consider demonstratives in English:

	NOMINAL DEMONSTRATIVES		ADVERBIAL
	SINGULAR	PLURAL	DEMONSTRATIVES
NEAR SPEAKER	this	these	here
AWAY FROM SPEAKER	that	those	there

All dictionaries list each of these terms. Under *this*, for instance, some (but not all) mention that its plural is *these*, a few mention *here*, just a few relate it to *that*. No dictionary which I have consulted provides the full matrix, even in an indirect manner. Yet demonstrative *this* only has significance in its spatial contrast with *that*, in its number relationship with *these*, and in its referential link with *here*.

Personal pronouns are discussed individually, with no referral to the complete system. *The* is described as 'definite' article, only occasionally contrasted with *a(n)*. Trying to deal with grammatical systems as if their terms were odd sorts of lexemes is a little like cutting off each node from a three-dimensional model and laying them flat on a table.

Grammar encompasses not only systems but also structures. Recall, from page 65, the diagram of basic noun phrase structure:

SLOT	determiner	modifier(s)	head of noun phrase
	↑	↑	↑
FILLER	articles, nominal demonstratives, possessive pronouns (all are closed systems)	adjectives (open class)	noun (open class)

This shows that a noun phrase in English can include only one item in the determiner slot – an article, a nominal demonstrative, or a possessive pronoun.

Suppose that a speaker of Portuguese wished to improve their rudimentary knowledge of English. In their native language, a noun phrase can include both demonstrative and possessive pronoun: *esse minha faca*, literally 'this my knife'. They expect that it should be possible to say, in English, *this my knife*. To be certain, they look up *my* and *this* in a good dictionary; there is no indication that demonstrative and possessive pronoun may not co-occur (and that one should in fact say *this knife of mine*).

Of course, the dictionary was the wrong place to look. Or, to cater for such eventualities, the dictionary should provide reference to appropriate sections of a grammar where structural patterns are discussed (in the way that Capell's dictionary of Fijian does).

A dictionary is concerned with lexical words and a grammar with grammatical forms and patterns. If a dictionary opts to include grammatical items it is trying to do too much. And, within the traditional dictionary format, it cannot do justice to them (we get: not enough of the too much).

The excuse could be given as follows: a dictionary deals with words and some grammatical forms are words. Indeed, some of them are written as words and pronounced with their own stress, including *this*, *I*, *down*, and *among*. However, as explained on pages 12–14, dozens of grammatical terms are written as separate words but generally pronounced as clitics. That is, they do not themselves bear stress but attach to a following word (proclitic) or a preceding word (enclitic). *To* is generally pronounced as /tə=/, *your* as /yə=/, *or* as /ə=/, and *the* as /ðə-/, so that *to your town or the city* is spoken as /tə=yə=taun ə=ðə='siti/. Grammatical clitics may be written between spaces, but they are not pronounced anything like lexical words (they do not bear stress).

There is no mistaking the identity of affixes, which are indisputably the province of grammar, not of dictionary. English has around 200 derivational affixes, about 110 of them suffixes and ninety or so prefixes. For example, *dis-*, *mis-*, *anti-*, *ante-*, *post-*, *para-*, *-ish*, *-able*, *-eer*, *-ist*, and *-ly*. The way in which these affixes derive new words was illustrated on page 18 with *true → tru-th → tru-th-ful → tru-th-ful-ness → un-tru-th-ful-ness*.

Some derivational affixes are 'productive'; that is, they are constantly being used to create new words. Others occur in a large number of existing words but are no longer being regularly employed in making new ones; they are 'non-productive'.

It is interesting to compare suffixes which derive adjectives from nouns. Suffixes *-y* and *-ous* have similar effect; compare *anger/angr-y* with *fury/furi-ous*, and *gossip/gossip-y* with *humour/humor-ous*. However, only *-y* is truly productive in the present-day language; one is always hearing new coinages such as *He's a windbagg-y liberal*, and *She's an [open air]-y kind of girl*. Suffix *-ous* occurs in several score analysable nouns (such as *fam-ous*, *parsimoni-ous*, *glori-ous*) but it is unlikely to be added to new nouns in the everyday language today (although it is employed a good deal in specialised scientific nomenclature).

There are quite a few pairs such as *pain-ful* and *pain-less*, *power-ful* and *power-less*, *fear-ful* and *fear-less*, but the suffixes here vary in terms of productivity. Derivational suffix *-less* is fully productive, as in new formations such as *He leads a quiet e-mail-less existence*, and *Sadly, we're a [wealthy sponsor]-less club*. In contrast, adjective-deriving suffix *-ful* is no longer productive. (It must be distinguished from a quite different noun-deriving suffix *-ful*, meaning 'a full container/building (of)' as in *a cup-ful of acorns*; this is productive.)

When a dictionary tries to deal with derivational suffixes, these are accorded wooden treatment, as if they were funny lexemes rather than creative elements. A learner – or an established speaker who wishes to hone up on the details of their language – needs to be informed about which derivational affixes are and are not productive today. They need to know how to use existing words and also how to manufacture new words in a felicitous manner. That it is alright to say *He's a facebook-y sort-of person*, but not

◆*He's a facebook-ous sort-of person*, and so on. Dictionaries don't help at all with this. Not only is their inclusion of affixes inappropriate but their treatment of them lacks the insight which is stock-in-trade of the grammarian.

Suppose that a speaker wished to create a verb based on the name of some favourite politician or philosopher, meaning 'to act in accordance with that person's ideas'. They need an appropriate verbalising affix to add to the proper name.

English has half-a-dozen morphological processes which derive verbs from nouns or adjectives. There is suffix *-en*, as in *deep-en*, *black-en*, but this is no longer productive. Three others have only limited productivity today and are not used with proper names – suffix *-ate*, as in *hyphen-ate*; prefix *be-*, as in *be-jewell-ed*; and prefix *en-*, as in *en-code*.

There are two highly productive verbalising suffixes which create new verbs from all manner of adjectives, common nouns, and proper nouns. They are *-(i)fy*, from Latin, and *-ise* (alternatively written as *-ize*), which goes back all the way to Greek. These are seldom interchangeable. That is, there are clear principles determining their use, which the speaker must master if they are to produce new verbalisations in an acceptable way. The critical factor is the phonological form of the root to which the derivational suffix is to be added.

This can be illustrated with a sample of the conditioning factors:

		ADDED TO ADJECTIVE	ADDED TO COMMON NOUN	ADDED TO NATION ADJECTIVE
(a)	monosyllabic base – add -ify	fals-ify	class-ify	French-ify
(b)	disyllabic base, ending in a vowel – add -(i)fy	pretti-fy	glori-fy	Israeli-fy
(c)	disyllabic base ending in l, r, m, n, or ng – add -ise	urban-ise	union-ise	German-ise

If one wished to verbalise personal names *Bush*, *Trotsky*, and *Reagan*, the appropriate forms would be (a) *Bush-ify* 'make more closely conform to the ideas set forth by President Bush', and similarly (b) *Trotski-fy* and (c) *Reagan-ise*. Prefix *de-* 'divest of' can be combined with the verbalising suffixes. Talking about moving away from unwanted doctrines, one could use verbs (a) *de-Mao-ify*, (b) *de-Nazi-fy*, and (c) *de-Stalin-ise*.

Dictionary entries for derivational affixes tell none of this story. A foreign learner consulting just a dictionary – instead of a high-class grammar – might come up with ◆*Bush-ise*, or ◆*Reagan-ify*, or ◆*de-Nazi-ise*, which are infelicitous. The moral: dictionaries should not attempt to do what they cannot do properly.

There are other properties of derivational affixes which lexicographers ignore (perhaps they are not aware of them).

1. **Positioning.** Some prefixes generally occur immediately before the base. That is, they are very seldom preceded or followed by other prefixes. These include *mis-*, *mal-*, *infra-*, and *peri-*. At the other end of the scale, there are a dozen or more prefixes with considerable fluidity of combination. For example:

    un-re-integrated group   anti-extra-marital sex
    ex-under-secretary   auto-de-frosting refrigerator
    pseudo-pre-Inca relic   pre-proto-Indo-European root

2. **Scope.** Generally, a derivational affix attaches to a single word – noun, adjective, or verb. But this scope can be extended, with the prefix or suffix applying to a complete noun phrase (or even a coordination of noun phrases). A couple of examples have already been given: *She's an [open air]-y kind of girl* and *Sadly, we're a [wealthy sponsor]-less club*. At least twenty more affixes have this property. For example:

    I fell asleep during the post-[end of year celebration] drive home
    Betty usually comes home at [four or five o'clock]-ish
    He's an ex-[forger and swindler]
    Non-[army, navy or air force personnel] are not welcome here
    [[Pale and ashen] face]-ed, he listened to the sad news
    She's taken up an anti-[blow you Jack, I'm alright] attitude
    She was happiest in her pre-[treatment for cancer] days
    He behaved in an [out of his mind]-like manner

As described on page 8, each of the meaningful portions into which a word may be segmented is called a 'morpheme'. The word *un-tru-th-ful-ness* consists of five morphemes: root *tru(e)*, derivational prefix *un-*, and derivational suffixes *-th*, *-ful* and *-ness*. Some morphemes show a constant phonological form; this applies for *un-* /ʌn-/, *true* /truː/, *-ful* /-fəl/, and *-ness* /-nəs/. However, quite a few morphemes have a number of variant forms, called 'allomorphs'.

For example:

The prefix morpheme with negative meaning whose basic form can be taken as *in-* has the following allomorphs:

/im/ before a word commencing with a bilabial stop /p/, or /b/. Thus: *improper, imbalance.*

/i/ before a word beginning with /m/, /l/, or /r/. Thus: *immature, illegal, irreligious.*

/in/ elsewhere. Thus: *inappropriate, infinite, insincere, intolerable.*

Dictionaries deal with this orthographically, saying that the prefix has the form *im-* before *m*, *il-* before *l*, and *ir-* before *r*. Although an extra *l* is added in writing, as the language actually is spoken the prefix just adds /i/ (not /il/) to *legal* /'li:gəl/, forming *illegal* /i'li:gəl/; and so on. For this morpheme, dictionaries show how to *write* the allomorphic variants, not how to *pronounce* them.

Suffixes fare rather worse. Consider the regular plural inflection, which is written as *-s* or *-es* and has the following allomorphs:

- /-iz/ after a sibilant /s/, /ʃ/, /tʃ/, /z/, /ʒ/ or /dʒ/. Thus: *lace* /leis/, plural *laces* /'leisiz/; *church* /tʃə:tʃ/, plural *churches* /'tʃə:tʃiz/; *adze* /adz/, plural *adzes* /'adziz/; and *judge* /dʒʌdʒ/, plural *judges* /'dʒʌdʒiz/.
- /s/ after *p*, *t*, *k*, *f*, or *th* (non-sibilant voiceless sounds). Thus: *lap* /lap/, plural *laps* /laps/; *plant* /pla:nt/, plural *plants* /pla:nts/; *cake* /leik/, plural *cakes* /keiks/; *chief* /tʃi:f/, plural *chiefs* /tʃi:fs/; *smith* /smiθ/, plural *smiths* /smiθs/.
- /z/ elsewhere. Thus: *deed* /di:d/, plural *deeds* /di:dz/; *bin* /bin/, plural *bins* /binz/; *ladder* /'ladə/, plural *ladders* /'ladəz/.

The possessive suffix, which is written as 's (for example, *church's*, *judge's*) has the same allomorphy as plural, written as *-(e)s*. So too does the present tense on a verb with 3rd person singular subject; for instance, *she curses* /ʃi:'kə:siz/, *he fusses* /hi:'fʌsiz/, *it breaks* /it breiks/, *he sobs* /hi:sɔbz/.

Of the half-dozen good-sized dictionaries which I have consulted, only one (Merriam-Webster's Collegiate) has anything approaching an adequate treatment of these three homophonous suffixes. The reader might be told something about adding *-s* or *-es*, but little or nothing concerning their conditioned pronunciations. One more instance of purporting to deal with affixes and botching the task.

The Development of Linguistics

Linguistics began with study of the classical languages. About 500 BCE, the Indian grammarian Pāṇini composed an intricate and insightful grammar of Sanskrit. Over in Alexandria, Apollonius Dyscolus (in the second century CE) produced a thoughtful grammar of Classical Greek. His lead was followed, a little later, by the Latin grammars of Donatus and Priscian, which were entirely appropriate for the language spoken around them.

And there it halted. Latin was regarded as the acme of civilisation. During the Middle Ages – and beyond – Latin grammars were recast and refurbished. From about 1600 there came grammatical sketches of English, but written in terms of categories more appropriate for Latin. The best of these, by John Wallis (in 1653), was a grammar of English actually written in Latin. The ways in which English somehow resembled Latin were enunciated, while the ways in which it differed were scarcely explored.

The Christian religion was toted around the colonies and some missionaries attempted a grammar of a local language. Basically, they looked for reflections of what was in Latin. Some useful work was achieved but there did tend to be something of a Latinate straightjacket. A complete chapter might be:

> Chapter 8 – Prepositions
> There are no prepositions in this language.

During the nineteenth century there was remarkable scholarship (centred on Germany) concerning historical development. By painstaking comparison of forms and meanings across a selection of Indo-European languages, many features of their undocumented common ancestor – dubbed Proto-Indo-European – were reconstructed. Similarly for other language families in and around Europe.

It was not until around 1900 that there arose the properly scientific discipline of linguistics, seeking to provide a characterisation of the nature of human language and the ways in which meaning may be communicated from speaker to hearer.

Swiss linguist Ferdinand de Saussure maintained that a language is an intermeshing system (encompassing grammar, vocabulary, phonology, etc.) and that each aspect of it only has significance and meaning with regard to its role in the whole. Furthermore, he insisted on the importance of synchronic study; that is, describing a language system at a given point of time. Following on from this there can be diachronic study of how the overall system of a language changes between one point in time and another. What should be avoided is piecemeal historical study – looking at how some fragment of a language (be it a word or a grammatical formative) changes over time, without consideration of its role in the overall system of the language at every step along the way. This Saussurean doctrine informs the work linguists do today, and is the basis for all discussion in the present volume.

There are many languages spoken across the world, each different from the others in significant and interesting respects. American linguist and anthropologist Franz Boas pioneered the description of languages each in its own terms (rather than within a Latinate model). He emphasised that languages differ in respect of what sort of grammatical information *must* be provided to produce an acceptable sentence. Whereas English has a contrast between *this* and *that*, in Kwakiutl (spoken on Vancouver Island) it is necessary to make a choice from a six-term system:

visible near me	visible near thee	visible near him
invisible near me	invisible near thee	invisible near him

In addition, the 'evidence' for any statement should be stated – whether the speaker saw it themself, or knows it by hearsay, or by indirect evidence, or dreamed it.

Practitioners of linguistics seek to examine the possibilities for every grammatical category. All languages mark possession and negation, questions and commands, and have systems of pronouns and demonstratives; most (but not all) have systems of gender and tense; a fair number must indicate evidence (as in Kwakiutl). The cumulative theory of linguistics deals with the parameters of variation for each grammatical feature, and how it relates to the lexicon. A theoretical framework is provided in terms of which the grammar for each specific language can be cast, dealing with the appropriate categories and leaving aside those which are not relevant for that language. There is continual interflow – as more languages receive a thorough description, new variations on established patterns will emerge, to enhance the theory.

The Boasian plan was to provide – for each American Indian language – a volume of texts, a grammar, and a dictionary, the three of them interlinked. These principles were soon being applied worldwide. After producing his grammar of Fijian, in conjugation with Capell's dictionary of that language (page 185), C. Maxwell Churchward moved across to the Kingdom of Tonga. He first completed a grammar, in 1953, and then six years later a comprehensive dictionary; this mentioned grammatical words and affixes, each cross-referenced to its discussion in the grammar.

There are several thousand languages still spoken today across the continents. Good-class documentation has been produced for a few hundred of them, providing the basis for an overall characterisation of the nature of language as a central facet of human social behaviour. Each grammar of a particular language benefits from the perspective of the overall theory. Danish linguist Otto Jespersen published *The Philosophy of Grammar*, and these cogent theoretical guidelines were put to use in his seven-volume masterpiece *A Modern English Grammar*.

The last few pages have delineated the real business of linguistics, which goes on steadily and without any pomp. Alongside this there have been – beginning in the 1950s – a series of distractions. These consist of a plethora of self-styled 'theories', each of which claims to provide a window into the role of language in human cognition. Their practitioners consider it inappropriate to enunciate a full grammar of any language (each part interlocked into the whole). The habit is to adopt a limited hypothesis about some aspect of language, then examine bits of grammars for confirmation of this. What makes such enterprises unworthy of serious consideration is that each has a limited half-life. 'Rejoice in my new theory, it outdoes yours.' One theory palls after a while – rather like a trend in fashion – and it is invigorating to adopt another, until that too falls into obsolescence. We have had Transformational Grammar,

Systemic Grammar, Relational Grammar, Lexical-Functional Grammar, the Minimalist Approach, Dependency Grammar, Optimality Theory, Head-driven Phrase Structure Grammar, Construction Grammar, Parallel Architecture Grammar – a further dozen and more could be added.

The distractions – none of which is put forward by anyone who has made a sustained contribution to real linguistics – are proposed with pomp and attract a transient group of loud-voiced followers. Lexicographers of English have never had much to do with standard grammatical theory (unlike Boas, Churchward, and many others similar to them, working with lesser-known languages). They rightly cringe at the distractions, and their lack of relevance to the important task in hand.

What lexicographers do need to do is engage with the essential features of English grammar (without frills) as set out in this chapter.

The historical account was left off, in chapter 11, with completion of the monumental OED. It can now be taken up again.

14   Standing Still

During the twentieth century and into the twenty-first, much has evolved. People fly to faraway places rather than relying on boats. Telegrams and cables have been replaced by e-mail. We still have guns but also nuclear bombs which can halt all evolution in a flash. Documentation has jumped from the single dimension of pens, paper and books to the organised diversity of computer memory. Real linguistics has blossomed, with enhanced understanding of how and why language performs its social role.

Just a few endeavours have remained resolutely untouched. Sadly, these include dictionary-making. In the discipline of physics, Newton's Laws of Motion were augmented by Einstein's Theory of Relativity and more beyond. Lexicography adheres, in essence, to Samuel Johnson's plan – each entry is treated as an isolated word (a world unto itself); pronunciation; etymology (just a little way back); minimal grammatical information consisting of word class and transitivity; a definition (which is sometimes supposed to be substitutable for the head word) – whose meaning may be divided into senses – supported by quotations.

Lexicographers will howl in protest at the suggestion that dictionary-making has shown no significant advance in recent decades. They will point to innovations such as providing better etymologies, giving the date of first mention, adding proper names, including line drawings, replacing these by small photographs, occasionally adding a list of semi-synonyms and antonyms (but seldom with hints on relative use). Varying styles of dictionaries are being produced for different classes of users. Most vital of all, the modus operandi for lexicography has been reinvigorated by the use of computer corpuses. The old method of working with handwritten slips based on literary or other written materials has been replaced by vast bodies of easily accessible digital data covering spoken language as well as libraries of digitalised books and newspapers.

It is of course true that the modern lexicographer is better informed and can presumably produce better definitions. But the fact remains that these are all improvements *within* the Johnsonian model. It has not been replaced by anything better suited to helping the dictionary user choose which word it is most appropriate to use in a particular circumstance. Let us return to the analogy with transport. In the nineteenth century, international travel was by boat. The twentieth and twenty-first centuries could just have refined this in startling ways (as lexicographers have refined the Johnsonian model) – by new designs of boats, making them speedier, more accessible, more comfortable. But we didn't stick with boats. Except for heavy cargo, they have been replaced by planes: a completely new dimension, with achievements previously unthought. The message of this book is that it is now time for dictionary-making to sprout wings and to embrace a new agenda. The dictionary of the future should – let it be said for the umpteenth time – assist in deciding when it is appropriate to employ a certain word in preference to others of similar meaning.

In *The Lexicography of English* (published in 2010), Henri Béjoint sums up the established – and generally unquestioned – character of a dictionary. It is 'a series of separate paragraphs', and 'a dictionary is meant to be consulted, not read'. But surely a language is not just a collection of separate words. It is an integrated entity, each part of which only has significance with respect to the whole. In his acclaimed volume *Mother Tongue*, Bill Bryson remarks that 'A dictionary will tell you that *tall* and *high* mean much the same thing, but it won't explain to you that while you can apply either term to a building, you can apply only *tall* to a person'. Bryson is a typical dictionary user, wanting to be told not what each word separately 'means' but the conditions under which it is felicitous to use a particular word in preference to semi-synonyms. (And note that the discussion of semantic sets – as illustrated in chapters 3, 6, 9, and 12 – can be both consulted and read.)

Dictionary-producing concerns have varied in their adaptability (while basically still working along lines laid down by Johnson), and in their perception of the need to keep up-to-date not only with the evolution of the language but with the innovative nuances of their rivals. As will be described in this chapter, Merriam-Webster does rather well in this regard, while the OED appears to bask in self-satisfaction.

A notable advance has been the reinstatement of terms which were there originally, but were outlawed for a couple of centuries, and then gingerly allowed back in.

Rude Words

Starting off the era of 'including everything', John Kersey's minor compilation of 1702 didn't concern itself with words not quite proper. The first truly comprehensive dictionary was Nathan Bailey's of 1730 and this covered every part of the vocabulary. He did feel the need for a modicum of delicacy and utilised Latin in definitions of *fuck*, *cunt*, and *twat* – only educated people, it seems, were to be made privy to these meanings (probably those not versed in Latin would, in any case, be fully familiar with the terms). Straightforward definitions were provided for *vagina, vulva, clitoris* (in considerable detail), *glans, to shit(e)*, and other such words. Bailey's treatment of *penis* was a bit roundabout:

penis   a man's yard
yard   a long measure containing three foot; also the virile member of a man
virile   manly, flout

(This meaning of *yard* was prevalent in the seventeenth and eighteenth centuries.)

Samuel Johnson would have none of this; prudery prevailed. He did include a couple of items on the borderline of rude since they were found in the 'best writers' – *turd*, no quotation provided, and *fart*, with a quotation from Swift. (In fact, *fuck, cunt*, and *twat* had featured many times in good literature, but Johnson drew a curtain on them.) Not everyone followed this path. John Ash – who was a minister of the Baptist church – included every sort of word in his 1775 dictionary and did not feel the need to resort to Latin. For example: *fuck (v.t. a low vulgar word). To perform the act of generation; to have to do with a woman.*

Johnson was religious but matter-of-fact about it. In contrast, Webster's extreme piety coloured his work. Indeed, it commenced with a divine dedication: 'To that great and benevolent Being … [who has] given me strength and resolution to bring the work to a close. I would present the tribute of my most grateful acknowledgements'.

An American Dictionary of the English Language was intended as a model for Christian rectitude. Any word with the slightest tinge of crudity was excluded, even such minor offenders as *turd* and *fart*. Joseph Worcester, in 1830, more-or-less followed suit, but not with total consistency. He does give **glans**, *nut of the penis*, but there is no entry for *penis*! (However, **glans** was purged from Worcester's later edition, in 1860.)

The editors of the OED aimed to be comprehensive, and they certainly made inroads into the items cast aside by Johnson and Webster. There was no objection to words describing excretory functions, such as *shit, turd*, and *fart*. And it was considered appropriate to include terms referring to sexual organs and acts so long as these were used by respectable people (or perhaps one should amend this to: so long as the terms were regarded as respectable) – *penis, vagina, clitoris, vulva*, and a few more. But it was felt that a line had to be drawn. There were no entries for *cunnilingus* (which had been around for two hundred years) or *fellatio* (attested from 1887) – these were not really very nice activities, don't you know. And no mention of *cunt* or *fuck* in the fascicles published in the 1890s.

But, within letter 'T' (in 1916) there did appear – somewhat surprisingly – an entry for *twat*. However, the OED baulked at providing their own definition, saying simply '(See quot 1727.)'. This is to a Nathan Bailey dictionary and the definition there was *pudendum muliebre*. The current online entry for *twat* has added more recent quotations, including a raunchy one from Henry Miller and a lilting couplet from e.e. cummings:

> on Tuesday in Uhlan
> to her twat put his tool in

But still the 1727 definition is held to suffice, taking no account of the fact that many of Bailey's readers would have been familiar with Latin, as against only a tiny sprinkling of OED users today.

Then we come to Webster's Third, that huge dictionary of 1961. It does pretty well, including *cunnilingus, fellatio*, even *cunt* (and was energetically criticised for doing so). Everything, it seems, except for that naughty – yet much used, nay, overused – word *fuck*. In fact the editor, Philip B. Gove, had prepared an entry but it was excised at galley proof stage by the company's manager.

The swinging 1960s would not allow this word to escape the dictionary web. On 14 April 1969, the editors of *OZ Magazine* wrote to Oxford University Press saying that they had recently purchased the 1967 edition of the *Shorter Oxford English Dictionary* 'for use in our office'. The preface stated: 'It is hoped that both the student and the general reader will find in this work what they might reasonably expect to find in a historical dictionary of English compressed within 2,500 pages'. The letter ended: 'It does not contain the word "fuck". We would be interested to know the reason for this curious omission'.

The reply from D. M. Davin, on behalf of Oxford University Press, is notable for the fact that it avoided using *fuck*, referring instead to 'the word of whose omission you complain'. Delicacy is maintained. The reply suggested that if such 'sensitive words' were included, some people might choose not to buy the dictionary and indeed it might be banned in certain countries.

But the tide had turned. R. W. Burchfield, editor of the Second Supplement to the OED, was strongly against discrimination. Soon almost every dictionary treated rude words like all others. The aura of propriety – which had shrouded dictionaries in England since the eighteenth century (and indeed blanketed those in America) – was finally flung aside. Such is progress, sometimes going in circles.

Keeping Up

Murray and his co-editors were keen to include words from far-flung places and they particularly welcomed the publication, in 1898, of *Austral English: A Dictionary of Australasian Words, Phrases and Usages* by Edward E. Morris, who was Professor of English, French, and German languages and literatures at the University of Melbourne. Indeed, the OED fascicle published in June 1899 had *humpy, a native Australian hut*, with acknowledgement to Morris. Later fascicles included *mallee, any one of several scrubby species of eucalyptus which flourish in the desert areas of South Australia and Victoria ...*, and *mulga, an Australian tree Acacia aneura*, among others. Morris's book arrived after letters 'A-E' of the OED had been published, and so his *brumby, a wild horse*, had to await the First Supplement to the OED, in 1933.

Following the demise of Murray (in 1915) and Bradley (in 1923), William Craigie took charge for completion of the OED. However, this involved commuting from the University of Chicago, where he had moved in 1925. Craigie immediately began work on *A Dictionary of American English on Historical Principles* (DAE), dealing with distinctively American words and phrases, and with special senses of established words; this was published by the University of Chicago Press in four volumes, 1938–44. The DAE was modelled on the OED, with dated quotations and the like. Oddly, it only included words which had been introduced before 1900.

Noah Webster had prided himself on producing an *American* dictionary; however, there were quite a few early words he had missed and the DAE now provided full details. For example: *ancon, a former breed of sheep having a long body and short, crooked legs* (attested from 1811), and *banjo, a stringed musical instrument of the guitar kind, popular among Negroes of the South, played by plucking the strings with the fingers* (from 1774).

Craigie combined being co-editor of the OED Supplement (1928–33) and working on a *Dictionary of the Older Scottish Tongue* with co-editing the DAE. One of the Assistant Editors, Mitford M. Mathews, strongly criticised Craigie for not according sufficient acknowledgement to the work done by his staff.

After Craigie's return to England, the University of Chicago Press commissioned Mathews to produce *A Dictionary of Americanisms on Historical Principles*, which came out as two large volumes in 1951. This was essentially a shortening and updating of the DAE, but concentrating on words and phrases which had first appeared in the USA, including those by then obsolete. (However, it didn't include words which had come from England, later become obsolete there, but survived in America.)

A few entries from the DAE were omitted by Mathews, such as *daffodil* (included by Craigie for Virginia daffodil). Others were added, including *davenport, a large upholstered sofa* (which had been around since 1897). For many words, Mathews simply used a shortened form of the DAE entry. Thus, the DAE had *dahlgren, a smoothbore gun, shaped somewhat like a bottle, invented by Lieutenant Dahlgren in 1856*, plus six quotations. Mathews just enlarged the final portion to *invented in 1856 by Lt. J. A. Dahlgren of the U. S. N.*, retaining the first and last of Craigie's quotations (from 1862 and 1901) and adding one more, from 1910. He also added a helpful drawing of the gun, showing it to be something like a small cannon. (The DAE, like the OED, and Johnson before, had eschewed illustrations.)

Sometimes Mathews revised an entry. Compare the headings in two treatments of the noun *deadfall*:

A Dictionary of American English: deadfall

1. A trap for large animals, consisting essentially of a heavy log or weighted board which falls upon and crushes the prey.
2. *transf.* Anything which is suggestive of a trap of this sort; esp. a low saloon or gambling dive. *colloq,* or *slang.*
3. An area in a forest encumbered with blown-down trees; a windfall.

A Dictionary of Americanisms: deadfall

1. A saloon or low gambling dive. *Slang.*
2. An area in a forest encumbered with blown-down trees; also a tree that has fallen across a trail.

Mathews used two of Craigie's five quotations for sense 2, and the sole quotation for sense 3, adding one more in each instance. Craigie's sense 1 was discarded, probably because it originated in England, although the DAE provided five American quotations. The way Craigie organised the entry, sense 1 – which is oldest – is taken as the basis, and the reader can see how senses 2 and 3 evolved from this. In Mathews' revision, his two senses seem quite disparate.

Meanwhile, the Webster rollercoaster went from strength to strength. After Webster's death, the Merriam company took over his second edition (see page 156). There were revisions at regular intervals, each employing a team of lexicographers to update and improve every aspect of the work. The fine new edition of 1864 was dubbed 'unabridged', indicating its comprehensiveness as compared with smaller compilations. Noah Webster's label 'American' was replaced by 'International' in 1890. Then came *Webster's New International Dictionary* in 1909, with a second edition in 1934 and the third in 1961. Affectionately known as 'Webster's Third or just "W3"', it is said to have involved 757 editor-years by a team of lexicographers. This is a daunting document – 2,662 large pages, each with three columns of very small type (about the size used in Charles Richardson's dictionary of 1835–7). It was bound as a single volume, weighing more than 6 kg or 13½ pounds. A magisterial work, epitome of the Johnsonian model. But daunting and absolutely non-user friendly.

W3 was lauded by scholars, and by critics in England. However, a reactionary media in America directed a vituperative barrage, fuming against the permissiveness of W3, how it went against the conventions of good grammar.

Believe it or not, the loudest outcry was that W3 accepted the use of *ain't*. Absolutely shocking!

Getting down to basics, it is instructive to compare entries in Webster's 1828 dictionary with those 133 years later in Webster's Third. On page 152 there was comparison of definitions by Bailey, Johnson, Webster, and Worcester of the rather recondite noun ***pickthank***. We can now take this forward.

Webster 1828: **pickthank**
An officious fellow who does what he is not desired to do, for the sake
of getting favor; a whispering parasite.   *South.*

Webster's Third 1961: **pickthank**
Archaic: one who tries to curry favour by flattery, sycophancy, or talebearing
<smiling ~s and base newsmongers – Shak.>

Webster's definition of ***pickthank*** was only a minor variant of Johnson's but, of the four quotations in Johnson's first edition, none are by anyone whose name begins with *South*. Webster was original here (but one cannot tell whether *South* refers to the English sermon-writer Robert South, 1674–1716, or the English poet Robert Southey, 1774–1843).

The quotation in Webster's Third was shortened from one of those in Johnson:

Many tales devis'd
Oft the ear of greatness needs must hear,
By smiling pickthanks and base newsmongers.   *Shakesp.*

For quotations from Shakespeare, Johnson sometimes gave the name of the play (but not act and scene numbers), othertimes just *Shakespeare* or *Shakesp.* (see the entry for *hot* quoted on page 95). W3 features more than 2,000 quotations from Shakespeare, all identified just as *Shak.* (In point of fact, this quotation is from *Henry IV, Part 1*, act 3, scene 2.)

Now consider a more frequently occurring word, the noun *coward*:

Webster 1828: **coward**
A person who wants courage to meet danger; a poltroon; a timid or
pusillanimous man.

A *coward* does not always escape with disgrace, but sometimes
loses his life.   *South.*

Webster's Third 1961: **coward**
One who shows ignoble fear; a basely timid, easily frightened, and easily daunted person. <a ~, irresolute, impulsive in any crisis – Walter de la Mare> <is an arrant ~ and shows the white feather at the slightest display of pluck in his antagonist – John Burroughs>

In this instance, Webster's definition was quite different from Johnson's, but his single quotation is one of the six given by Johnson (and this is from Robert South, the cleric). The 1961 dictionary has a new definition, and more recent quotations.

Note the difference of layout. Johnson had good-sized type and full quotations (often a whole verse of a poem), each on a separate line. Noah Webster employed a smaller typeface, but still easily readable; he used less quotations, and often shortened those he took from Johnson, but still had each on a new line. Webster's Third opts for maximum economy, running quotations on and using '~' for the head word. Full details of a source – which would enable a reader to follow up on a quotation – are not considered necessary. And no dates are provided.

From mid-century, a number of new companies entered the market, and competition hotted up.

The Battlefield

Dictionaries can be roughly divided into:

- **Massive** – just the OED.
- **Large**, what are called **Unabridged.** Compendious volumes that the reader will refer to for a special enquiry. Well-regarded but only attaining moderate sales.
- **Medium-sized**. Accessible and ideal for day-to-day reference. Of a size to fit on the corner of a desk, and thus often called **Desk** dictionaries. These sell extremely well and keep the publishers in profit.

Most publishers also put out a range of smaller versions, suitable for use in schools, when travelling, of a size to fit in a (largish) pocket, and so on. These also sell well.

Johnson's large dictionary of 1755 would be called Unabridged (if the term had been in use then). The following year an 'abridged' Desk edition was put out; this did not include the literary quotations (just the names of authors quoted in the larger book). Webster's 1828 dictionary was of Unabridged size; it sold poorly. Much more financially successful was a Desk version in 1829, with quotations and most etymologies omitted, definitions abridged, and a few new entries added. (This was edited by Chauncey A. Goodrich, Webster's son-in-law, and Joseph Worcester; Webster himself declined to work on it and then criticised the product.)

As mentioned earlier, the G. and C. Merriam company put out a series of Unabridged dictionaries, culminating in 1961 with Webster's Third. Alongside these they introduced, in 1898, *Webster's Collegiate Dictionary* as their Desk volume. The eleventh edition in 2003 – now called *Merriam-Webster's*

Collegiate Dictionary, for reasons soon to be explained – describes itself as 'America's best-selling dictionary'.

Oxford University Press had sunk a great deal of money into the OED, and they got it back largely from the spin-offs. *The Shorter Oxford Dictionary on Historical Principles* is of Unabridged size; from its inception in 1933, it has sold steadily. But the real winner has been Oxford's Desk volume *The Concise Oxford Dictionary*, first issued in 1911 (when the OED itself was struggling through letter 'S') and with revised editions every ten years or so.

Up in Scotland, W. and R. Chambers had pioneered a multi-volume encyclopaedia in 1859 and added a Desk-sized dictionary in 1872; this had reached its twelfth edition by 2011. Back in the States, Funk and Wagnalls commenced their Desk dictionary in 1893, and added an Unabridged one in 1913 (this was revised up to 1943). *The Century Dictionary* (1889–91) was an Unabridged volume, followed by a Desk version, *The New Century Dictionary*, in 1927. As mentioned before (pages 137–8 and 156) Random House bought the rights to this and in 1947 put out a revised version as their Desk volume, the *American College Dictionary*, which came to be steadily revised and reprinted.

Those affluent pre-computer days were a halcyon era for sales of Desk dictionaries. Competition became intense. One reads of the 'dictionary war' in America in the mid-nineteenth century between succeeding editions of works by Worcester and Webster. During the last decades of the twentieth century, there was, in America, a veritable battle for sales between Desk dictionaries which were in fact all rather similar to each other. Generally, each user had their favourite and would purchase a new edition of it every ten years or so. The aim was to persuade people to switch allegiance (a bit like inveigling voters to switch party loyalty in a political election).

There developed a sort-of one-upmanship – adding a feature which was really pretty peripheral and extolling its magnificence. For the ninth edition of their Collegiate, in 1983, Webster's included the date of first-known citation for each word. However, this did not always produce the most useful results since the predominant current sense of a word may have developed relatively recently, with the original sense being now quite minor. For example, the entry for verb *want* in the Ninth Collegiate provides a date '13c' and this is appropriate for the first sense quoted 'be needy or destitute'. However, the predominant modern sense is '2a: to have a strong desire for', and the dictionary user would surely be interested to know (but is not told) that it developed only around 1700 (see page 169).

New dictionaries are produced for a variety of reasons. The rationale behind *The American Heritage Dictionary of the English Language* (published in 1969 by Houghton Mifflin) was outrage at the permissiveness of

W3 – *ain't* and all that. The American Heritage editor, William Morris, was enjoined to employ strict guidelines, using a panel of conservative-minded experts to advise on what ought to be included, and what should be said about critical words.

There also were new features. Whereas the Collegiate included a few line drawings of things, and had appendices of 'biographical names' and 'geographical names', American Heritage placed proper names in the dictionary itself and, in the margin, photographs of things, people and places mentioned on that page.

American Heritage's major innovation was to extend etymologies back as far as possible – to Proto-Indo-European (PIE), for words coming through Indo-European languages. There was an Appendix of Proto-Indo-European roots, by Calvert Watkins, the pre-eminent scholar in the field. (This was also issued as a separate booklet.)

The etymologies for *merry* and *brief* can be repeated here from page 148. They are taken from American Heritage.

from PIE root **mreghu* 'short' there developed:

- PIE zero grade form **mregh*
- giving Proto-Germanic **murgja* 'short, pleasant, joyful'
- which became Old English *myrge* or *mirge* 'pleasant, delightful'
- this developed into Middle English *merri*, and then modern *merry*

- PIE suffixed form **mregh-wi*
- giving Latin *brevis* 'short; of small extent'
- which became Old French *bref* 'taking a short time'
- this was borrowed into Middle English in the late thirteenth century, as *bref*, which has become present-day *brief*

From its fourth edition, in 2000, American Heritage added similar material on roots in Proto-Semitic and how they gave rise to modern English words.

Lexicographers copy others' definitions. On page 137, Landau was quoted: 'we worked in a large open space at desks without partitions, a row of dictionaries propped before each of us'. As time went by, there were more dictionaries to prop up.

In view of this, it is a little surprising that the major dictionaries failed to take up their rivals' 'innovations'. For example, American Heritage did not see fit to add dates. And nobody else would take their etymologies back to PIE.

We can examine how a couple of dictionaries deal with etymologies for *merry* and *brief*:

	merry	brief
Random House Unabridged 1987	bef. 900; ME *meri(e)*, *myrie, murie*, OE *myr(i)ge, mer(i)ge*, pleasant, delightful	1250–1300. ME *bref* < AF, OF < L *brevis* short
Merriam-Webster Collegiate 2003	ME *mery*, fr OE *myrge, merge*; akin to OHG *murg* short – more at BRIEF (bef. 12c)	ME *bref, breve*, fr, AF *bref, brief*, fr, L *brevis*; akin to OHG *murg* short, Gk *brachys* (14c)

One feels for the Collegiate etymologist, who plainly knew that these two adjectives go back to the same PIE root. Presumably, there had been a directive from on high not to refer to PIE. The etymologist tries to indicate the relationship with 'akin to' but it just isn't clear.

In 1966 Random House greatly expanded their Desk dictionary and labelled it 'Unabridged'. There were only about half as many entries as Webster's Third, plenty of example sentences but no sourced quotations. And, unlike Webster, it did include proper names. While Webster's continued to reprint their 1961 Unabridged edition, Random House forged ahead. Work on a second edition began in the early 1980s, and – having heard that the Ninth Collegiate would include dates – Random House added a date of first mention for each word. As exemplified on pages 141–2, in many instances they simply took the OED's date and made it into a time span; for example, the OED's 1374 for *centre* became 1325–75. The Ninth Collegiate made it into bookstores first and, by the time Random House's second edition actually appeared, in 1987, their boast could then only be: 'This is the first *unabridged* American dictionary to list the dates of entry …' (my italics).

Random House's Unabridged second edition added forms from regional dialects and paid attention to the etymology of words from non-Indo-European languages. There was an account on pages 140–1 of how I supplied source details for *kangaroo, boomerang*, and eighty more words taken from the indigenous languages of Australia. The relevant information was quickly copied into the Collegiate and American Heritage (but ignored by dictionaries in Britain).

These competing dictionaries carried on in the same old way, treating each word as a lonesome citadel of meaning, not caring to explain under what circumstances it should be appropriately used in preference to another word with similar meaning. Random House did occasionally include a list of 'synonyms' (really, of course, semi-synonyms) after an entry, but in an inconsistent way (see page 107). Little or no help was provided for choosing when and how to employ each word.

Attitudes to this matter can be stupefying. In *Dictionaries: The Art and Craft of Lexicography*, Sidney J. Landau states rather emphatically that 'English as a Second Language and bilingual dictionaries do not include synonym discriminations, since such rarefied distinctions are quite beyond the skills of their users and altogether irrelevant to their purpose'.

Is it sufficient for a foreign learner to be told that *big* means *large* and *large* means *big*? Wouldn't it be relevant to let them know that it is more felicitous to say *a large number of cakes* rather than ♦*a big number of cakes*, and that *She's a big boss* explains her importance whereas *She's a large boss* simply draws attention to her corpulence? (See chapter 6.) Would such things be 'beyond their skills'? There seems to be an assumption that foreigners wanting to learn English are of low mental capacity. In fact, the 'semantic sets' approach advocated throughout this volume would be absolutely invaluable – and not at all difficult – for such dictionary users.

Then the battlefield erupted with a new ploy. When Random House brought out a new edition of their Desk dictionary, in 1991, it was called the *Random House Webster's College Dictionary*, in the expectation that adding *Webster's* in the middle of the title would increase sales. The name Webster's had long been declared out of copyright and there had been several non-Merriam dictionaries using it. But Random House went further, copying Merriam's 'trade dress' – the use of nearly identical colours and lettering on the dust jacket.

And what had been called *The Random House Unabridged Dictionary* was rebranded *Random House Webster's Unabridged Dictionary* There was no difference to all in the content, just *Webster's* inserted in the middle of the title.

This impudence by one of their major rivals was just too much for Merriam. They sued and won, but this judgment (and the $4 million award) was overturned on appeal. Merriam already included a statement, opposite the contents page of the Collegiate, which reads (with slight variations):

A GENUINE MERRIAM-WEBSTER

The name Webster alone is no guarantee of excellence. It is used by a number of publishers and may serve mainly to mislead an unwary buyer.

Merriam Webster™ is the name you should look for when you consider the purchase of dictionaries or other fine reference books. It carries the reputation of a company that has been publishing since 1831 and is your assurance of quality and authority.

What Merriam now did – in addition – was to adjust the title of their desk volume: *Webster's Ninth New Collegiate Dictionary*, in 1983, was succeeded by *Merriam-Webster's Collegiate Dictionary, Tenth Edition*, in 1993 (and then the eleventh in 2003). Before too long, Random House was floundering while Merriam-Webster continued to flourish, albeit in a steadily contracting market.

And new Desk volumes were emerging across in Britain. *The Penguin English Dictionary*, in 1965, was the first since John Ash in 1775 to include *fuck* and its risqué congeners. In 1971 came *The Encyclopedic World Dictionary*. edited by Patrick Hanks, a somewhat anglicised version of Random House's *American College Dictionary* (see pages 138–9); a slightly trimmed and mildly Australianised version of this came out in 1981 as *The Macquarie Dictionary*. Hanks then went on to produce *The Collins English Dictionary*, in 1979. And 1978 saw the arrival of the *Longman Dictionary of Contemporary English*; no etymologies but boasting of employing a 'defining vocabulary' of just over 2,100 words (this was discussed on pages 110–13).

Then came innovation with the Collins Birmingham University International Language Database. A bit of a mouthful and so the Desk dictionary it produced in 1987 was just called COBUILD. (Patrick Hanks turns up once again, as Managing Editor.) There were hardly any proper names, no illustrations, but it was based on a mammoth 500-million word corpus covering many genres of the language (but excluding poetry!). Also, instead of standard definitions, each head word was placed in an explanatory sentence. As discussed on pages 112–13, this is very often just a definition made longer. For instance:

brief   Something that is brief lasts only for a short time

A standard definition, *lasting only for a short time*, is shorter and just as effective. Despite appearance, Cobuild is only a mild variant on the standard format, That is, it does not explain the circumstances in which to employ a certain word rather than others of similar meaning.

Its strength lies in use of the database. Useful colloquial sentential examples (but with no source stated) are provided for every numbered sense within each entry. But the list of senses often seems endless – for example, twenty-eight for *cover*, forty-five for *life*, no less than ninety-four for *way* – and there is no division into sub-senses as happens in other dictionaries. In addition, the order in which senses are given seems arbitrary.

Cobuild doesn't include etymologies; this is alright if the book is aimed at a readership which doesn't want such information. But what is absolutely unacceptable is that it merges homonyms. There are in English two words *ear*. One refers to the organ of hearing and comes from OE *ēare*, a development from PIE **ous-* 'ear'. The other is the seed-bearing bud of a cereal plant, which is from *ēar* in OE and **ak-* 'sharp' in PIE. These become just one word in Cobuild; the cereal plant meaning is given as sense 4, the organ of hearing meanings are dealt with by senses 1–3 and 5–17. The same merging into a single entry links verb *pine (for)* and the tree type *pine*. Everything spelt the same way is – almost always – all one word.

There are two words *fast*, with distinct etymologies: (a) abstain from food; and (b) main meaning today (b-i) at considerable speed, and minor – but original – meaning (b-ii) firm, fixed (see chapter 9). Cobuild conflates all this into one entry; their senses 1–4, 8 and 11–13 relate to meaning (b-i), 5–7 and 10 to (b-ii), and 9 to (a). Not only merged but truly muddled.

The Ninth Collegiate, published in 1983, sold more than a million copies in its first year and was on the *New York Times* bestseller list for more than 155 weeks. Then the great dictionary boom in America abated. Sales fell, gradually at first and then more rapidly as the Internet took hold. It is now possible to consult all manner of dictionaries, of decidedly varying quality, with a click. Good bookshops used to have shelves of dictionaries; now there is only a handful, and those largely editions for schools.

Whereas dictionary publishers previously derived their income from hardcopy sales, it now comes largely from searches of the website; the idea is to draw people to its website and keep them there for as many page-views as possible. Number of page-views sets the rate for advertisement, which is the major source of revenue

The habit had been to produce a new edition of an Unabridged dictionary every twenty or thirty years, and of the Desk model about every ten years. Random House's Unabridged was introduced in 1966 and had a second edition in 1987. That was it. And Random House stopped revising their Desk dictionary in 1999. Webster's 'New International' Unabridged had its first edition in 1909, second in 1934, and third in 1961. The focus now is on the online version. Between 2012 and 2016 there were five releases of additions and revisions (about 11,000 new entries and 4,000 new senses).

This company's Desk volume, the Collegiate, had new editions in 1983, 1993, and then the eleventh in 2003. This is available as hard-copy and on the web. There are currently no plans for a hard-copy twelfth edition.

Oxford continues to be world leader and appears to be in reasonable shape. Their Unabridged volume, the Shorter Oxford, had its fifth edition in 2002 and sixth in 2007; however, there are currently no plans for a seventh edition. Their flagship Desk dictionary, the Concise Oxford, has produced new editions in quick succession, from the eighth in 1990 through 1995, 1999, 2004, to the twelfth in 2011.

But what about that battleship of a dictionary, the OED? We can take up the story where it was left off at the end of chapter 11.

The OED Putters On

James Murray had begun work on the OED in 1879; the first fascicle appeared in 1884, and the twelfth and final volume was completed in 1928. However, many more quotations had come in and were begging to be taken account of.

A Supplement was undertaken, edited by Craigie (from Chicago) and Onions, dealing just with new words and new senses. (They were instructed not to revise existing entries, otherwise it might take another forty-four years!) The Supplement came out in 1933. That was *it*, as far as Oxford University Press was concerned. Their smaller dictionaries continued to be revised, taking account of new developments in the language. But as for the OED, it was 'done'.

Correspondents continued to send in quotation slips and many people wrote with suggestions or requesting opinions concerning correct usage. The Press dealt with all this; however, it was not until 1957 that a decision was made to, in effect, resuscitate the OED. But in what manner? Revise the whole compilation, word by word? No, that would be far too great a task. Instead, Robert W. Burchfield was appointed as editor for a Second Supplement of 'new words, important new meanings and phrases'. This was expected to be completed within ten years; in the end the project ran to four volumes published between 1972 and 1986 (having taken twenty-nine years). Then in 1989 there came the second edition of the OED (in twenty volumes), merging the original twelve volumes and the two Supplements, plus about 5,000 new words and phrases which had come into view since the respective volumes of the Second Supplement.

The next step was for the entire OED behemoth to be keyboarded and, in 2000, put online (with a non-trivial fee charged to access it). The intention was to undertake a thorough revision, letter by letter, commencing at 'M', with an estimate of ten years to complete the task. This plan was abandoned in 2010, by which time the end of letter 'R' had not quite been reached (it was then realised that forty years would have been a more realistic estimate). Now the 'more than seventy editors' work on selected topics. Every three months there is an 'update' bulletin listing the new entries, meanings, phrases, 'compounds', and derivatives added during that period.

The OED is indeed a magnificent historical document, an unmatched inventory of quotations. The website is ideally organised. One can easily search for a word or phrase. And for an entry which has been recently revised, it is often (although not always) possible to see the earlier entry (but only as far back as the second edition in 1989). Everything is quantified. The website states that, as of 16 May 2016 there were 277,226 entries, which included 163,455 nouns, 32,004 verbs, 83,433 adjectives, 256 pronouns, and 442 prepositions (this last figure seems a little generous – a reason for it will be disclosed in a few pages' time). One is continually reminded – at the top of each entry – that the OED is 'The definitive record of the English language'.

Okay, leaving aside the hype, how does the present-day OED measure up as a dictionary? First, how well does it accord with James Murray's original vision? How does it perform as an up-to-date record of English vocabulary?

How does it compare with its competitors? Does it take on board their useful innovations? And, in the light of progress in the grammatical study of English over the past century, to what extent has it allowed itself to benefit from this?

William Craigie worked for four years as assistant to Bradley and then to Murray before being appointed, in 1901, as third co-editor, taking charge of 'N', 'Q' and then 'R'. Craigie had his own ideas concerning what should go in the OED, rather different from Murray's. On reviewing Craigie's entry for *railway*, which included many 'combinations' such as *railway porter*, Murray wrote an acerbic letter stating that his 'treatment of the attributive use of these words' was 'not in accordance with the principles and method of the Dictionary, and that much valuable space appears in consequence to be consumed on what is of no practical value.' Murray's point was that knowing the meanings of *railway* and *porter*, the reader would be able to put the two words together so that a sub-entry for this combination (with an accompanying quotation) was not needed.

Craigie paid no attention, continuing to include dozens of such combinations, and instructing that the proofs of his entries should not in future be sent to Murrray. The same practice was continued in the 1933 Supplement, in Burchfield's Second Supplement, and most particularly in the online edition today.

The entry for *railway* in the 1989 second edition included more than sixty of the combinations which Murray considered were 'of no practical value', things like *railway accident, railway bookstall, railway excursion, railway journey, railway passenger, railway ticket, railway worker*, and dozens more. No definitions or explanations were provided for the combinations, just quotations which were often not at all informative.

Nearly all of these are retained in the current version but they are now oddly termed not combinations but 'compounds' (despite not satisfying the normal criteria for being a compound). Just a few have been discarded, including *railway act, railway bill*, and *railway stock* (one wonders why, since this is a historical dictionary), while *railway passenger, railway shed, railway terminal*, and *railway travel* have been added. The 1989 edition lacked definitions (presumably because the meanings are obvious, which was Murray's point) but included one quotation for each combination, occasionally more. The 2008 revision still lacks definitions and generally has three quotations for each 'compound', sometimes including the 1989 one(s), sometimes not. We get, for *railway traveller*:

Second Edition, 1989

1891   *Murray's Handbk. India & Ceylon.* p xv. In Bombay, the Indian *A. B. C. Guide* and the *Indian Railway Travellers' Guide* give the railway routes for all India.

1980   G. M. FRASER *Mr American* xxvi 552. The vaguely hostile silence of the British railway traveller.

Online Edition, Updated in June 2008

1836   *Times* 4 June 6/6. His Honour doubted whether that was a proper phrase to apply to the railway travellers.

1925   W. H. DAWSON *S. Afr.* xix. 374. Relating this incident to a well-informed fellow railway traveller, he commented, 'I can well believe it.'

2008   *Western Morning News* (Plymouth) (Nexis) 21 February, 6. Britain's railway travellers pay some of the highest fares in Europe.

Plainly, a lot of effort has gone into assembling these quotations – and many thousands more like them. Do they tell the reader any more about the meaning of the combination/'compound' *railway traveller* than they knew already from the meanings of *railway* and of *traveller*? What *would* Murray have said?

However, there is one combination involving *railway* which has a special connotation and social role in Britain today. Unlike the others, this is worthy of inclusion. **Railway sandwich** refers to a sandwich which is several days' old, so that the top has hardened and the triangular corners curled up. It is typically encountered at railway buffets but the term is used for a second-rate sandwich found anywhere. The phrase has become something of an icon, in conversation and in literature. There was even a radio comedy skit entitled 'The collapse of the British railway sandwich system'. Despite this, all one finds in the OED is a bare heading, plus two quotes in the 1989 edition (one more added in 2008). No definition or comment on cultural salience (in the one place within the lengthy *railway* entry where this is needed).

It might be argued that, since the OED is now online, space is unlimited, so why not put in as much as possible? Note that space *was* at a premium for the printed works – the first edition, the supplements, and the second edition. Murray's objection to Craigie's practice was only partly about space; in essence, he wished the dictionary to be concise, well-ordered and informative.

It is instructive to examine an entry which originated from Murray himself. **Boy** was in his third fascicle, in March 1887, and was revised in December 2008. Murray's first sense (on historical principles) was *A male child below the age of puberty* and his third *A servant, slave*. The revision reverses these, having as first sense *A male servant, slave, assistant, junior employee, etc.* and as third *A male child or youth*. There is cogent, scholarly discussion of the reasons for this change, involving reassessment of fourteenth-century manuscripts.

This is good. But what about the treatment of combinations? Murray identified a number which indicated sex, such as *boy-child*, *-cousin*, and *-elephant*, and others relating to immaturity, including *boy-actor*, *-bridegroom*, and *-king*. The 2008 revision lists a couple of dozen of these (now called 'compounds'), in alphabetical order with three (or more) quotations for each. Thus, *boy baby* is followed by *boy-bridegroom*, lacking Murray's explanation that the first specifies sex and the second immaturity. And why this set of combinations and not any of the many others which are in use today? A quick corpus search turns up: *boy entrant* (to the Royal Navy), *boy TV star*, *boy pig* (alongside *girl pig*) and *boy singer* (the OED revision has *boy alto* and *boy soprano* but not *boy singer*). Scores more could be added. Why not include them all? Or, better, none. The meaning of *boy alto* is obvious; quotations such as *He became well known as a boy alto* (from *The Times* of 28 June 1967, following a quotation of 1872) add nothing and are a waste of everybody's time and patience.

Combinations are filed according to their first element, rather than in terms of the semantic head. A *boy choir* is a sort of choir, not a sort of boy, yet it is listed under **boy** (not even cross-referenced under **choir**). Such a mechanical approach (also followed by dictionaries other than the OED) obscures the basic meanings involved. But, anyway, the dictionary user will infer (or is assumed to be able to infer) that a boy choir is a choir made up of boys, so in any case the whole exercise lacks value.

Wanting to see how Webster's treatment had evolved over the years, I picked *coward* (a common word with a shortish entry). The difference in definition and quotations between Noah Webster in 1828 and Webster's Third in 1961 (133 years later) was presented on page 200. Then I looked to see how the OED's treatment of the same word had evolved between James Murray's entry of May 1893 and the current online version 123 years later. There was no change – the same headings, sub-headings and quotations (just a couple of the dates have been silently adjusted, such as *Hamlet* from 1602 to 1603). There has been added one so-called 'compound':

coward-tree *n.* a tree under which men who show fear in battle are killed, in accordance with the custom of some Zulu tribes.
    [with one quotation, from 1904]

Apart from this, the latest quotation is from 1884. The OED website informs us that this entry 'has not yet been fully revised'. This same comment applies for more than half the entries. 'The definitive record of the English language' – huh! For about half the vocabulary, the definitive record is from about a century ago. Yet, for entries that are revised, great effort is expended on providing (usually) three examples for each of a great number of obvious and redundant 'compounds'. Surely priorities need to be rethought.

Things do happen outside of the OED's bastion. They often seem unaware of them or perhaps they just don't care. Providing dates was the OED's innovation. As shown on page 142, in many instances Random House's Unabridged of 1987 simply copied these, converting a year into a time span. Four years earlier, Webster's Ninth New Collegiate had added dates but on a more original basis. And with each new edition, these have been reassessed. We can look at three words from the table on page 142:

	OED 1887	OED 2016	Ninth New Collegiate 1983	Eleventh Collegiate 2003
bland, adjective	1596	1596	1661	1565
blight, noun	1611	1611	1669	1578
bollard, noun	1844	1844	1795	1775

Sources for the earlier dates now given in the eleventh Collegiate are as follows. *Bollard* is an entry in John Ash's dictionary of 1775. A search of 'Early English Books Online' shows *bland* used in 1565. And the date for *blight* comes from occurrence within another entry in the OED. Go to the OED webpage (which is not free), search for *blight*, click on 'quotations'. There will appear 313 tokens of *blight* throughout the dictionary. Click on 'time' to put them into chronological order. The earliest token is then seen to be within the entry for:

† **brantcorn**. n. *Obs*. Blight, smut (*Uredo segetum*)
1578   H. LYTE tr. R. Dodoens *Niewe Herball* IV. xvii.471. Blight or Brandtcorne…insteede of a good eare, there cometh up a black burnt eare, ful of blacke dust or powder.

This was in Murray's fourth fascicle, in June 1888, fifteen months after the third fascicle, which included the entry for *blight*.

One of the most significant innovations in lexicography during the twentieth century was that from American Heritage, taking etymologies (for words from Indo-European languages) back as far as possible, to the reconstructed Proto-Indo-European (PIE). They referred to established scholarship of good quality.

American rivals – such as Merriam-Webster and Random House – decided not to follow suit. But what about that ultimate dictionary, the OED? Generally, no mention is made of PIE, even in those entries which have been thoroughly revised. There are just occasional exceptions.

A straightforward etymology for adjective *sweet* was given on page 148, from OE *swēde*, which came from Proto-Germanic **swōtja*, which in turn came from PIE **swōde* 'sweet, pleasant'. The OED entry has the typical, tangential (and unnecessary) list of cognate forms in other Germanic languages plus Greek and Sanskrit, but it does include '< Indo-European *swād-* (with variant *swăd-*)'. (Note the omission of 'Proto-'.)

This is unusual. Mostly there is no mention of PIE even when a clear etymological chain has been established by scholars in the field. Sometimes there may be a side-comment; for instance, the lengthy etymological discussion for noun *poet* includes '< the same Indo-European base as Sanskrit *cinoti* he collects, assembles', but the PIE root is not stated. In fact, it is recognised to have been *k^wei 'to pile up, build, make', which gave rise to Greek *poiein* 'to make, create' with derived form *poiētēs* 'maker, composer', borrowed into Latin as *poēta*, which developed into French *poète*, this being borrowed into ME.

To ensure comprehensive coverage, Samuel Johnson scoured specialist dictionaries of the time – for medical, legal, gardening terms, and so on (see page 95). One would imagine that, once a new dictionary of technical terms appeared, one of the many OED editors would be deputed to go through it, crafting entries for words not already included. This appears not to happen. Take, for example, *The Concise Oxford Dictionary of Linguistics* by P. H. Matthews. Terms within the range 'M–R' seem to be included but many others are lacking. They include *antipassive*, *atelic*, *back shifting*, *catenative*, and *circumfix* (to look no further than letter 'C'); these are all established terms in wide circulation.

And the OED would do well to pay attention to Matthews's professional treatment of words they do already include. ***Ergative***, for example, first appeared in the first volume of the Second Supplement (1972), with a definition which only related to a minor sense. For the second edition, in 1989, this was improved but is still inadequate. No revision has been undertaken since. Surely it would be a straightforward matter to just use Matthews' definition (after all, his dictionary is from the same publisher), which was the sort of thing Johnson did. As matters stand now, I would advise a student who does not have access to Matthews to consult the excellent entries in Merriam-Webster's Collegiate or the Unabridged Random House.

Murray and his co-editors made use of the information on words from Australia and New Zealand in Morris's 1898 volume *Austral English*, sometimes just copying them. Many of the words were from Aboriginal languages. Since, at that time, the 250 individual languages of Australia had not been fully documented, etymologies were mostly just 'Native Australian name'. And the same for all other dictionaries until in 1987 the second edition of the Unabridged Random House had proper etymologies which I was able to supply – the Australian language each loan word came from (and its location) plus the original form and meaning in that language (see pages 140–1). Other American dictionaries copied this information.

Then, in 1988, came *The Australian National Dictionary*, edited by W. S. Ramson (published by Oxford University Press), which included about 400 English words that have been taken from an Australian language. Two years later a book was published which I co-authored, *Australian Aboriginal Words in English: Their Origin and Meaning*, also with Oxford University Press (this corrected some errors in Ramson's volume). A second edition in 2006 added

further loans, bringing the total number up to about 435. One might ask: did
the OED pay due attention? No, not really.

If Samuel Johnson or James Murrray were currently in charge of the OED
revision, they would surely not allow thirty years to pass without taking full
cognisance of this new information. The entry for *wombat* has in fact been
properly revised. But not those for *boomerang, dingo, koala, humpy, kangaroo*, and dozens more. The current etymology for *kangaroo* reads: 'Stated
to have been the name in an Australian Aboriginal language'. This is a pretty
important word. Shouldn't the OED feel a trifle embarrassed at not yet having
revised this, when the current edition of the Collegiate has:

> Guugu Yimidhiir (Australian aboriginal language of northern
> Queensland), *gaŋurru.*

The OED would no doubt respond that they haven't yet got around to revising the entry for *kangaroo*. But shouldn't some priority might be accorded to
revising poor entries for quite common words?

Of course, Oxford isn't just the OED. There are many commercial dictionaries for which each entry is reassessed for every new edition. In 1996 I purchased a Desk volume, *The Oxford English Reference Dictionary*, and noticed
that for *kangaroo* it said 'generic name of a specific kind of kangaroo in an
extinct Aboriginal language of N. Queensland'. (What on earth is a 'generic
name' for something specific?)

I wrote to the editor suggesting that it would be appropriate to name the
kind of kangaroo (large black or grey kangaroo, *Macropus robustus*) and the
language concerned (anyway, Guugu Yimidhirr is not extinct). I mean, a loan
from Italian wouldn't be described as being 'from a language of southern
Europe'. The editor did reply, stating that this omission had been deliber-
ate since 'our readers would not be interested in such detail'. (Note that the
readers of comparable Desk dictionaries in America are believed to be so
interested.)

On page 1–2 and also on page 178, it was pointed out that although most
adjectives can either modify a noun or function as copula complement (one
can say both *that clever girl* and *That girl is clever*), some adjectives only
have one of the two functions. How does the OED deal with this? Looking
at *rife* (a fully revised entry), the only grammatical information is 'adj', with
no indication that it may not function as modifier. A dictionary user will see
the statement *Corruption was rife in both political parties* and might attempt
to relay this information to a friend by saying ♦*Rife corruption was present
in both political parties*. This is unacceptable, but you wouldn't know it from
the OED.

It was emphasised in the preceding chapter that derivational affixes are the
province of grammar and ought to receive just a cross-reference in a dictionary.

If a dictionary should insist on having entries for affixes (as most do) they should at least treat them comprehensively.

Derivational prefixes and suffixes generally attach to a word. But, as exemplified on page 189, there are quite a few which may be attached to a complete noun phrase. One could say:

pre-war	pre-lunch lessons
pre-[the first world war]	pre-[late lunch] lessons
pre-[the war to end all wars]	pre-[mid-morning break] lessons

The OED does have some recent quotations with *pre-* added to a multi-word phrase, such as *pre-[my being in office]*. For the OED, it appears, this cannot be a prefix since it is added to a phrase. What then can it be? As from its Second Supplement, the OED has decided that such instances of *pre* are prepositions! Thus, *pre-* is presumably regarded a prefix in *pre-lunch*, but a preposition in *pre-[late lunch]*. Such instances of mal-analysis are certainly one reason why the OED recognises such an inflated number of 'prepositions'.

Another prefix which may attach to a phrase is *non-*, as in *non-[beer drinking] man* and *non-[teacher training college] students*. I cannot find an example of this in the OED. At least they avoid having to say that *non* is a preposition. Nor can I find examples of a derivational suffix being added to a phrase (although these do abound). How would *He usually comes home at [four or five o'clock]-ish* be dealt with? Would *ish* be called a postposition here, the first instance of this word class in English?

The OED has specialist editors covering every kind of science – except, apparently, there is no one with expertise in modern linguistics, and no one conversant with current work on Indo-European etymology. Also, the organisation seems unaware of recent work on the structure of English; they appear to be operating in terms of the 'traditional grammar' which was taught in schools a hundred and more years ago.

The March 2016 OED 'Update' lists new entries, which include more than twenty combinations commencing with *football*, such as *football boot, football coach, football fan,* and *football team* – all obvious and unnecessary. In place of such activity, more effort could be devoted to revising entries such as *applause, coward,* and *kangaroo* (there are tens of thousands more). If James Murray had celestial access to the OED website today, it can be guessed what (rude) words might pass his lips.

One wonders – now that going through the alphabet has been abandoned – how the seventy editors choose what to work on, and how they go about it. On 9 January 2016 I received a message from an 'OED Consultancy administrator' saying that 'one of our editors' wanted to ask me about the etymology of *callop*. I replied:

Really! It is all there on p. 90 of the second edition of *Australian Aboriginal Words in English* by Dixon et al. 2006. Don't you have this book, published by OUP?

The reply came back: 'Apologies from our editor who had forgotten that our library has the book'. (Callop is an alternative name for golden perch and is likely to come from *galaba* in Ngayawang, a language formerly spoken on the Lower Murray River in South Australia.)

Taking everything into consideration, the overall impression has to be that, since the OED was revived in 1957, it has regressed, and continues to do so. The OED is indeed an English institution, self-proclaimed as 'the definitive record of the English language'. It is, without doubt, extremely useful as a historical resource. But simply as a dictionary it could be so much more effective with up-to-date planning, priorities, and expertise.

The OED does not attempt what should surely be a main goal of every kind of dictionary – to provide advice on when to use a particular word rather than others of similar meaning. But wait! There is a further tool, integrated into the OED's website, a Historical Thesaurus. It will be instructive to see how this deals with *ample*, *enough*, and *sufficient*, words whose similarities and difference of meaning and of use were examined in chapter 6.

The Historical Thesaurus is modelled on Roget (see pages 105–6). Whereas Roget operated with six overarching classes, the Historical Thesaurus has just three – The external world, The mind, and Society, each with many divisions, sub-divisions, sub-sub-divisions, and so on. Locating a word through this hierarchical spider-web is impractical. With Roget, one uses the index as direction to paragraphs including a given word. In similar fashion, here one types in a word to obtain a list of the semantic sets in which it occurs. The Historical Thesaurus goes beyond Roget in providing a brief definition for each item in a set and its date of first use.

We find that *enough* is in five semantic sets and *sufficient* in thirteen, with some overlap. For instance, the set identified by 'the external world > relative properties > quantity or amount > sufficient quantity, amount or degree > [noun]' includes:

enough ... That which is sufficient; as much as is requisite or desired...
sufficience The quantity or condition of being sufficient or enough; sufficient supply, means or resources.

This (and related sets) will scarcely inform the reader about the circumstances in which to use one word rather than the other. And what about *ample*? This is traced to nine semantic sets, none of which also includes *enough* or *sufficient* (or their derivations).

The limitations of *Webster's New Dictionary of Synonyms* (a book from 1973) were outlined in chapter 8. But it is of more use than this web-based successor.

As the twentieth century rolled into the twenty-first, the basic methodology of dictionary compilation had changed little. Sure, a number of accessories have been added – differing ones by different publishers – including date of first attestation, and full and pithy etymologies. But these are tangential to the main business of a dictionary.

New features have been added (again, publishers vary) including names of important people (sometimes with potted biographies); names of places (sometimes with a small map) and of battles; name of plays, novels, poems, and important speeches; a diagram of geologic name scale; a table listing American Presidents (together with the religious affiliation of each). Some Desk dictionaries have become like encyclopaedias, which perhaps takes attention away from the fact that they are not really doing such a good job as dictionaries.

Grammatical information provided is minimal – little more than word class. Definitions are seldom properly structured. Lexicographers should seek generalisations rather then just providing a list of disparate senses. If the definitional approach is utilised it should at least be done well, focusing first on the central meaning of a word, and then bringing in metaphorical and other extensions in a principled way.

The overarching purpose of a dictionary – as has been said many times on earlier pages – should be to assist the user in deciding when to use one word rather than another with similar meaning. Definitions do not easily achieve this aim. A truly effective dictionary would integrate comparative discussion of words in semantic sets, linked to a clear and up-to-date grammatical description (casting aside the echoes of Latin grammar), as tentatively illustrated in chapters 3, 6, 9, and 12.

Sales of hard-copy dictionaries rose dramatically during the twentieth century, and then swiftly fell away, under competition from the worldwide web. The web supplies many dictionary-type resources, some good but others plain awful.

However, there is another side to things, which could not be brighter. The potentialities of computers are just what are needed for a great jump forward, outlined in the next chapter.

15   The Way Forward

Previous chapters have recounted the story of monolingual dictionaries. Samuel Johnson established English lexicology, and only minor improvements have been made since his time. Johnson combined erudition, imagination, and application. He also had a sense of perspective, according to each word a length of entry appropriate to its role in the language. Legal, medical, and agricultural terms were taken – with acknowledgement – from standard works. Highly technical terms were avoided, these being accessible in specialist manuals.

Johnson's innovations included recognising several senses for those words which have a wide range of meaning, including quotations to demonstrate how a word was used by the 'best authors', plus basic grammatical information concerning word class, and transitivity value for verbs.

His work has been criticised for not paying sufficient attention to usage in everyday discourse. This is only partly justified. Johnson did confine his quotations to the 'best authors', but his definitions would have been informed by the conversational round in London for which he was a central figure. (The same could not be said of his predecessors and successors.) Another (justified) criticism is that the senses within a definition could have been more thoughtfully organised, around a 'central meaning', with extensions in different directions from this.

What Johnson absolutely failed to do was make any attempt to contrast words of similar meaning, providing criteria and clues concerning the circumstances in which it would be more felicitous to use one word rather than another. Each word was regarded as an isolated entity, its definition autonomous.

Johnson's definitions were original, avoiding the 'theft' of unattributed plagiarism. The same applied for Charles Richardson in 1835–7, but his huge tome lies a little outside the mainstream. The OED worked in its own way, although it sometimes did utilise elegant portions of Johnson, shown by '(J)'. For example, how could the meaning of *swift* be better characterised than by 'moving far in a short time (J)'?

Leaving aside these two exceptions we can return to the self-description of how a lexicographer works with 'a row of dictionaries' propped on the desk. It is worth revisiting quotations already given in chapter 10. In *Dictionaries: The Art and Craft of Lexicography*, Sidney J. Landau relates how:

Dictionaries have always copied from one another … Although phrased differently, the definition of a given sense usually covers the same ground in all major dictionaries. Dictionary editors look at each other's books, and though each editor may form his own opinion about what ground should be covered, he dare not depart too far from the area laid out by his competitors.

Similar comments are made by Bo Svensén in *A Handbook of Lexicography: The Theory and Practice of Dictionary-Making*:

Compilers of dictionaries have always utilized each other's work to a greater or lesser extent … The survival instinct causes lexicographers to consult all dictionaries relevant to their own work in order to make sure that they have not overlooked anything important.

But what if there is something important which has been neglected by *all* competitors (as they continually copy from each other)?

The 'battle' between Desk dictionaries during the second half of the twentieth century was mentioned in the previous chapter. Some of the protagonists attempted to woo buyers through a special feature – date of first mention, far-back etymologies, employing a 'defining vocabulary' of two thousand or so words. These may have sounded good but they were really of little interest for the great majority of users. Leaving the extras aside, in their essential nature the dictionaries were all minor variants of each other. This was illustrated by the set of definitions for ***congratulate*** given on pages 143–5. All are pretty similar (and all are unsatisfactory, there being an important sense which they *had all* neglected).

The boom in sales of hard-copy dictionaries was extinguished by the advent of electronic media. There is a profusion of dictionary-type sources on the web – some require subscription, others are difficult to manipulate. A number are overly 'democratic' (with no quality control), including everything which anyone suggests, even odd formations by non-native speakers which would be judged as inadmissible by standard dictionaries.

All this is unfortunate but perhaps in some ways appropriate. The very tool which has impaired the sales and thus the well-being of traditional dictionaries is ideally suited as conduit for the new approach.

As has been repeated throughout this volume, what a dictionary user needs is advice on the semantic – and grammatical – differences between words of similar meaning, and the circumstances in which one should be preferred over the others. Traditional dictionaries scarcely fulfilled this aim.

My suggestion is that an entirely new approach is needed, radically departing from the Johnsonian paradigm. The new-style dictionary involves a number of interlocking 'semantic sets' (such as those tentatively outlined in chapters 3,

6, 9, and 12), the whole being linked to a clear and accessible grammar. These will be integrated within an electronic matrix.

A user of the new dictionary keys in their word of interest and is directed to semantic sets which reflect each nuance of its meaning. They learn when and where it may be employed, and the pragmatic implications of using this word rather than another.

How is the new dictionary constructed? Does one examine what old-style dictionaries have said, and build on this? Absolutely not, or this would simply perpetuate the established cycle of unoriginal plagiarism.

The lexicographer requires native-speaker (or near-native-speaker) knowledge of the language. A set of words with similar meanings is selected. As a starting step, the lexicographer ruminates long and hard, jotting down sentences in which each word may be used. They then examine occurrences in one or more corpuses, which serves to extend the database. The next step is to consider each context in which word X appears, and check whether word Y or word Z (and so on) may be substituted for it. If not, why not? (There will be a mix of grammatical and semantic reasons.) If substitution is acceptable, what are the implications of using Y rather than X in a given frame?

One does not begin by consulting existing dictionaries since this would prejudice the endeavour. The intention is to start from scratch. But when the investigation is more-or-less complete, then and only then should dictionary sources be scanned, to see if they contain anything which has so far been missed. (In my experience, it is rather rare for anything new to turn up in this way. But, in order to be complete, this final step should be included.)

The empirical method can be illustrated for three verbs with overlapping meanings – *suggest*, *propose*, and *recommend*.

Contrasts in Context

It is always useful to get a bit of background knowledge on anything one wishes to examine. The fact that the three verbs have main stress on a non-initial syllable, and an initial syllable relating to a prefix in Latin, indicates that they are of Romance origin:

- *recommend* /ˌrekəˈmend/ was a loan in the fourteenth century from Mediaeval Latin *re-* 'again' plus *commendāre* 'entrust, commend', this going back to Proto-Indo-European (PIE) *man-* 'hand'.
- *propose* /prəˈpouz/ came in the fourteenth century from French *proposer*. This was a development from Latin *prōpōnere* 'set forth', made up of prefix *pro-*'forth' added to verb *pōnere* 'put', this going back to PIE *apo-* 'off, away'.
- *suggest* /səˈdʒest/ came into English in the early sixteenth century from Mediaeval Latin *suggerere*, which involved prefix *sub-* added to verb *gerere* 'carry' (no earlier etymon is known).

There is overlap between the contexts in which these verbs occur. For instance:

(1)   Mr Jones recommends (that) Smithers should be fired
(2)   Mr Jones proposes (that) Smithers should be fired
(3)   Mr Jones suggests (that) Smithers should be fired

Each of (1–3) puts forward the idea that Smithers' employment should be terminated but they have different implications concerning the role of Mr Jones. Hearing (1), the most likely inference is that Mr Jones is an outside consultant who has been hired to advise on improving the company's performance. If Smithers is fired, Mr Jones will have no direct role in this.

Sentence (2) could be interpreted in the same way but it is far more likely that Mr Jones is a manager in the company who would personally implement the dismissal. In contrast, sentence (3) is neutral and could be used in either circumstance.

The grammatical object of the three verbs is a THAT complement clause (see page 7) in (1–3). It could, alternatively, be a noun phrase (NP), such as *the amalgamation of the two companies* or *a bonus scheme for good performance* or *a Christmas party*. Or the verbs could simply introduce direct speech: *Mr Jones recommends/proposes/suggests: 'Smithers should be fired'*.

We can now look at the possibilities for what may be in subject and object slots for each verb, and examine whether the other two verbs are substitutable for it. For *suggest*, the subject may be an NP with human reference, such as *Mr Jones* or *the committee*. Or it may be a complement clause as in (4), or an NP with non-human reference, as in (5–7):

(4)   (The fact) that his work is sloppy suggests (that) Smithers should be fired
(5)   The complaints made about him suggest (that) Smithers should be fired
(6)   Weather reports suggest (that) a storm is imminent
(7)   Experience does suggest (that) we should proceed cautiously

Neither *propose* nor *recommend* could be used in place of *suggest* in sentences such as (4–7). For these two verbs, the subject must be an NP with (individual or collective or indirect) human reference. *Propose* and *recommend* indicate an idea which emanates from a person or persons. *Suggest* may also be used in this way, but it can also indicate an idea which is brought to light from some state of affairs, as in (4–7).

When *suggest* takes a THAT complement clause, it frequently includes *should*. However, other modals also occur. In place of *should* in (3) there could be – for instance – *must, could, might*, or *will*. Or there need not be any modal at all, as in (6) and:

(8)   Circumstantial evidence suggests (that) it was Fred who robbed the bank
(9)   The explorer suggests (that) insufficient food has been provided

Whereas *suggest* simply indicates an idea that has been put forward (or come to light), both *propose* and *recommend* imply that the idea should be acted on. In keeping with this, their THAT complement clauses overwhelmingly include *should*. And, unlike *suggest*, they may both take a (FOR) TO complement clause which describes purpose or intention (see page 8).

For *propose*, the subject of the main clause is generally the same as the subject of the (FOR) TO clause, and it is omitted from this clause. For example:

(10)   Mr Jones proposes to fire Smithers
(11)   The government proposes to pay off the debt within two years

Just occasionally, main and complement clauses have different subjects:

(12)   She proposes for James to do it
(13)   The committee proposed for everyone to pay off their individual debt

Recommend is a little different. When discussing (1), it was pointed out that Mr Jones must here be an outside consultant, telling others what to do but not doing it himself. In keeping with this, *recommend* only takes a (FOR) TO complement clause whose subject is different from the subject of the main clause. That is, *recommend* could substitute for *propose* in (12–13) but not in (10–11).

Typical examples with *recommend* are:

(14)   Mr Jones recommended (for) the company to fire Smithers
(15)   The analyst recommended (for) shareholders to accept the offer
(16)   Central office recommends (for) teachers to use the new edition of the textbook
(17)   What would you recommend (for) me to read?

Whereas *for* is normally included after *propose* in sentences such as (12–13), it is often omitted after *recommend* in sentences such as (14–17).

Suggest may not be used with any type of (FOR) TO clause. That is, it is not substitutable into any of (10–17)

Parallel to (14–17) are constructions where *recommend* is followed by '*to* X' and then a THAT complement clause whose subject has the same reference as X. For example, *Mr Jones recommended to the company that they should fire Smithers*. In this construction, *suggest* (and *propose*) could replace *recommend*.

We can return to the question of what may be the subject. The subject of a (FOR) TO complement clause for *recommend* and for *propose* – when it is typically the same as the subject of the main clause – must have human reference, and be able to control the implementation of the idea which is recommended or proposed. This will be *the government* in (11), *James* in (12), *teachers* in (16), and so on. The same applies for the subject of a THAT complement clause after these verbs.

Main clause subject for *recommend* and *propose* generally has human reference. Or it can refer to something that reflects the opinion of humans. For example:

(18) The (specialist's) report recommends (for) the children to drink more milk

In contrast, the kind of report which is purely factual, such as *weather reports*, cannot be the subject for *recommend* or *propose*, as it can be for *suggest* in a sentence such as (6). Both main clause and complement clause subject for *suggest* may lack any reference to humans or to control, as in:

(19) Those minor tremors suggest that a considerable earthquake is imminent

The contrasting characteristics of the three verbs may be summarised in a table:

	suggest	*propose*	*recommend*
plain NP as object, e.g. *a Christmas party, new projects*	yes	yes	yes
THAT complement clause	often includes *should*, but wide possibilities	almost always includes *should*	almost always includes *should*
(FOR) TO complement clause with same subject as main clause	no	common	no
(FOR) TO complement clause with different subject from main clause	no	infrequent but acceptable	common
main clause and complement clause subjects	wide range (NP or complement clause)	NP with human reference	NP with human reference

There is a nominalisation corresponding to each verb. *Recommendation* was borrowed from Mediaeval Latin in the fourteenth century, not long after *recommend*. *Suggestion* entered the language, from the same source, in the fourteenth century a couple of hundred years before *suggest*. *Proposal* was coined within English in the early sixteenth century.

Basically, a recommendation, proposal, or suggestion is something which is recommended, proposed, or suggested. These nominals may be followed by complement clauses just like their parent verbs. Sentences (1–3) could be rephrased:

(20)   Mr Jones put forward a recommendation/proposal/suggestion that
       Smithers should be fired

Corresponding to (11) and (16), one could say:

(21)   The proposal is for the government to pay off the debt within two years
(22)   There is a recommendation (for) teachers to use the new edition of the
       textbook

Suggestion is more limited than *suggest* in that the nominalisation does
require human agency. Sentence (9) can be restated:

(23)   There is a suggestion from the explorer that insufficient food has been
       provided

However, sentences such as (4–8) could not be rephrased with *suggestion*.

When the three verbs take a plain NP as object, the nominalisation generally
marks this with *for* (a different *for* from that marking a (FOR) TO complement
clause). It occurs commonly with *proposal*, occasionally with *suggestion* and
recommendation. For example:

(24)   They propose a new theatre   There is a proposal for a new theatre
(25)   They suggested a tax hike   There was a suggestion for a tax hike
(26)   She recommended action   Her recommendation was for action

Corresponding to *suggest/suggestion* and *recommend/recommendation*,
the nominalisation for *propose* would be expected to be *proposition*. There
is such a word and while it can have a very similar meaning to *proposal*
(relating to verb *propose*) it also has a range of quite distinct senses. Among
other uses, the noun *proposition* can describe a planned activity, as in (27);
it can be an aphorism, as in (28); or a mathematical or logical statement,
as in (29):

(27)   We decided that mushroom-farming should be a profitable proposition
(28)   They discussed the proposition that all men are created equal
(29)   The syllogism involves two propositions: 'All humans are mortal' and
       'Athenians are humans'

Noun *proposition* already had this range of meanings in French, being borrowed into English – with the span of meanings – in the fourteenth century,
at about the same time as *propose*. The fact that *proposition* does not semantically match *propose* was undoubtedly the trigger for a new nominal to be
created within English which would more closely correspond to the verb *propose*. Nominalising suffix -al had been adopted from French and came to be
used in English to form nouns from verbs, mostly of Romance origin (*arriv-al*,
revers-al) but a few Germanic (*betroth-al*, *withdraw-al*). In the early sixteenth
century it was added to *propose* to give *propos-al*.

On the basis of the discussion so far, the characteristics of our three verbs can be briefly summarised.

I   **Recommend**. A human (or human agency) puts forward an idea to a person (or people) such that they can implement the idea, with control over it. It can be followed by a THAT or a (FOR) TO complement clause. Or just by an NP; for instance:

(30)   Hector recommended the new seafood restaurant (to Freda)

Hector has set forth the idea of eating at this restaurant, which Freda can put into practice. Without the *to Freda* this would be a general recommendation, to anyone who is listening (or reading it).

II   **Propose**. The most common sense is of a human putting forward an idea which they themselves can then implement, with control over it. Alternatively, it can be like *recommend,* putting forward an idea to someone else. Like *recommend*, it can be followed by a THAT or a (FOR) TO complement clause or an NP.

One use of *propose* is to put forward a person's name for some office, as in *I (hereby) nominate Felix Brand to be our new treasurer.* Or to put forward a topic for debate, such as *I would like to propose the motion 'Some people are more equal than others'.*

Verb *propose* and both its nominalisations have special senses relating to procreation. *Propose* and *proposal* generally refer to a formal offer, as in:

(31)   Robin proposed (marriage) to Alex
       Robin made a proposal of marriage to Alex

Note, though, that someone may make *an indecent proposal*, which would be sex outside marriage. Noun *proposition* is typically used for an indecent proposal; and – unlike the other nominalisations – it functions as its own verb, as in *Spike propositioned Sheila.*

III **Suggest**. A person or some situation or abstraction (e.g. experience) leads to an idea. There is no implication that it necessarily be implemented – the suggester may say 'It was just an idea' – which is why, unlike *recommend* and *propose, suggest* does not take a (FOR) TO complement clause, only a THAT clause or an NP. Compare (30) with:

(32)   Hector suggested the new seafood restaurant

Sentence (30), with *recommend*, implies that Hector understands this to be a good restaurant, whereas (32), with *suggest*, just points out the existence of the restaurant as a possible dinner venue (perhaps without knowing very much about it).

A common mistake from foreign learners is to use a TO clause after *suggest*, saying *I suggested her to go* when it should be *I suggested (that) she (should) go*. In a number of modern European languages, a verb similar in meaning to English *suggest* does take a TO-type clause, and this leads to the error when speaking English. Study of the discussion provided here will indicate the appropriate way to use *suggest*.

All that has been attempted here is an illustration of the methodology which may be followed. Select a set of words with similar meanings and grammatical possibilities and assemble a corpus of typical instances. For each sentence involving one of the verbs, check whether the others may replace it there. If they may not, what is the semantic reason for this? If they may, what are the semantic and pragmatic differences associated with using alternative verbs in the same frame?

Note that the summary characterisations of the three verbs are not intended to be self-standing but need to be appreciated in association with the discussion of the example sentences. This brief outline would be a preliminary to producing a full account of the semantic set. It focuses on central meanings of the verbs and their nominalisations; there will of course be extensions of various kinds from these.

Also needed are cross-references to related sets. *Recommend* has similar meaning and grammar to *advise* and *urge*; *propose* to *intend*, *plan*, and *aim*; and *suggest* to *indicate* (also to *hint*, although the meaning here restricts the available frames).

The aim throughout is to provide advice to a dictionary user concerning when to use one of a related set of words rather than the others.

The Vision

My suggestion – nay, recommendation – is for an entirely new approach to lexicography. Relegate tradition to the background. Abandon reliance on definitions of one-word-at-a-time. Realise that the scanty grammatical information which Samuel Johnson provided (word class, plus transitivity value for verbs) was merely a first step. Two and a half centuries later, and with modern understanding of the subtleties of English grammar, much much more is needed.

The enterprise must be descriptive, dealing with how the language is used, rather then prescriptive, demanding that certain pedantic principles be followed. It should, of course, conform to the accepted and respected usage of native speakers, avoiding half-baked coinages from half-taught outsiders.

The scheme presented towards the end of chapter 8 (pages 118–21) can be recapitulated. Nobody would approach any kind of monolingual dictionary if they had absolutely no knowledge of the languages. One can **assume** some sort of superficial knowledge of the vocabulary, and of basic grammatical patterns.

They are likely to know that *little* and *small* have overlapping meanings. The **purpose** of the new dictionary is to illustrate contexts – when only one of the adjectives may be used, when it is more felicitous to use one rather than the other, and when either may be employed. (This was the topic of chapter 6.)

When a word under enquiry is keyed into the new-style dictionary, the user will be referred to a semantic set (or perhaps to a choice of several, if the word has a wide range of meaning). The **basis** of the endeavour is that each semantic set is explained within a 'conceptual template', involving notions which a dictionary user would be expected to have some familiarity with. These would be made fully clear through the sentential examples in the discussion of the semantic set. (For example, the examination of *suggest*, *propose*, and *recommend* was (in part) in terms of 'idea' and 'to implement'.) There is further illustration in chapters 3, 6, 9, and 12.

The new dictionary implies a new – and much healthier – attitude towards lexicography. Think of what the traditional method must be like. Having a row of dictionaries before you, concocting a definition which is different from that in any one dictionary but similar to those in them all. Each entry on its lonesome. Word after word, day after day. William Craigie, an editor of the OED and much else besides, confided: 'It cannot be denied that dictionary work, for most of the time, is very dull and boring'.

My experience has included working on thesaurus-based bilingual dictionaries for two of the indigenous languages of Australia, plus researching full details of the 430 or so words borrowed from Australian languages into English. All of this work was engrossing and entirely satisfying. Producing drafts of the four semantic sets in chapters 3, 6, 9, and 12 was as enjoyable a task as any I have undertaken. (And I have never embarked on any academic task unless it was alluring in prospect and fulfilling as it progressed.) Work on the new dictionary will be an intellectual challenge, involving concentration and dedication. And it will be fun.

The new dictionary is interactive, each part being linked to other appropriate sections. A query will be partly explicated in one place, then a click will bring forth a related exposition and so on, as needed (moving back and forth at will). This is, of course, only possible through the aegis of computers. (It would be impractical if one only had printed books.) A new technique in the new age.

Dictionaries have always been constrained by space, time, and money. Space will no longer be a critical issue. However, abundance should not be permitted to override prudence. A user does not want to have to wade through fifty pages when it could all be said more concisely in fifteen. Clarity and succinctness typically go together, and this must be a guiding principle.

The new dictionary will be a considerable task. First, a director needs to be appointed. A youngish person who is prepared to devote ten or fifteen years to the project, someone who combines linguistic intuition and knowledge (lexical and also grammatical) with organisational ability. They will appoint teams of appropriately trained lexicographers.

Work will commence with the most common twenty or thirty thousand words (which make up 99 per cent or so of tokens in text). These will be items which a dictionary user is likely to look up and require instruction on how to use. They will be words which the lexicographer will know how to employ, and have intuitions about, words for which there are plentiful examples in corpuses. The words will be grouped into (overlapping) semantic sets, as illustrated in chapters 3, 6, 9, and 12 here. The director will exercise oversight over all of this work. Each piece of analysis by one lexicographer will be read by several others for comment and refinement so that the new dictionary is essentially a group effort. The lexicographers will meet to discuss semantic parameters and descriptive strategies. It is essential that the whole work be consistent and – to a large extent – homogeneous.

The new dictionary will be, in a sense, complementary to the OED which seems to emphasise cataloguing every obscure word rather than focusing on the important ones (let alone contrasting their meanings and uses). In its initial stages the new dictionary would not expect to deal with words of the lowest frequency; for example, *inveigle* or *otiose*. The latter is more-or-less a hyponym of *useless*, which occurs about 300 times more frequently. Eventually, of course, every word should be included in the semantic matrix. But those most used require primary attention if the dictionary is to fulfil its purpose, of explaining to its audience when to use one word rather than others of similar meaning. Bear in mind that it is the commonest words which have the widest ranges of meaning and function, thus requiring the most careful explication. Their central meanings need to be pin-pointed, and extensions from these explained (not just a list of senses in any old order). The pragmatic dimension is vital – suitable circumstances for use, and the social implications of using a word outside of its appropriate time and place.

Money is always a factor in dictionary-making. A large investment will be required, extending over a considerable period. The ideal situation would be for one of those people who has made untold billions out of computational tools to feed a few tens of millions back. There seems to be no chance of this – philanthropy is invariably directed at helping poor people in undeveloped countries, rather than towards matters intellectual in the first world. A government (or several) could decide that this sort of thing would be a beneficial investment, but they never have and probably never will. The only likely scenario is for several universities and publishers to get together, linking support and facilities.

How long will it take to get the first stage of the new dictionary up and running? It all depends on how many lexicographers work on it. Money is of course a factor here – they do have to be paid. However, the most critical requirement is being able to find the right sort of people (who will be as different from editors working on traditional dictionaries as the choicest cheese is from the cheapest chalk). They need to be imaginative scholars, thoughtful and well-read, with an understanding of contemporary grammatical analysis, semantically attuned, intensely curious, and devoted to the project.

Results will be more than worthwhile, the new dictionary providing satisfaction for the compilers, and – the sine qua non – conveying insight and understanding to its users.

Sources and Notes

Some historical accounts of English lexicography appear not to have involved detailed study of the dictionaries discussed, or of the source literature. As a consequence, there are a number of items of misinformation, which get repeated.

For instance, one reads that Charles Richardson, in his 1835–7 volumes, made 'a dictionary without definitions or explanations of meaning, or at least with the merest rudiments of them, but illustrating each group of words by a large series of quotations' (Murray 1900: 29). This is quite untrue. Richardson did include many quotations but, in addition, he almost always provided a separate definition, sometimes quite lengthy. Richardson gave a single definition for each word (including its derivations), with no recognition of sub-senses, following John Horne Tooke's principle that each word has, and always has had, a single basic meaning (see pages 149–51 and 154).

In another well-regarded text we read: 'An assistant on Webster's 1828 *American Dictionary of the English Language*, Worcester had in the process – at least so Webster contended – been appropriating words and definitions for his own 1830 dictionary (Mugglestone 2011: 46–7). In fact, Worcester did not work on Webster's 1828 dictionary. He had been compiling his own dictionary for many years. Webster's volume was compendious and sold poorly. A shorter, and better-selling version – omitting quotations and most etymologies, abridging definitions, and adding some new entries – was edited by Chauncey A. Goodrich, Webster's son-in-law, and Worcester in 1829. Webster himself declined to work on this and then criticised the product. In no sense was Worcester ever an assistant to Webster. As for the charge of appropriation, this was solidly refuted – see Micklethwait (2000: 223–30) and pages 155–6 here.

Prologue: The Work in Advance

- Quotations from Thomas (1587), Cawdrey (1604), and Bailey (1730).
- Entries for *choose, select, widow, dog* are from Allen (1990), identical to those in Moore (1999).

230

- For discussion of *choose, select,* and other hyponyms of *choose* see Dixon (1991a: 138–40, 254–5; or 2005a: 143–6, 274–5).
- Entries for *ask, answer,* and *reply* from Fowler and Fowler (1951).

Chapter 1: How the Language Is Made Up

Comparative Constructions

- The account here of conditions for using *-er* or *more* is slightly simplified. There is a full account in Dixon (2005b/2011).

Complement Clause Constructions

- Just the essentials of the three main types of complement clause constructions in English are given here. A more complete account will be found in Dixon (1991a: 33–50, 124–266; or 2005a: 36–53, 131–206, 230–85).
- Note that some speakers place *'s* on the subject of an -ING complement clause, giving *John likes [Mary's singing the blues]* and *[Mary's singing the blues] pleases John]*.
- There can be a TO complement clause after *abhor*, but this is rather uncommon.
- It must be borne in mind that the grammatical principles outlined here are the basic template employed by educated native speakers. There can be considerable variation on this, by various dialectal and social groups, and especially by foreign learners.

Orthography and Phonology

- The only English textbook I know of which uses a phonemic orthography is Palmer (1924, 1939), revised as Palmer and Blandford (1969).

What Is a Word?

- For a full account of clitics in English, see Dixon (2007).

Two Approaches

- Quotation from Svensén (2009: 143).

Chapter 2: What a Dictionary Needs to Do

Derivation

- Full details of *un-, -ful, -ness, -hood, -dom, -y, -ous,* and about 190 further derivational affixes in English are in Dixon (2014).

Only Half the Story

- Detailed discussion of nominalisations is in Dixon (2005a: 217–322) and of adverbs in Dixon (2005a: 375–445).

Investigating Meaning

- Quotation from Malinowski (1935:17).
- Entries for *finish*, *cease* and *stop* from Allen (1990), repeated in Moore (1999).

Chapter 4: Explaining Hard Words

This and following chapters only mention a selection of English glossaries and dictionaries, sufficient to provide a general picture of what was happening.

Bilingual Dictionaries

- For early glossaries and bilingual dictionaries (discussed in this chapter and the next), see Stein (1985), Starnes (1954), Healey (2012), also Mathews (1933), Mugglestone (2011), and the comprehensive bibliography in Alston (1966). See also Stein (2014) and Considine (2014) on Elyot, and Stevenson (1958) on Thomas.

Early Word Lists

- This section is based on Schäfer (1989).

Monolingual Dictionaries

- Another contribution to the apotheosis of Cawdrey as 'the first English dictionary' is that Alston (1966) begins his bibliography of English dictionaries with Cawdrey, while Coote is relegated to the bibliography of 'spelling books' (Alston 1967).
- In an insightful study 'The beginnings of English lexicography' (written in 1935 but unfortunately not published until 2003), Allen Walker Read acknowledges Coote's list, at the end of his primer, as essentially the first bilingual dictionary. Read states that Cawdrey produced 'the first purely English dictionary to be issued as a separate work' although it was, in fact, 'a mere adaptation' of Coote's list.
- Coote's 1596 volume underwent more than sixty-four new editions and reprints up to as late as 1742 (Alston 1967). Cawdrey's 1604 volume went into four editions until 1617; Bullokar's 1616 volume went through nineteen editions, in London, Cambridge, and Dublin, until 1775 (Alston 1966).
- Major sources on early monolingual dictionaries are Mathews (1933) and Starnes and Noyes (1946); also Schäfer (1970). More recent overviews

include Béjoint (2010), and chapters in the volume edited by Cowie (2009).

Chapter 5: Putting Everything In

More Hard Words

• Blount's *Glossographia* went through five editions, until 1681. Edward Phillips' *The New World of English Words* had eight editions, until 1720 (the sixth, in 1706, revised by John Kersey). *An English Dictionary*, by Elisha Coles, had thirteen editions, until 1732. There were four editions of *The Complete English Dictionary*, by John Wesley, from 1753 to 1790.

All Encompassing

• *A New English Dictionary*, by John Kersey, went through eight editions, until 1772. *An Universal Etymological English Dictionary*, by Nathan Bailey, had twenty-eight editions, from 1721 in London until 1800 in Edinburgh and York. Bailey's *Dictionarium Britannicum* was published in 1730 and had just one further edition, in 1736.

The Other Words

• There is fuller information on English noun phrase structure in Dixon (2005a: 26–7). Quotations are from the translation of Wallis (1972).

Rationale

• *A Vocabulary or Pocket Dictionary*, by John Baskerville, had a single printing, in 1765.

Chapter 7: Spreading Wings

• Allen (1978: 37–8) states: 'The pronunciation of the *i*-consonant [in Latin] presents no basic problems; it is the same type of semivocalic sound as the English *y* in *yes*, etc. We should expect such a value from the fact that it is written in Latin with the same letter as the *i*-vowel, the difference between vowel and semi-vowel being simply that the former stands at the nucleus and the latter at the margin of a syllable. ... The traditional English pronunciation of the Latin *i*-consonant like the English *j* [dʒ] has no basis in antiquity. It probably goes back to the teaching of French schoolmasters after the Norman conquest, when this pronunciation was current in France both for Latin and for borrowings from Latin. In the thirteenth century it changed to [ʒ] in France, but the earlier pronunciation has survived in English borrowings from French (e.g. *just*, beside French *juste*)'.

Samuel Johnson, Lexicographer

- Quotations from the preface to the dictionary (pages unnumbered) and from the *Plan*, page 4.
- Conversation with Dr Adams from Boswell's *Life*, entry for 1748.
- Samuel Johnson is something of an icon; much has been written about him and his dictionary enterprise. The most useful of the many works I have consulted include Mugglestone (2015), Hüllen (2004: 170–97), Clifford (1979), and Kolb and Sledd (1953).
- Johnson's dictionary was published in 1755 and had a great number of subsequent editions; for the fourth edition, in 1773, there were significant revisions by Johnson. A cheaper abridged edition first came out in 1756, without the quotations, just the names of authors quoted.

The Method

- See Brewer (2012) for an account of Johnson's quotations from Lennox and other female writers.

The Results

- Comparison of head words commencing with 'L' in Bailey and Johnson is in McCracken (1969).
- The statement that more than 80 per cent of the occurrences of *hot* relate to 'having heat' is based on West (1953: 239) and my own corpus searches.

Grammar

- In his 1749 volume *Lingua Britannica Reformata*, Benjamin Martin marked word class sparingly, just to distinguish homonyms. For example: *Prior*, *sub[stantive], the head of a priory*; and *Prior*, *adj[ective], antecedent, or before*.
- The use and development of the term 'neuter verb' is detailed in Michael (1970: 94–9, 380–8).

Chapter 8: Semantic Organisation

'Synonym' Lists

- Information on early synonym(s) lists from Hüllen (2004: 199–228).

- Quotations from Trusler (1766: 5–6), from Piozzi (1794, I: 110–11, II: 170–1), from a modern edition of *Roget's Thesaurus* (Dutch 1962: 142), from *Reader's Digest Use the Right Word* (1969: 327), and from *Webster's New Dictionary of Synonyms* (Gove 1973: 749, 127).

Definitions

- 'Principles of defining' based on Zgusta (1971: 257–8) and Landau (1984: 124).
- Noun **hope** is defined as *expectation and desire combined* in Fowler and Fowler (1951: 574) and Allen (1990: 568).
- There is an excellent history of the England-based movement for utilising a limited 'defining vocabulary' in Cowie (1999).
- Swahili entry from Johnson (1939: 76).
- Entries for *quick* and *fast* from *Collins Gem Dictionary and Thesaurus* (2009).

The Tradition

- The volume *Electronic Lexicography* (2012), edited by Granger and Paquot provides a useful overview of recent application of computers for a range of dictionary-making endeavours. However, all are firmly within the Johnsonian paradigm.

Chapter 10: No Need to Keep Re-inventing the Wheel

How It Is Done

- Quotation from Landau (1984: xi).
- Comparing the *American College Dictionary* (ACD) with the *Encyclopedic World Dictionary* (EWD) and the *Macquarie Dictionary*, we find many of the entries are identical or very nearly so. However, the Macquarie differs from its predecessors in three important respects.
  - (a) The ACD includes many small illustrations with informative captions. For example, the first illustration bears the caption: 'Aardvark, *Orycteropos afer* (Overall length 5 to 6 ft., tail 2 to 2½ ft.)'; and the caption to the second illustration is 'Chinese abacus (Each vertical column = one integer; each bead in group A = 5 when lowered; each bead in group B = 1 when raised; value of this setting is 203,691,500.)' The EWD repeats the drawings and captions exactly. The Macquarie retains the illustrations but their captions are simplified to a single word: 'aardvark' and 'abacus', respectively. (And similarly throughout the volume.)

(b) The ACD includes entries for countries and major cities across the world, with information on their population and many small but useful maps. These are repeated (with population figures updated) in the EWD. All such information is omitted from the Macquarie.

(c) After a number of common words, the ACD and the EWD provide several lines of synonyms, and sometimes also antonyms, with discussion of their meaning and use. All these are omitted from the Macquarie.

- Quotations from Burchfield (1982, 1989: 153).

How Far Can One Go?

- Quotations from Landau (1984: 296–7).
- The mis-spelling of the source for *pademelon* as *gadimalion*, introduced into the second edition of the Macquarie Dictionary in 1991, was maintained in the fourth edition, of 2005. The initial *g* was changed to *b* in the sixth edition (2013) once I had pointed out the error in a 2008 paper.

Keep with the Familiar

- Quotations from Svensén (2009: 428) and Landau (1984: 172).
- Oxford's Desk dictionaries, such as the Concise and the Advanced Learner's stand quite apart from the OED, and did – like works from other publishers – take part in the merry-go-round of copying; see the entries from two editions of the Concise in the tabulation on pages 143–4.
- Of the several dozen dictionaries I have consulted, only the American Heritage includes the further sense of *congratulate*, saying: *to express joy or acknowledgement, as for the achievement or good fortune of (another).* The crucial element is 'or acknowledgement' (without any necessary accompanying joy).

Chapter 11: The Nineteenth Century

- Wheatley (1865) has an annotated list of 143 dictionaries published by 1864.

Etymology

- Proto-Indo-European etymologies from Watkins (1985, 2000), based on Pokorny (1959).
- Horne Tooke's opinion of Americans from Stephens (1813, 2: 227).
- Examples from pages 141, 370, 485, 374–6 of Horne Tooke (1786).
- James Mill's comments on HorneTooke from Aarsleff (1967: 93).

- The anonymous review of *The Diversions of Purley* was published in *Blackwood's Edinburgh Magazine* (47: 484–96, 1840). See also the commentary by Ostler (2008).

Over in America

- Comparison of Webster and Johnson for entries commencing in 'L' is in Reed (1962).
- It is interesting to compare the entries for **stupid** quoted from Bailey, Johnson, Webster, and Worcester with that in Richardson (1835–7). As usual, he simply provides a long list of semi-synonyms (with no division into senses): 'like a log or block; hard or difficult to receive impressions or perceptions; inapprehensive; insensitive; dull, obtuse, thick, heavy, sluggish, inert'. This was followed by twenty original quotations.
- Quotation from Byron's *Dan Juan* Canto XIII, stanza lxxxix.
- The exchanges between Webster and Worcester are set out in Micklethwait (2000: 223–30).
- Lester quotation from Micklethwait (2000: 1). Quotation 'Noah Webster was instrumental …' from McDavid (1984).

The Oxford English Dictionary

- Much has been written about the history of the OED; particularly useful accounts are in Murray (1979), Winchester (2003), Brewer (2007), and Gilliver (2016). Great caution should be exercised when consulting Ogilvie (2013).
- Quotation from Black (1984: 162–3).
- Impressions of Furnivall by people at Cambridge from Murray (1979: 148–9).
- Murray dealt with letters *A–D*, *H–K*, *O–P* and *T*; Bradley covered *E–G*, *L–M*, *S–Sh*, and *W–We*; Craigie was responsible for *N*, *Q–R*, *Si–Sq*, *St*, *U–V*, and *Wo–Wy*; Onions did *Su–Sz*, *Wh–Wo*, and *X–Z*. It would be interesting to compare entries by the four editors, examining points of difference; this would be a fine topic for a PhD thesis.
- For further discussion of 'combining form' see Dixon (2014: 12–13). The definition of *stupid* is taken from the current online edition of the OED.

Chapter 13: The Role of Grammar

Not Enough

- A comprehensive treatment of adverbs is in Dixon (2005a: 375–431).
- Note that, for instance, the OED's quotations for *really* include instances of it being used in all five adverb functions, mixed together without comment or

understanding of the grammatical frames involved (which are not available for other adverbs).
- Quotation from Landau (1984: 88).
- *The Oxford Advanced Learner's Dictionary of Current English* was first produced by A. S. Hornby in 1948 and has been revised several times since. There are instructive historical accounts of English dictionaries which are addressed to foreign learners in Cowie (1999) and Béjoint (2010: 163–200).

Too Much (and Also Not Enough)

- A full account of English derivational affixes is in Dixon (2014); see also Jespersen (1942) and Marchand (1969).
- Only a part of the conditioning for verbalising suffixes -(i)fy and -ise is given here; for a fuller account (which relates a good deal to stress placement) see Dixon (2014: 178–218), also Lieber (1998, 2004) and Plag (1999).
- For combinations of prefixes, and for affixes added to noun phrases, see Dixon (2014: 393–4, 53).

The Development of Linguistics

- Information on Kwakiutl from Boas (1911: 40–3).
- Churchward's volumes are *Tongan Grammar* (1953) and *Tongan Dictionary (Tongan–English and English–Tongan)* (1959).
- Jespersen's volumes are *The Philosophy of Grammar* (1924) and *A Modern English Grammar, on Historical Principles*, vols. I–VII (1909–49).
- Classic expositions of the theory of scientific linguistics include – besides Boas (1911) – volumes each entitled *Language* by Sapir (1921) and Bloomfield (1933). Aikhenvald's *The Art of Grammar: A Practical Guide (2015)* and my three-volume work *Basic Linguistic Theory* (2010a, b; 2012) constitute summations of the cumulative development. Seminal studies of genders and classifiers, of evidentials, and of imperatives and commands are in Aikhenvald (2000, 2004, 2010).

Chapter 14: Standing Still

- Quotations from Béjoint (2010: 10) and Bryson (2008: 143).

Rude Words

- The correspondence between *OZ Magazine* and Oxford University Press concerning *fuck* is quoted in full in Burchfield (1972).

Keeping Up

- For a short account of Craigie's work and character, and his difficulties at Chicago, see Brewer (2007: 20–4) and the further references in her note 31.
- For detailed accounts, and documentation, of the attacks on Webster's Third, see Sledd and Ebbitt (1962) and Morton (1994).

The Battlefield

- There had been one earlier dictionary with a list of Proto-Indo-European roots. This was *Webster's International Dictionary of the English Language* (the first to have 'International' in place of 'American') published by the Merriam company in 1890. It had a seven-page 'List of Indo-Germanic roots found in English' (by the prominent German linguist August Flick), in two columns of minute-size type. Unfortunately, words in the body of the dictionary were not cross-referenced to this list. The list was not included in the first *Webster's New International Dictionary*, published in 1909. (This information was provided by James L. Rader.)
- Quotation on synonym discrimination from Landau (1984: 110).
- One of many Desk dictionaries using the name Webster but having no connection with the Merriam company is *Webster's New World Dictionary*, put out by Simon and Schuster from 1980.
- Cobuild does sometimes keep homonyms apart, as with nouns **bank** (for money) and **bank** (e.g. of a river). However, this is an exception. It may be that editors dealing with different sections of the alphabet applied varying policies, with no overall direction having been provided.

The OED Putters On

- Brewer (2007) provides an excellent account of the OED in the twentieth century, which I have drawn on here.
- Extracts from Murray's letter of complaint to Craigie are in Murray (1979: 287–8) and Burchfield (1989: 194–5).
- The 520-million-word Corpus of Contemporary American English (COCA; corpus.byu.edu/coca) has 83,800 instances of *boy*. I checked

just the first 1,000 of these to come up with the four new combinations mentioned here.

- Criteria for being a compound are in Matthews (2014: 21) and, more fully, in Aikhenvald (2015: 122–4, 178). The OED appears to recognise no limits concerning what it may label a 'compound'. For example, under *radio* we find *radio talk show host*, with two quotations.
- Dixon (2008/2011) provides an account of how all sorts of dictionaries have dealt with the etymologies of words borrowed from Australian Aboriginal languages.

Chapter 15: The Way Forward

- Quotations from Landau (1984: 296–7) and Svensén (2009: 428).

The Vision

- Craigie quotation from Wyllie (1961: 287). Although Samuel Johnson defined **Lexicographer** as *A writer of dictionaries; a harmless drudge, that busies himself in tracing the original, and detailing the signification of words*, the enjoyment one obtains from perusing Johnson's dictionary suggests that he obtained enjoyment from compiling it. The 'drudge' comment was simply one of his playful asides.
- The bilingual thesaurus-based dictionaries of Australian languages which I have worked on are Dixon (1991b) on Yidiny, and an almost completed work on Dyirbal. Compilations of words borrowed into English from Australian languages are Dixon et al. (1990, 2006).
- The 520-million-word Corpus of Contemporary American English (COCA; corpus.byu.edu/coca) has fifteen instances of *otiose* as against 5,157 of *futile* and 2,055 of *useless*. It has fifteen instances of *inveigle* as against 5,431 of *persuade*.

Acknowledgements

A considerable debt is owed to Rob Pensalfini for help with editions of Shakespeare, and to James L. Rader for insights into many aspects of modern-day lexicography. Kate Burridge, Clare Allridge, Brigitta Flick and Jolene Overall read a draft and provided useful suggestions for improvement. Alexandra Aikhenvald discussed every aspect of this book with me, then read the chapters as they were drafted, providing cogent and compelling suggestions; she could be called the patron of this work.

I have greatly benefited from access to the Macquarie Corpus website, courtesy of Pam Peters, making use of several corpuses there, most particularly the Lancaster–Oslo/Bremen corpus. The gigantic Corpus of Contemporary American English was also a fine resource.

Recommendation

Colleagues who have observed me surrounded by many dictionaries invariably ask which is the pick of the crop. This is a difficult question to answer – each dictionary has different pluses and minuses. The ideal dictionary would be a blend of several. But, putting everything together, I'd have to opt for Merriam-Webster's Collegiate. (This despite the fact that my own background is British and Australian.)

Chronological List of Dictionaries and Glossaries Mentioned

Unless otherwise stated, dictionaries are monolingual in English. Generally, just the date of the first edition is given. Works are listed under author until 1850, after that by title. Abbreviated titles are given here; see the list of references for fuller titles of editions quoted from.

c725	Corpus Glossary. Latin to Latin, Old English, and Old French.
c1000	Aelfric's Glossary. Latin to Old English.
1499	Anonymous. *Promptorium Parvalorum* [ms version in 1430]. English to Latin.
1500	Anonymous. *Hortus Vocabularum* [ms version in 1440]. Latin to English.
1535	Ambrogio Calepino. *Dictionarium Latinae Linguae*. Monolingual Latin.
1538	Thomas Elyot. *Dictionary*. Latin to English.
1552	Richard Huloet. *Abecedarium Anglo-Latinum*. English to Latin.
1565	Thomas Cooper. *Thesaurus Linguae Romanae & Britannicae*. Latin to English.
1573	John Baret. *An Alvearie or Triple Dictionarie*. English, Latin, and French.
1582	Richard Mulcaster. *Elementarie*. [List of English words with no definitions.]
1587	Thomas Thomas. *Dictionarium*. Latin to English.
1596	Edmund Coote. *The English Schoole-maister*.
1604	Robert Cawdrey. *A Table Alphabeticall*.
1613	Academia della Crusca. *Vocabulario*. Monolingual Italian.
1616	John Bullokar. *An English Expositor*.
1623	Henry Cockeram. *The English Dictionarie*.
1656	Thomas Blount. *Glossographia*.
1658	Edward Phillips. *The New World of English Words*.
1676	Elisha Coles. *An English Dictionary*.
1694	Académie française. *Dictionnaire*. Monolingual French.
1702	John Kersey. *A New English Dictionary*.

1721	Nathan Bailey. *A Universal Etymological English Dictionary.*
1730	Nathan Bailey. *Dictionarium Britannicum.*
1749	Benjamin Martin. *Lingua Britannica Reformata.*
1753	John Wesley. *The Complete English Dictionary.*
1755	Samuel Johnson. *Dictionary.*
1765	John Baskerville. *A Vocabulary, or Pocket Dictionary.*
1773	William Kenrick. *A New Dictionary of English.*
1775	John Ash. *The New and Complete Dictionary.*
1798	Samuel Johnson, Junr. *A School Dictionary.*
1828	Noah Webster. *American Dictionary.*
1830	Joseph Emerson Worcester. *Comprehensive Dictionary.*
1835–7	Charles Richardson. *A New Dictionary of the English Language.*
1847–50	John Ogilvie. *The Imperial Dictionary.*
1872	*Chambers's English Dictionary.* Robert Chambers and William Chambers.
1888–1928	*Oxford English Dictionary.* James A. H. Murray et al.
1889–91	*The Century Dictionary and Cyclopedia.* William Dwight Whitney.
1893–5	*A Standard Dictionary.* Isaac K. Funk. [Later known as Funk and Wagnalls.]
1898	*Webster's Collegiate Dictionary.* [No editor stated.]
1898	*Austral English.* Edward E. Morris.
1909	*Webster's New International Dictionary.* William Torey Harris and F. Sturgis Allen.
1911	*The Concise Oxford English Dictionary of Current English.* H. W. Fowler and F. G. Fowler.
1927	*The New Century Dictionary.* H. G. Emery and K. G. Brewster.
1933	*The Shorter Oxford English Dictionary.* C. T. Onions.
1935	*The New Method English Dictionary.* Michael West and James Endicott.
1938–44	*A Dictionary of American English.* William A. Craigie and James R. Hulbert.
1947	*The American College Dictionary.* Clarence Barnhart.
1948	*The Oxford Advanced Learner's Dictionary.* A. S. Hornby.
1951	*A Dictionary of Americanisms.* Mitford M. Mathews.
1965	*The Penguin English Dictionary.* George N. Garmonsway.
1966	*The Random House Dictionary Unabridged.* Jess Stein.
1969	*The American Heritage Dictionary.* Anne H. Soukhanov.
1971	*Encyclopedic World Dictionary.* Patrick Hanks.
1978	*Longman Dictionary of Contemporary English.* Paul Proctor.
1979	*Collins English Dictionary.* Patrick Hanks.

1981	*The Macquarie Dictionary*. Arthur Delbridge.
1987	*COBUILD English Dictionary*. John Sinclair.
1988	*The Australian National Dictionary*. W. S. Ramson.
1995	*The Oxford English Reference Dictionary*. Judy Pearsall and Bill Trumble.
1999	*The Australian Oxford Dictionary*. Bruce Moore.

This is just a selection of English dictionaries, and glossaries. There were more in every period, and many more from the eighteenth century onwards. Useful listings of early works are in Stein (1985), Starnes (1954), Starnes and Noyes (1946), Alston (1966), Mathews (1933), Wheatley (1865), Worcester (1830), and Murray (1900).

References to Printed Materials

Generally, the edition(s) I have referred to are given.

DICTIONARIES AND GLOSSARIES

Allen, R. E. 1990. Editor of *The Concise Oxford Dictionary of Current English*, 8th ed. Oxford: Clarendon Press.

American College Dictionary, see Barnhart.

American Heritage Dictionary, see Soukhanov.

Annandale, Charles. 1882. *The Imperial Dictionary of the English Language*, revised edition. Glasgow: Blackie.

Anonymous. 1499. *Promptorium Parvalorum sive Clericum*. London: Richard Pynson.

Anonymous. 1500. *Hortus (or Ortus) Vocabulorum*. London: Winard de Worde.

Ash, John. 1775. *The New and Complete Dictionary of the English Language*. London: Edward and Charles Dilly, and R. Baldwin.

Austral English, see Morris.

Australian National Dictionary, see Ramson.

Australian Oxford Dictionary, see Moore.

Bailey, Nathan. 1721. *A Universal Etymological English Dictionary ....* London: E. Bell, J. Darby, A. Bettesworth et al.

   1730. *Dictionarium Britannicum: Or a More Compleat Universal Etymological English Dictionary than any Extant ....* London: T. Cox.

Baret, John. 1573. *An Alvearie or Triple Dictionarie, in Englishe, Latin and French....* London: Henry Denham.

Barnhart, Clarence L. 1947. Editor of *The American College Dictionary*. New York: Random House.

Baskerville, John. 1765. *A Vocabulary, or Pocket Dictionary,... to which is Prefixed, a Compendious Grammar of the English language*. Birmingham: John Baskerville.

Blount, Thomas. 1656. *Glossographia, or a Dictionary Interpreting all such Hard Words, ... as are now Used in our Refined English Tongue ....* London: Tho. Newcomb, sold by Humphrey Moseley and George Sawbridge.

Bullokar, John. 1616. *An English Expositor: Teaching the Interpretation of the Hardest Words used in our Language. With Sundry Explications, Descriptions, and Discourses*. London: John Legatt.

Calepino, Ambrogio. 1535. *Dictionarium Latinæ Linguæ*. Basle: ex officio Ilan[nis] Valderi.

Capell, A. 1941. *A New Fijian Dictionary*. Sydney: Australasian Medical Publishing Company.

Cawdrey, Robert. 1604. *A Table Alphabeticall, conteyning and teaching the true writing and vnderstanding of hard vsual English wordes, borrowed from the Hebrew, Greeke, Latine, or French, etc.* ... London: John Roberts for Edmund Weaver. [And see Simpson 2007.]

Century Dictionary and Cyclopedia, see Whitney.

Chambers, Robert and Chambers, William. 1872. *Chambers's English Dictionary*. Edinburgh: W. and R. Chambers.

Churchward, C. Maxwell. 1959. *Tongan Dictionary (Tongan–English and English–Tongan)*. Tonga: Government Printing Press.

COBUILD Dictionary, see Sinclair.

Cockeram, Henry. 1623. *The English Dictionarie: or, an Interpreter of Hard English Words* .... London: Edmund Weaver, and London: Nathaniel Butter.

Coles, Elisha. 1676. *An English Dictionary, explaining the difficult terms that are used in divinity, husbandry, physick, phylosophy, law, navigation, mathematicks, and other arts and sciences* .... London: Samuel Crouch.

Collegiate Dictionary, see Mish.

Collins English Dictionary, see Hanks.

Collins Gem Dictionary and Thesaurus. 2009. Glasgow: HarperCollins.

Concise Oxford Dictionary, see Allen; Fowler and Fowler.

Cooper, Thomas. 1565. *Thesaurus Linguæ Romanæ & Britannicæ* .... London: Quondam Bertheleti, cum priuilegio Regiæ Maiestatis, per Henricum W. Vykes.

Coote, Edmund. 1596. *The English Schoole-maister, teaching all his scholers, of what age soeuer, the most easie, short and perfect order of distinct reading and true writing our English tongue* .... London: Joan Orwin for Ralph Jackson and Robert Dexter.

Craigie, William A. and Hulbert, James R. 1938–44. Editors of *A Dictionary of American English on Historical Principles*. Chicago: University of Chicago Press.

Delbridge, Arthur. 1981. Editor of *The Macquarie Dictionary*. Sydney: Macquarie Library.

—— 1991. Editor of *The Macquarie Dictionary*, 2nd ed. Sydney: Macquarie Library.

Dictionary of American English, see Craigie and Hulbert.

Dictionary of Americanisms, see Mathews.

Elyot, Sir Thomas. 1538. *The Dictionary of Sir Thomas Elyot knyght*. London: Thomas Berthlet.

Emery, H. G. and Brewster, K. G. 1927. Editors of *The New Century Dictionary*. New York: Appleton-Century-Crofts.

Encyclopedic World Dictionary, see Hanks.

Flexner, Stuart B. 1987. Editor-in-chief of *The Random House Dictionary of the English Language Unabridged*, 2nd ed. New York: Random House.

Fowler, H. W. and Fowler, F. G. 1951. Original editors of *The Concise Oxford Dictionary of Current English*, 4th ed., further edited by E. McIntosh. Oxford: Clarendon Press.

Funk, Isaac K. 1893–5. *A Standard Dictionary of the English Language upon Original Plans*. New York: Funk and Wagnalls.

Garmonsway, George N. 1965. Editor of *The Penguin English Dictionary*. Harmondsworth: Penguin.

Gove, Philip B. 1961. Editor-in-chief of *Webster's Third New International Dictionary of the English Language Unabridged*. Springfield, MA: Merriam-Webster.

Hanks, Patrick. 1971. Editor of *Encyclopedic World Dictionary*. London: Paul Hamlyn. 1979. Editor of *Collins English Dictionary*. Glasgow: Collins.

Hornby, A. S. 1948. *Oxford Advanced Learner's Dictionary of Current English*. Oxford University Press.

Huloet, Richard. 1552. *Abecedarium Anglo-Latinum*. London: Gulielmi Riddel.

Imperial Dictionary, see Annandale; Ogilvie.

Johnson, Frederick. 1939. *A Standard Swahili-English Dictionary*. Oxford University Press.

Johnson, Samuel. 1755. *A Dictionary of the English Language* .... London: J. and P. Knapton, T. and T. Longman, C. Hitch and L. Hawes, A. Millar, and R. and J. Dodsley.

Johnson, Samuel, Junr. 1798. *A School Dictionary: Being a compendium of the latest and most improved dictionaries*. New Haven: Edward O'Brien.

Kenrick, William. 1773. *A New Dictionary of the English Language: Containing not only the explanation of words ... but likewise, their orthopoepia or pronunciation* .... London: John and Francis Rivington, William Johnston, et al.

Kersey, John. 1702. *A New English Dictionary; or, a Complete Collection of the Most Proper and Significant Words, Commonly used in the Language; with a Short and Clear Exposition of Difficult Words and Terms of Art* .... London: Henry Bonwicke and Robert Knaplock.

Longman Dictionary of Contemporary English, see Proctor.

Macquarie Dictionary, see Delbridge.

Martin, Benjamin. 1749. *Lingua Britannica Reformata: or, a New English Dictionary,* .... London: J. Hodges, S Austen, J. Newbery, et al.

Mathews, Mitford M. 1951. Editor of *A Dictionary of Americanisms on Historical Principles*. Chicago: University of Chicago Press.

Merriam-Webster's Collegiate Dictionary, see Mish.

Mish, Frederick G. 1983. Editor-in-chief of *Webster's Ninth New Collegiate Dictionary*. Springfield, MA: Merriam-Webster. 1993. Editor-in-chief of *Merriam-Webster's Collegiate Dictionary, Tenth Edition*. [And also *Eleventh Edition*, 2003.] Springfield, MA: Merriam-Webster.

Moore, Bruce. 1999. Editor of *The Australian Oxford Dictionary*. Melbourne: Oxford University Press.

Morris, Edward E. 1898. *Austral English: A Dictionary of Australasian Words, Phrases, and Usages*. London: Macmillan.

Mulcaster, Richard. 1582. *The First Part of the Elementarie which entreateth chefelie of the right writing of our English tung*. London: Thomas Vautroullier.

Murray, James A. H., Bradley, Henry, Craigie, William, A., and Onions, C. T. 1888–1928. Editors of *A New English Dictionary on Historical Principles, Founded Mainly on the Materials Collected by the Philological Society*. Oxford: Clarendon Press. [Later re-titled, by the publisher, the *Oxford English Dictionary*.] *Supplement* 1933, edited by Craigie and Onions. *Second Supplement* 1972–86, edited by Robert W. Burchfield. 2nd edition 1989, edited by John Simpson and Edmund Weiner.

New Century Dictionary, see Emery and Brewster.

New Method English Dictionary, see West and Endicott.

Ogilvie, John. 1847–50. *The Imperial Dictionary of the English Language*. Glasgow: Blackie.

Onions, C. T. 1933. *Shorter Oxford English Dictionary on Historical Principles*. Oxford University Press.

Oxford English Dictionary, see Murray.

Oxford English Reference Dictionary, see Pearsall and Trumble.

Pearsall, Judy and Trumble, Bill. 1996. Editors of *The Oxford English Reference Dictionary*, 2nd ed. Oxford University Press.

Penguin English Dictionary, see Garmonsway.

Phillips, Edward. 1658. *The New World of English Words: or, a General Dictionary* .... London: E Tyler for Nath. Brooke.

Pokorny, Julius. 1959. *Indogermanisches Etymologisches Wörterbuch*. Bern: Francke.

Proctor, Paul. 1978. Editor-in-chief of *Longman Dictionary of Contemporary English*. Harlow: Longman.

Ramson, W. S. 1988. Editor of *The Australian National Dictionary: A Dictionary of Australianisms on Historical Principles*. Melbourne: Oxford University Press.

Random House Dictionary Unabridged, see Flexner; Stein.

Richardson, Charles. 1835–7. *A New Dictionary of the English Language*. London: William Pickering.

Shorter Oxford English Dictionary, see Onions.

Simpson, John. 2007. Editor of *The First English Dictionary, 1604, Robert Cawdrey's A Table Alphabetical*. Oxford: Bodleian Library.

Sinclair, John. 1987. Editor-in-chief of *Collins COBUILD English Dictionary for Advanced Learners*. Glasgow: HarperCollins.

Soukhanov, Anne H. 1992. Executive editor of *The American Heritage Dictionary of the English Language*, 3rd ed. Boston: Houghton Mifflin.

Stein, Jess. 1966. Editor-in-chief of *The Random House Dictionary of the English Language Unabridged*, 1st ed. New York: Random House.

Sweet, Henry. 1896. *The Student's Dictionary of Anglo-Saxon*. Oxford: Clarendon Press.

Thomas, Thomas. 1587. *Dictionarium Linguæ Latiæn et Anglicæ*. Cambridge: University Press.

Watkins, Calvert. 1985. *The American Heritage Dictionary of Indo-European Roots*. Boston: Houghton Mifflin. [2nd ed. in 2000.]

Webster, Noah. 1828. *An American Dictionary of the English Language*. New York: S. Converse.

Webster's Collegiate Dictionary, see Mish.

Webster's Third, see Gove.

Wesley, John. 1753. *The Complete English Dictionary, explaining most of those hard words, which are found in the best English writers* .... London: W. Strahant, sold by J. Robinson, T. Trye, T. James, and G. Englefield.

West, Michael P. and Endicott, James G. 1935. Editors of *The New Method English Dictionary*. London: Longmans, Green and Co.

Whitney, William Dwight. 1889–91. *The Century Dictionary and Cyclopedia*. New York: Century.

Worcester, Joseph E. 1830. *A Comprehensive Pronouncing and Explanatory Dictionary of the English Language*. New York: Collins and Hannay.

1860. *A Comprehensive Dictionary of the English Language*. Boston: Brewer and Tileston.

OTHER REFERENCES

Aarsleff, Hans. 1967. *The Study of Language in England, 1780–1860.* Princeton: Princeton University Press.

Aikhenvald, Alexandra Y. 2000. *Classifiers: A Typology of Noun Categorization Devices.* Oxford University Press.

2004. *Evidentiality.* Oxford University Press.

2010. *Imperatives and Commands.* Oxford University Press.

2015. *The Art of Grammar: A Practical Guide.* Oxford University Press.

Allen, W. Sidney. 1978. *Vox Latina: A Guide to the Pronunciation of Classical Latin,* 2nd ed. Cambridge University Press.

Alston, R. C. 1966. *The English Dictionary: Bibliography of the English Language from the Invention of Printing to the Year 1800.* Vol. 5. Leeds: E. J. Arnold.

1967. *Spelling Books: Bibliography of the English Language from the Invention of Printing to the Year 1800.* Vol. 4. Bradford: Ernest Cummins.

Anonymous. 1840. 'The Diversions of Purley', *Blackwood's Edinburgh Magazine* 47: 484–96.

Béjoint, Henri. 2010. *The Lexicography of English: From Origins to Present.* Oxford University Press.

Black, Michael H. 1984. *Cambridge University Press, 1584–1984.* Cambridge University Press.

Bloomfield, Leonard. 1933. *Language.* New York: Holt.

Boas, Franz. 1911. 'Introduction', pp. 1–83 of *Handbook of American Indian Languages,* Part 1, edited by Franz Boas. Washington: Smithsonian Institution.

Brewer, Charlotte. 2007. *Treasure House of the Language: The Living OED.* New Haven: Yale University Press.

2012. 'A goose-quill or a gander's? Female writers in Johnson's *dictionary*', pp. 120–39 of *Samuel Johnson: The Arc of the Pendulum,* edited by Freya Johnston and Lynda Mugglestone. Oxford University Press.

Bryson, Bill. 2008. *Mother Tongue: The English Language.* Melbourne: Penguin. [First published in 1990.]

Burchfield, Robert. 1972. 'Four-letter words and the OED', p. 1233 of *The Times Literary Supplement,* 13 October 1972.

1982. 'Opening Words: Review of *The Macquarie Dictionary*'. *The Age* (Melbourne) 1 March 1982, 'Monthly Review Section', pp. 10–11.

1989. *Unlocking the English Language.* London: Faber and Faber.

Chambers, Ephraim. 1728. *Cyclopaedia: or, a Universal Dictionary of Arts and Sciences.* London: James and John Knapton.

Churchward, C. Maxwell. 1941. *A New Fijian Grammar.* Sydney: Australasian Medical Publishing Company.

1953. *Tongan Grammar.* London: Oxford University Press.

Clifford, James L. 1979. *Dictionary Johnson: Samuel Johnson's Middle Years.* New York: McGraw-Hill.

Considine, John. 2014. 'Sir Thomas Elyot makes a dictionary', *International Journal of Lexicography* 27: 309–18.

Cowie, A. P. 1999. *English Dictionaaries for Foreign Learners: A History.* Oxford: Clarendon Press.

2009, Editor of *The Oxford History of English Lexicography,* 2 vols. Oxford University Press.

Cowell, John. 1607. *The Interpreter: or Booke Containing the Significance of Words*. Cambridge: John Legate.

Dixon, R. M. W. 1991a. *A New Approach to English Grammar, on Semantic Principles*. Oxford: Clarendon Press.

1991b. *Words of our Country: Stories, Place names and Vocabulary in Yidiny, the Aboriginal language of the Cairns-Yarrabah Region*. St Lucia: University of Queensland Press.

2005a. *A Semantic Approach to English Grammar*, 2nd ed. Oxford University Press.

2005b. 'Comparative constructions in English', *Studia Anglica Posnaniensia* 41: 5–27. [Reprinted as pp. 472–93 of Alexandra Y. Aikhenvald and R. M. W. Dixon. 2011. *Language at Large: Essays on Syntax and Semantics*. Leiden: Brill.]

2007. 'Clitics in English', *English Studies* 88: 574–600.

2008. 'Australian Aboriginal words in dictionaries: A history', *International Journal of Lexicography* 32: 787–817. [Reprinted with minor revisions as pp. 539–53 of Alexandra Y. Aikhenvald and R. M. W. Dixon. 2011. *Language at Large: Essays on Syntax and Semantics*. Leiden: Brill.]

2010a. *Basic Linguistic Theory*, Vol. 1, *Methodology*. Oxford University Press.

2010b. *Basic Linguistic Theory*, Vol. 2, *Grammatical Topics*. Oxford University Press.

2012. *Basic Linguistic Theory*, Vol. 3, *Further Grammatical Topics*. Oxford University Press.

2014. *Making New Words: Morphological Derivation in English*. Oxford University Press.

Dixon, R. M. W., Ramson, W. S., and Thomas, Mandy. 1990. *Australian Aboriginal Words in English, their Origin and Meaning*. Melbourne: Oxford University Press.

Dixon, R. M. W., Moore, Bruce, Ramson, W. S., and Thomas, Mandy. 2006. *Australian Aboriginal Words in English, their Origin and Meaning*, 2nd ed. Melbourne: Oxford University Press.

Dutch, Robert A. 1962. *Roget's Thesaurus of English Words and Phrases*, new edition completely revised, modernized and abridged. London: Longmans.

Gilliver, Peter. 2016. *The Making of the Oxford English Dictionary*. Oxford University Press.

Girard, Abbé Gabriel. 1736. *Synonymes françois, leurs significations et le choix qu'il en fait pour parler avec justesse*. Paris: Laurent d'Houry.

Gove, Phillip B. 1973. Editor-in-chief of *Webster's New Dictionary of Synonyms, A Dictionary of Discriminated Synonyms with Antonyms and Analogous and Contrasted words*. Springfield, MA: G. and C. Merriam.

Granger, Sylviane and Paquot, Magali. 2012. Editors of *Electronic Lexicography*. Oxford University Press.

Healey, Antonette diPaulo. 2012. 'Old English glossaries: Creating a vernacular', pp. 3–12 of *Ashgate Critical Essays in Early English Lexicographers*, Vol. 1: *Old English*, edited by Christine Franzen. Farnham, UK: Ashgate.

Hill, John. 1751. *A History of the Materia Medica*. London: T. Longman, C. Hitch and L. Hawes.

Hüllen, Werner. 2004. *A History of Roget's Thesaurus: Origins, Development, and Design*. Oxford University Press.

Horne Tooke, John. 1786. *Epea pteroenta or, the Diversions of Purley*, Part I. London: J. Johnson.

Jespersen, Otto. 1909–49. *A Modern English Grammar, on Historical Principles*, Parts I–VII. Heidelberg: Winter (Parts I–IV), Copenhagen: Munksgaard (Parts V–VII).

1924. *The Philosophy of Grammar*. London: Allen and Unwin.

1942. Part VI, *Morphology*, of *A Modern English Grammar, on Historical Principles*. Copenhagen: Munksgaard.

Johnson, Samuel. 1747. *The Plan of a Dictionary of the English Language*. London: J & P. Knapton.

Kolb, Gwin J. and Sledd, James H. 1953. 'Johnson's *Dictionary* and lexicographic practice', *Modern Philology* 50: 171–94.

Landau, Sidney J. 1984. *Dictionaries: The Art and Craft of Lexicography*. New York: Charles Scribner's Sons.

Lennox, Charlotte. 1752. *The Female Quixote, or, the Adventures of Arabella*. London: A. Millar.

1753. *Shakespeare Illustrated*. London: A. Millar.

Lester, C. Edwards. 1883. *Lester's History of the United States*. New York: P. F. Collier.

Lieber, Rochelle. 1998. 'The suffix *-ize* in English: Implications for morphology', pp. 12–33 of *Morphology and its Relation to Phonology and Syntax*, edited by Steven G. Lapointe, Diane K. Brentar, and Patrick M. Farrell. Stanford: CSLI.

2004. *Morphology and Lexical Semantics*. Cambridge University Press.

McCracken, David. 1969. 'The drudgery of defining: Johnson's debt to Bailey's *Dictionarium Britannicum*', *Modern Philology* 66: 338–41.

McDavid, Raven. Jr. 1984 'Noah Webster', *Encyclopædia Britannica*, 15th ed., 19: 720–1.

Malinowski, Bronislaw. 1935. *Coral Gardens and their Magic*, Vol. II, *The Language of Magic and Gardening*. London: George Allen and Unwin.

Marchand, Hans. 1969. *The Categories and Types of Present-day English Word-formation, a Synchronic-diachronic Approach*, 2nd ed. Munich: C. H. Beck.

Mathews, M. M. 1933. *A Survey of English Dictionaries*. London: Oxford University Press.

Matthews, P. H. 1997. *The Concise Oxford Dictionary of Linguistics*. Oxford University Press. [New editions in 2007, 2014.]

Michael, Ian. 1970. *English Grammatical Categories, and the Tradition to 1800*. Cambridge University Press.

Micklethwait, David. 2000. *Noah Webster and the American Dictionary*. Jefferson, NC: McFarland.

Miller, Philip. 1732. *The Gardener's Dictionary Containing the Methods of Cultivating and Improving the Kitchen Fruit and Flower Garden*. London, printed by G. Rivington for the author.

Morton, Herbert C. 1994. *The Story of Webster's Third: Philip Gove's Controversial Dictionary and its Critics*. Cambridge University Press.

Mugglestone, Lynda. 2011. *Dictionaries: A Very Short Introduction*. Oxford University Press.

2015. *Samuel Johnson and the Journey into Words*. Oxford University Press.

Murray, James A. H. 1900. *The Evolution of English Lexicography*. Oxford: Clarendon Press.

Murray, K. M. Elisabeth. 1979. *Caught in the Web of Words: James Murray and the Oxford English Dictionary*. Oxford University Press.

Ogilvie, Sarah. 2013. *Words of the World: A Global History of the Oxford English Dictionary*. Cambridge University Press.

Ostler, Rosemary. 2008. 'Are prepositions necessary? John Horne Tooke and the origin of words', *Verbatim* 32: 1–5.

Palmer, H. E. 1924. *A Grammar of Spoken English on a Strictly Phonetic Basis*. Cambridge: Heffer. [2nd ed. in 1939.]

Palmer, H. E. and Blandford, F. G. 1969. *A Grammar of Spoken English*, 3rd ed., revised and rewritten by Roger Kingdon. Cambridge: Heffer.

Piozzi, Hester Lynch. 1794. *British Synonymy; An Attempt at Regulating the Choice of Words in Familiar Conversation* .... London: G. G. and J. Robinson.

Plag, Ingo. 1999. *Morphological Productivity: Structural Constraints in English Derivation*. Berlin: Mouton de Gruyter.

Reader's Digest Use the Right Word. Modern guide to synonyms and related words, lists of antonyms, copious cross-references, a complete and legible index. 1969. The editors of The Reader's Digest and the Funk and Wagnalls Dictionary staff.

Read, Allen Walker. 2003. 'The beginnings of English lexicography', *Dictionaries: Journal of the Dictionary Society of North America* 24: 187–226.

Reed, Joseph W. Jr. 1962. 'Noah Webster's debt to Samuel Johnson', *American Speech* 37: 95–105.

Roget, Peter Mark. 1852. *Thesaurus of English Words and Phrases, classified and arranged so as to facilitate the expression of ideas and assist in literary composition*. London: Longman, Brown, Green and Longmans.

Sapir, Edward. 1921. *Language*. New York: Harcourt Brace.

Schäfer, Jürgen. 1970. 'The hard word dictionaries: A reassessment', *Leeds Studies in English* 4: 51–68.

    1989. *Early Modern English Lexicography*, Vol. I, *A Survey of Monolingual Printed Glossaries and Dictionaries 1475–1640*. Oxford: Clarendon Press.

Sledd, James and Ebbitt, Wilma R. 1962. *Dictionaries and THAT Dictionary*. Chicago: Scott, Foreman.

Starnes, De Witt T. 1954. *Renaissance Dictionaries: English-Latin and Latin-English*. Austin: University of Texas Press.

Starnes, De Witt T. and Noyes, Gertrude E. 1946. *The English Dictionary from Cawdrey to Johnson 1604–1755*. Chapel Hill: The University of North Carolina Press.

Stein, Gabriele. 1985. *The English Dictionary before Cawdrey*. Tubingen: Max Niemeyer.

    2014. *Sir Thomas Elyot as Lexicographer*. Oxford University Press.

Stephens, Alexander. 1813. *Memoirs of John Horne Tooke, Interspersed with Original Documents*. London: J. Johnson.

Stevenson, Allan. 1958. 'Thomas Thomas makes a dictionary', *The Library*, 5th series, 13: 234–46.

Svensén, Bo. 2009. *A Handbook of Lexicography: The Theory and Practice of Dictionary-Making*. Cambridge University Press.

Trusler, John. 1766. *The Difference, between Words, Esteemed Synonymous, in the English Language; and the Proper Choice of them Determined: Together with, so much of Abbé Girard's treatise, on this subject, as would agree with our mode of expression. Useful, to all, who would, either, write or speak, with propriety, and elegance*. London: J. Dodsley.

Wallis, John. 1653. *Grammatica Linguae Anglicanae....* Oxford: Leon Lichfield.

    1972. *Grammar of the English Language ....* Translated and with commentary by J. A. Kemp. London: Longman.

Webster's New Dictionary of Synonyms, see Gove.

West, Michael. 1953. *A General Service List of English Words, with Semantic Frequencies ....* London: Longmans.

Wheatley, Henry B. 1865. 'Chronological notes on the dictionaries of the English language', *Transactions of the Philological Society for 1865*, pp. 218–93.

Winchester, Simon. 2003. *The Meaning of Everything: The Story of the Oxford English Dictionary.* Oxford University Press.

Wyllie, J. M. 1961. 'Sir William Craigie, 1867–1957', *Proceedings of the Royal Society* 47: 273–91.

Zgusta, Ladislav. 1971. *Manual of Lexicography.* The Hague: Mouton; and Prague: Academia.

Index

Note that only lexical words which are afforded semantic-grammatical discussion, and a few others which recur, are included in the index.